Richard Blackmore · Essays upon Several Subjects

Anglistica & Americana

A Series of Reprints Selected by
Bernhard Fabian, Edgar Mertner,
Karl Schneider and Marvin Spevack

164

1976

Georg Olms Verlag
Hildesheim · New York

Richard Blackmore

Essays
upon Several Subjects
(1716)

1976
Georg Olms Verlag
Hildesheim · New York

Note

The present facsimile is reproduced from a copy in the possession of the Staatsbibliothek, Stiftung Preußischer Kulturbesitz, Berlin.

Shelfmark: Nh 3488-1.

B. F.

Nachdruck der Ausgabe London 1716
Printed in Germany
Herstellung: Strauss & Cramer GmbH, 6901 Leutershausen
ISBN 3 487 05931 2

ESSAYS
UPON
Several SUBJECTS.

BY
Sir RICHARD BLACKMORE, *Kt. M.D.*
and Fellow of the College of Physicians
in *London*.

LONDON:
Printed for E. CURLL at the *Dial* and *Bible*,
and J. PEMBERTON at the *Buck* and *Sun*,
both against St. *Dunstan*'s Church in *Fleet-
street*. M.DCC.XVI.

THE
PREFACE.

AN *Essay* is an instructive Writing, either in Prose or Verse, distinguish'd from compleat Treatises and voluminous Works, by its shorter Extent and less accurate Method. It is natural for Men to desire the Acquisition of Knowledge by the most easy and expeditious Ways, and therefore few Persons have been so patient of Labour and Application, as to be delighted with prolix Compositions, in which, the main De-

fign of the Author being long fuſ-
pended, the Difcourfe grows ſo tedious to many, that they imagine
it will never be finiſh'd. But the
Difrelifh of ſuch diffufive Pieces in
theſe Times is more univerſal, and
carry'd ſo far, that great Books are
look'd on as oppreffive, and by their
Bulk, concluded to be dull and ſpi-
ritlefs; while thoſe in which the
principal End, as well as the Sentiments of the Author, are contracted
into a narrower Compafs, if well
writ, meet with general Approbation. And if it happens that a large
Volume is well receiv'd in the preſent Age, it muſt be adorn'd with
Variety of Matter, as well as pure
Diction, and wrought up to a great
Degree of Perfection, otherwife the
Reader is difcourag'd, and throws it
by as too painful a Task to be undertaken.

WHE-

The Preface.

Whether this Delicacy proceeds from a more refin'd and elegant Taste, or an indolent and unactive Temper of Mind, I shall not here examine; but in Fact, the Observation is so just, that not only long and methodical Systems of Divinity, Natural Philosophy, Morals and Medicine are grown disagreeable, but likewise voluminous Romances, the Delight of the past Age, are no longer demanded, but lie by as neglected Lumber in the Shops, while short Novels and Tales are become the common Entertainment of those who are pleas'd with Fictions of that Nature. And should it be granted, that this arises from a greater and more universal Relish of Polite Literature, I am afraid that the principal Interests of Learning, and the Advancement of solid Knowledge will suffer by it. There is that

that Connexion, Dependence, and beautiful Order of the Parts in a perfect Body of Science, that it is impossible to contemplate the whole Structure but in a lame and imperfect View, when the Members of it are fever'd and disunited, as they are in small Discourses. If the relation of one Proposition to another, and the coherent Train of Conclusions are not discern'd by the Mind, there must follow a great Confusion and Obscurity of Ideas; and at best those Men, for want of full and comprehensive Conceptions of Things, will only perceive some scatter'd Branches of Truth, and form but a dim and defective Sketch of any Art or System of Knowledge.

Should a barbarous *Indian*, who had never seen a Palace or a Ship, view their separate and disjointed Parts drawn by the Pen or Pencil,

and

The PREFACE.

and observe the Pillars, Doors, Cornishes, and Turrets of one, and the Prow, Stern, Ribs, and Masts of the other, he would be able to form but a very lame and dark Idea of either of those Inventions. In like manner those, who contemplate only the Fragments or Pieces broken off from any Science, dispers'd in short unconnected Discourses, and do not discern their relation to each other, and how they may be adapted, and by their Union procure the delightful Symetry of a regular Scheme, can never survey an entire Body of Truth, but must view it as deform'd and dismember'd; while their Ideas, which must be always indistinct and often repugnant, will lie in the Brain unsorted, and thrown together without Order and Coherence. But since the Taste of the Times is so nice and delicate, and their Temper so impatient of long Application, those who would convey Instruction to their Minds, must accommodate their Writings to this prevailing Inclination, must possess themselves of those Avenues that lie open and lead with ease to their Understanding, and change their Method of Address when it grows disagreeable, for another that meets with a better Reception. He must be a very morose Physician, that when the Form of his Medicines begins to grow ungrateful and nauseous, will not alter it, or direct a new Vehicle, by which they may be taken down with less Reluctance.

And since Discourses contracted into a narrow room, if they are wrote with Strength and Perspicuity, and contain Variety of good Sense, are more acceptable to Readers, by not putting them to too much Labour and Attention; it must for that Reason be acknowledg'd, that their
use-

The Preface. ix

usefulness is more diffusive than that of long and elaborate Volumes; and tho they do not exhibit Truth in such a clear and perfect Scheme, nor set it in so full a Light, as it appears in a large and methodical System, they are, however, very beneficial, and promote the Interests of Literature and Vertue. And since, as I have said, most Men take greater delight in this manner of Writing than in prolix and unweildy Productions, whose enormous Size puts them in a Fright, to gratify the general Taste, as well as to avoid all Affectation of the Air of the Schools, and Ostentation of Learning, many Gentlemen have apply'd themselves to write in a more concise and elegant, tho a less instructive and scholastick manner.

The most celebrated *English* Authors of Essays are, the Lord *Verulam*

lam and Sir *William Temple*; and tho Mr. *Locke* has given that Appellation to his Book on *Human Understanding*, yet that Title seems to be prefix'd from a real or an affected Modesty; for by its Extent, as well as accuracy and methodical Composure, it may justly be reckon'd among large and compleat Treatises.

MEN by Writing in this close and short way, prevent their being tedious to the Reader, who desires often to take Breath, and to be reliev'd from Satiety by frequent Rests: And as they find, that not being fetter'd by Terms of Art and the Method and Rules of School-men, they are at liberty to write in a more polite and ornamental Stile, so they are able to infuse into a contracted Work more Life and Energy, while, like the Chymist, by evaporating the superfluous and insipid Phlegm, they

The Preface.

they can draw into a little Room the pure and active Spirit.

Believing that I am oblig'd to employ my Talents, such as they are, for publick Good, I have, in conformity to the prevailing Disposition of the People, express'd my Sentiments on the several Subjects of the following Dissertations in a less extensive manner, than otherwise I should have done; in which I have impartially pursu'd the Interests of Truth and Vertue, without a Design of pleasing or provoking Any.

Some Gentlemen have objected to my former Writings, and they will have no less reason to object against a great Part of these, that they contain too great a Mixture of Religion, without which predominant and disagreeable Ingredient, in their Judgment, my Performances would

would have met with a more universal Approbation; while others censure them not so much for introducing Divine Subjects, but for treating them in too Technical a way, that is, by coming too near the Manner proper to the Gown, and the Air of the Pulpit. To the first I make this Reply, That the Books which gave Offence to some, by having too high a Seasoning of Religion in general, and too strong a Taste of Christian Sentiments, were the Epick Poems which I have given to the Publick.

But if Gentlemen would reflect and enter into the Nature of an Epick Poem, they would soon be convinc'd that Pious and Divine Subjects are essential and necessary to this sublime Species of Poetry, which was invented and constituted for the Praise and Honour of the Gods and God-like Men, to celebrate the admirable

mirable Works and Perfections of the one, and the great Atchievements and beneficial Inventions of the other. *Homer*'s *Iliad* and *Ulysses* are at least as full of the Heathen, as my Poems are of the Christian Theology; yet I never heard he was censur'd for introducing Divine Subjects and Actors; tho for transgressing the Bounds of Decency and Probability in the Conduct of his Machines, he has been condemn'd.

The essential Character of *Virgil*'s *Hero*, is Piety; and lest you should not discover it by his Actions, he frequently tells you so himself, *Sum Pius Æneas*, *I am pious Æneas*. If then the principal Quality of the Hero may be Piety, the Poet will be oblig'd through his whole Work, to exhibit him to the Reader under that Idea; which cannot be done, but by introducing him
always

always speaking and acting in such a divine Manner, as keeps up the uniformity of the Character in which he first appear'd: And this *Virgil* has for the most part observ'd, and where at any Time he has neglected to do so, he has transgress'd an indispensable Rule of Epick Poetry. Now should any Poet in this Age, in imitation of *Virgil*, chuse to celebrate a Hero under the Idea of Pious, must he not represent him as such, and make his Poem all over Religious? And if it fell out that this Poet was a Christian, and wrote in a Country where that Institution was establish'd, must he not acquit himself according to his own Scheme of Theology, as the ancient Poets wrote according to theirs? *Homer* and *Virgil* writ up to the full Measure of Divine Knowledge which they had acquir'd, and in conformity to the Notions of Religion which then obtain'd

The Preface.

tain'd in the World; and by a parity of Reason, a Christian Poet is oblig'd to observe the same Rule. But I shall dismiss this Subject here, and not anticipate the Positions I have advanc'd in the following Essay on Epick Poetry.

I am conscious that three sorts of Persons have been displeas'd with my Writings upon the Account before-mention'd; the Impious in Principle, that denies the Divine Being; the Unbeliever, who renounces the Christian Institution; and the Libertine, who professes his Belief of that reveal'd Religion, but refuses Obedience to its Precepts.

As to the first, it is to me an unaccountable Paradox why an Atheist, to whom all Religions are alike, should not be as well entertain'd with the Beauties of a Poem contriv'd according

cording to the Christian, as of one that is written upon the Plan of the Heathen Theology. But the Infidel, who disclaims the Belief of Divine Revelation, while he asserts the Existence of a Deity, has, I acknowledge, Reason to dislike and decry the Poems that are form'd upon the Scheme of the Christian Institution; for that being in his Judgment an imaginary and groundless System, he looks upon himself oblig'd to oppose it with his utmost Efforts: And this, perhaps, is the true Reason, why many Gentlemen cannot bear the Introduction of Christian Machines into Heroick Works, nor the Mixture of that Religion in any other Species of Poetry; but insist with great Vehemence, that let Poets be ever so much Christians in their Opinion and Practice, they ought however to be Pagans in their Writings; and not to take their Machines,

The PREFACE. xvii

chines, or borrow their Ornaments from that Theology which they believe to be true, but from that which they are sure is false; becaufe in that, say they, a Poet may shine, but must be very heavy in the other. Admirable Reasoning! who can resist the Force of such a clear and convincing way of arguing?

As to the third sort, it is at first View surprizing that any Man, who owns the Truth of the Christian Institution, should disrelish any Performance on this Account, that it is design'd to promote the Honour of that Religion which he himself professes; but if we search the Matter deeper, the reason of this will appear very evident; many, who acknowledge the Divine Authority of Revelation, have no Taste of the Vertues enjoyn'd by it, but live in open Defiance and Contradiction to its Laws,

that

that is, they believe like Christians but act like Atheists, they cannot therefore read a Writing with satisfaction, which causes in their Minds uneasy Reflections, and upbraids them with the great dissimilitude and difformity between their Profession and their Actions; upon this account they deride the Works of Gentlemen which recommend Piety and Vertue, as Cant and Hypocrisy, and give them the Name of *Preaching*, which in their Opinion is an ignominious Term, and very unbecoming the Character of a Christian Gentleman.

But, I have another Reply to the above-mention'd Objection, namely, that I look upon it as an Expence of Time, for which I should not be able to account, if the Propagation of just Notions of Religion, and a Conformity of Manners to such Notions, were not the

prin-

The PREFACE.

principal End that engag'd me in Writing; were I ever so capable of the Province, I should not esteem it a valuable Consideration for my Labour, only to entertain the Fancies of Men with Wit, and make them laugh with facetious Conceits. To communicate to the Minds of others noble and elevated Ideas, to inspire them with pious Ardor and Divine Passions, and push them on to a vigorous Resolution of engaging and persevering in a Series of vertuous Actions, becoming the Dignity of their Nature and the Precepts of their Religion, is a praiseworthy Province; for this is to be employ'd about the most excellent Objects for the Attainment of the most important Ends; and I would chuse rather in this Sense to be the Author of Good, tho but to ten Persons, than by the happiest strains of Wit and the most pleasant Humour to divert and recreate ten Thousand; notwithstanding I were sure to make many Enemies by the first, and by the last to gain universal Applause. It was for this reason I began to write, and shall be well pleas'd to die with my Pen in my Hand, asserting the Honour of the Divine Being and the Interest of Mankind, which I know I am doing while I vindicate the Cause of Religion and Vertue. I have been impell'd by a disinterested and undesigning Principle to engage on the Side I have taken, and if I had entertain'd any indirect and mean Views, I should have chosen other ways to accomplish my End, than by Writing on such Subjects and in such a manner, that I was well assur'd would draw upon me the Resentments of great Numbers of no inconsiderable Figure. These Gentlemen should, however, be induc'd

The PREFACE.

duc'd to pardon a well-meant Zeal; while to do them the highest Service, by setting their Judgments right in a Matter of the greatest Concern, I have adventur'd to incur their Displeasure, whose Favour and Countenance might have done me Honour, protected my Reputation, and promoted my Interest: It is because I as really wish their Felicity as I do my own, that I attempt to cure their erroneous Principles, which, if not rectify'd, must be attended with the most fatal Consequence.

Being fully convinc'd that no solid Satisfaction can be attain'd, but that which arises from a consciousness of doing Good, and the expectation of a Future Reward, and (it is with great Satisfaction that I certainly foresee that all Men living, whatever they think now,

now, will in a short Time be of the same Opinion) I shall still employ what Capacities I have, and for which I am accomptable, in pursuit of the same Ends to which I have all along directed my Aim; and if for adhering stedfast to the Divine Cause of Religion I am vilify'd by Gentlemen of impious or unchristian Maxims, I am so hard and impenitent that I shall still endeavour to be viler, being ambitious to merit their Displeasure to a greater Degree, and recommend my self yet more to their Contempt.

The more I advance in Years, and the nearer the Future State is presented to my View, the more I am pleas'd with reflecting on what I have written on Divine and Moral Subjects; and whatever Appellation of Reproach Men of pleasantry Humour think fit to give
to

The PREFACE. xxiii

to this Difpofition of Mind, they cannot enjoy fo great Satisfaction in deriding it, as the Poffeffion of it gives to me. Tho I defpair of changing the Judgments of the determin'd and inflexible Leaders of Impiety, yet I am not without hopes of being ufeful to younger Men, who are only wavering and unfettled in their Opinions, or in whofe Minds loofe and unchriftian Principles are not deeply rooted.

THIS was always look'd upon as a good natur'd Nation, well difpos'd to Religion and receptive of vertuous Impreffions; and tho one cannot without Aftonifhment fee the wonderful Progrefs that Profanenefs and Immorality have made among us, yet I flatter my felf that it is but an acute and temporary Diftemper, being fo much againft the native Conftitution of the People, that I hope is still strong enough to throw off by degrees this malignant Ferment, which if it be unable to do, the Event muſt be deplorable. We cannot but be ſenſible how much we owe our preſent Sufferings and Calamities to the prevailing Power of Irreligion and Vice, that have in ſo terrible a degree over-ſpread a Kingdom once renown'd for Piety and ſober Life; and if I am not miſtaken, ſhould impious Maxims and their genuine Fruit, diſſolute Manners, which Heaven avert, be carry'd yet to a greater Height, and ſpread their unreſtrain'd Influence to a greater extent, the Conſequence, to our ſad Experience, will prove deſtructive. But I ſhall not enlarge on this Head, intending to publiſh a Diſcourſe, in which I ſhall trace the Origin of Atheiſm, and deduce the Succeſſion of its Aſſertors and Patrons through

every

The Preface.

every Age to thefe Times. I fhall make it appear, that Impiety has a direct tendency to fubvert the Foundations of all human Societies, and expofe the falfe Reafoning of Mr. *Bayle,* who maintains the contrary Opinion.

Besides, let Gentlemen of Irreligious Principles reflect on the freedom which they themfelves ufe: Have they a Right to deride and affront Religion? fo have I to defend its Honour: Are they at liberty to profelite Chriftians to Paganifm? fo am I to convert Pagans to Chriftianity: In maintaining and fpreading their Opinions have they no unwarrantable Ends in view, no Vanity, no irregular Paffions, no voluptuous Appetites to gratify? I am compell'd to boaft, no more have I. Seeing then they believe they are privileg'd to expofe Religion and

and Vertue among their Acquaintance, for the Peace and Happiness of the Nation; for that, as they pretend, is the Mark at which they aim; why should I offend by asserting religious Maxims and the Divine Authority of the Christian Institution, the establish'd Worship of the Country where I live, which I look upon as so conducive to the Publick Good, that without their Assistance the strongest Pillars of Civil Communities must be destroy'd.

If it be said that there is a venerable Order of Men appropriated to this sacred Office, of instructing the People in the Notions of Religion, and persuading them to yield Obedience to Moral and Christian Obligations; and that therefore it is owing to a presumptuous Curiosity, that I have taken a Fancy to trouble

ble my self about Affairs of this nature; I answer, that notwithstanding there is such an establish'd Order separated from secular Employment to attend the Service of the Altar, of whom many by their excellent Labours and exemplary Lives have propagated Religion, adorn'd the Church, and been the Authors of great Good to their Country; yet that does not hinder but others, who have competent Talents, may employ them in their Station, for the Instruction and Improvement of Mankind in Piety and Moral Goodness. It is every Man's Duty in his private Sphere, as well as the Divine in his publick and more extensive Capacity, to promote religious Knowledge and a Love of Vertue; but let it be consider'd, that notwithstanding the venerable Clergy are appropriated to this Province, yet many eminent Persons of that
Order

Order have in all Times believ'd, that without any sacrilegious Violation of their holy Function, they might alienate a great part of their Lives from the Service of the Church, to which they are consecrated, while they attended on secular Affairs: Many have held great Offices of State, and many have been Publick Ministers in foreign Countries, and several have for many Years in other Employments discontinu'd the Duties of their sacred Calling, and have nevertheless preserv'd, at least in their own Opinion, their indelible Character; and not a few of the Reverend Clergy give their Neighbours Advice in Cases of Physick and Law, as well as in those of Conscience. Now if the Guides of the Church condescend to take such Care of our Welfare in secular Concerns, why may not a Lay-man, in his Turn, express his Gratitude and

Good-

Good-will by serving the Church in Matters of Religion. Besides, it should be consider'd, that a Gentleman has this one Advantage over the Clergy, That when he writes for the Instruction and Improvement of the People in Religion and Vertue, he is look'd upon as undesigning and disinterested; and it cannot be suspected that he writes for a Party, or that he is Mercenary, and aims at Riches and Promotion.

For my farther Vindication it may be alledg'd, that in the Pagan World before the Christian Revelation, *Pythagoras*, *Socrates*, *Plato*, *Plutarch*, *Cicero*, and all the eminent Writers on Divine and Moral Subjects were learned Men, not consecrated to the Service of the Temple; and after the Christian Worship was instituted, many Lay-

Lay-Profeſſors of it, in the Primitive Times, as well as Multitudes in the Modern, have, with great Approbation and Applauſe, vindicated the Truth of their Religion, and promoted the Intereſts of Vertue by their valuable Labours. How many, beſides the Clergy, have given to the Publick Expoſitions on the Sacred Volumes, as well as Moral and Divine Contemplations, which are receiv'd with great Eſteem; nor did I ever hear, that any Gentleman has been condemn'd for Writing on ſuch Subjects, how many ſo ever have been cenſur'd for not Writing well.

As to the ſecond Objection mention'd at the beginning of this Diſcourſe, That when I introduce Divine Subjects, I am too Technical, and do not obſerve the faſhionable Stile of a Gentleman, but approach too

too near to the manner of the Gown;
I must own, that if some of my former Writings have been obnoxious to this Censure, I have reason to apprehend that many Places in the following ESSAYS will lie more expos'd to that critical Observation, and therefore I shall here make the same Apology for the one and the other. It will appear to the judicious Reader, that I have not imitated the Method, nor us'd the Phrases appropriated to the Discourses of the Reverend Clergy and the Eloquence of the Pulpit, but have vary'd the one, and frequently cast the other into different Forms of Diction; but if the Objectors mean, that I am too warm and appear too much in earnest, that I affect the Language of the Heart, and do not strive to please the Imagination with delicate Touches, spriteful

ful Turns of Expreffion, and new Speculations which only hover in the Brain, without finking deep enough to difturb the Reader with uneafy Reflections, excite Divine Paffions, and produce generous Refolutions to engage in the Practice of Vertue; if, I fay, the Objectors mean that this is the way of Writing becoming a Gentleman, I freely acknowledge that I do not aim at that Honour; I am not ambitious of the Character of a Polite but a ufeful Writer; which I imagine I cannot be, if under the Confinements before-mention'd.

I HAVE heard a Clergy-man cenfur'd for faying, that he look'd upon it as a very uncivil Thing for a Divine in the Pulpit to fcare the Audience by mentioning Damnation, Hell, and other fuch Terms of Horror. This fine Orator muft furely surely think that the rude and boisterous way of Preaching, in which the Words and Phrases of the Sacred Writings are employ'd, ought to be left off by polite and well-manner'd Christians; and that notwithstanding the Apostles, who were rough and unrefin'd, and had little Taste of Elegance, good Breeding, and ingenious Conversation, might be allow'd such harsh and frightful Expressions, yet they would not become a modern civiliz'd Pulpit. Nevertheless one would think, that since these Men acknowledge that the Primitive Planters of Christianity were directed by an infallible Spirit, they should not be mistaken in the Nature of Evangelical Eloquence, and the right Art of Perswasion, and therefore that it would be a pardonable Condescention in such an accomplish'd Preacher if he thought fit to follow the Examples of Men under the Guidance of Divine Inspiration.

Mankind by their inbred Propensions, strengthen'd and improv'd by a Series of evil Actions, are so strongly prepossess'd in favour of forbidden Enjoyments, and so much prejudic'd against the disagreeable Practice of Vertue, while the Exercise of their Reason is suspended or corrupted, that the soft and gentle Persuasions and well-bred Address of a meer elegant Writer will make no more Impression on their Minds, than the Descent of a Feather upon the Ground, or a gentle Breeze upon a Rock. If a Man has a mind to combat Profaneness and Immorality, Enemies not easy to be vanquish'd, he must be furnish'd with Arms that will cut as well as glitter; and he might as well enter the Lists quite naked, as

pro-

The Preface.

provided only with bright but edge-less Weapons.

It is certain, that those do engage in a worthy and generous Design, who endeavour to reclaim Persons of disorderly and profligate Behaviour, and to make Vice appear so dangerous and detestable that it may be abhor'd, and Vertue so amiable, that it may exert its attractive Force and invite Mankind to the Practice of it: But then this is a Province attended with so many and great Difficulties, that setting aside the indispensable Obligations of Reason and Christian Charity, it would not be so discreet and prudent, as it is Heroick and Honourable to attempt it, while the Approaches to the Understandings of Men are generally so bar'd and guarded against Instruction, that for the most part they are inaccessible.

But notwithstanding it is a melancholy Truth, that the Depravity of Human Nature is so great that it is a very difficult Task to undertake the Cure, yet to give over Mankind as deplorable and uncapable of Moral Improvements is to carry the Matter too far: It is true, that Princes have the most effectual and extensive Power for this purpose, and the venerable Clergy, who are abstracted from the World, disengag'd from secular Employments, and set apart to this high Calling, have, next to Princes, the greatest Capacity and Advantages to sink the Reputation of Vice, and propagate the Esteem and Love of Vertue; nevertheless, private Persons may, in their circumscrib'd Station, be useful in promoting Religion and Morality, tho not to so great a degree; and if they may be so, so, who can excuse them if they do not attempt it?

As to the Means of procuring this End I am of Opinion, that the ingenious and polite Discourses upon Divine Subjects, in which the Authors endeavour to dissuade Men from the Practice of Vice, by shewing the unreasonableness of its Nature, and representing in a handsome manner, the Temporal Inconveniencies that attend it, as the loss of Honour, Health, and Riches, tho ever so elegant and entertaining, are not sufficient to reform a loose Age and recover the Power and Reputation of Divine Vertues. Degenerate Man has such a native Indisposition and Reluctance to the Practice of Religion, that in this respect he is often represented in sacred and profane Writings under the figurative Idea of a dead Person. Now is it in any degree probable, that such Men should owe a new Life and moral Resurrection to Discourses on religious Subjects, which, tho correct and polite, are wrote in a cold didactick and impassionate manner, and therefore never shake the false Notions and Prepossessions of the Offender; never awaken him with the Prospect of his Danger, nor work him up to a Resolution of parting with his forbidden Enjoyments. I acknowledge I cannot see any harm in these Discourses, wherein the Writers, besides their beautiful and ornamental Stile, have this peculiar Character of the Gentleman, that they make no body uneasy, but with great Tenderness and Caution avoid all Sentiments and harsh Expressions, that are likely to alarm and disturb the Criminal; nor can I discern their usefulness farther, than that they please and entertain.

THE inveterate Diseases of the Mind are as hard to be remov'd as those of the Body; and therefore their Cure requires as sharp and painful Applications. Will a Man in a profound Lethargy be awaken'd with Whispers and soft Musick, that can sleep in a Storm, and is undisturb'd with Thunder? Will a violent Fever yield to the Art of the Confectioner, after the Skill of the Physician is in vain exhausted? Or must a Surgeon who is employ'd to heal a mortifying Limb and stop the spreading Gangrene, be disarm'd of his cutting Instruments and corrosive Medicines, and be permited only to sooth the Suffering Part with scented Waters and pleasant Balsams? Is it likely that an immoral Person should become the Convert of a genteel Satire or an elegant Harangue, who is deaf and inexorable

able to the Tears and Entreaties of his Relations, and perseveres in his expensive Vices till he has finish'd the Ruin of his disconsolate Family? Is it credible, that a dissolute Youth that has given the Reins to his inordinate Appetites, and plung'd himself in forbidden Pleasures, should be reclaim'd by the Power of a polite offenceless Performance, who is not prevail'd upon by the terrible Consequences of his criminal Enjoyments? Can the Stings of Satire, and the Reproaches of a Man of Wit, pierce deeper into his Heart, than those of Remorse and conscious Reflection, and the painful Sense of wasting Diseases, the sad Fruits of his vicious Courses?

To conclude this Head. I am convinc'd that Discourses on Divine and Moral Subjects, let them be the Productions of ever so fine Imagination

The Preface.

nation and admirable Genius, and ever so valuable for Purity of Words, beautiful Expression, accurate Stile, and worthy Sentiments, if the Author does not strive to penetrate the Heart, and by the only prevalent Arguments taken from the endless Misery that attends the Practice of Vice in a Future Life; if he does not grapple and contend with the Criminal, and set his Danger before him in a strong Light, so as to disturb him in his presumptuous Opinions, wrest from him his false Hopes, and fill his Mind with just Fear of Divine Punishment, those Discourses, I say, must be unavailing, being incompetent and unequal to their End. It is evident, that the Menaces of Divine Displeasure and unspeakable Sufferings in a Future State, tho they prevail upon some, yet are ineffectual and unoperative upon the generality of Mankind; and therefore all other

other Means whatever that are employ'd to perſuade Men to be vertuous, which are infinitely of leſs force than thoſe, muſt certainly be fruitleſs and inſignificant.

And here I think it not improper to take Notice, that ſince all ſupream Magiſtrates guard their Laws by the Sanction of Puniſhment, by which they aim to ſecure the Obedience of the Subject, and in ſuch a proportion as they judge ſufficient to attain their End, the Divine Legiſlator of the World, by annexing to his Laws eternal Sufferings to deter Men from Diſobedience, has not exceeded a juſt Meaſure, ſince in Fact it ſadly appears that thoſe Puniſhments are inſufficient to prevail with the greateſt Part of Mankind to obey his Will; and therefore it is too evident that this threaten'd Penalty does not ſurpaſs a due

The Preface.

due Proportion; for whatever Means are too weak to acquire their End, cannot be said to be immoderate and excessive.

As to the following Essays, having prefix'd a particular Preface to that upon Epick Poetry, I shall in this Place, only admonish the Reader, that having laid down the Rules relating to a Writing of that Kind, I forbore to add many Examples out of the celebrated ancient and modern Poets, which might have illustrated and confirm'd those Precepts, lest the Essay should have swell'd to a larger Extent than I thought was proper to such a Writing, and by being prolix and diffus'd should have grown tedious, and perhaps it is too much so already.

Notwithstanding the unsuccefsful Efforts of Perfons of all Denominations, to ftop the licentious Tide of Impiety and Vice might, with Reafon, difcourage private Perfons from making any future Attempts, yet I am fo hardy as not utterly to defpair of being beneficial to the Nation by purfuing that Defign. I have therefore in my Essay upon Wit, reviv'd my old Controverfy with the Stage; the Entertainments of which, as they are ftill manag'd, are highly prejudicial to the Interefts of Religion and Vertue, as having an apparent tendency to produce profane Principles and Corruption of Manners. My chief Objection is againft the Comick Poems, for the Tragick are become for the moft Part, not only clean and inoffenfive, but in fome Inftances inftructive and ufeful, efpecially

Tamer-

The PREFACE.

Tamerlane, *Cato*, and the Lady *Jane Grey*; which besides their other great Beauties, abound with excellent Moral and Divine Sentiments. I have in the following Essay upon Wit, show'd how that Talent is abus'd and prostituted to unworthy Purposes in Dramatick Performances, and what a pernicious Influence it must needs have while so employ'd, on the Minds and Actions of Men. I know it is alledg'd in Defence of our Comedies, that they are proper to expose the Fool, and reform the Libertine, to recommend Decency and Vertue, and put Foppery and Immorality out of Countenance. But as to the Correction of Vice and propagating Sobriety of Manners, it is evident by long Experience, that it has not that Effect in any degree, and indeed it is not an adequate and competent Means for that End.

IF general Discourses, as I have shown on the Beauty and Benefits of Vertue, and the Turpitude and Inconveniences of Vice, that only float on the Surface of the Brain and please the Imagination, but do not warm the Heart and excite generous and Divine Passions, let them be writ with ever so much Elegance and Dignity, are insignificant, as being uncapable to reclaim a dissolute People; can it be thought that our modern Comedies will be more effectual?

IF the greatest Danger imaginable set before Men in the fullest View, and the most pathetick and importunate Manner will not deter them from Vice, what can we expect that Jest and Ridicule should do? These are not a Match for the criminal Inclinations

clinations of Nature ripen'd into Habits, and confirm'd by long Custom.

Tho a well writ Comedy may not only become an agreeable Diversion, and in some measure beneficial, by correcting the Indecencies and exposing the Follies and inferior Faults of Mankind; yet the Comick Poet must have a very sanguine Complexion, that can hope with such feeble and unequal Weapons, to triumph over Vice and Immorality. To endeavour to cure an Age over-spread with degenerate and licentious Manners by such ways, is to express great Ignorance of Human Nature, and the Power of inordinate Appetites. One may as well charge a Gyant with a Bull-rush, or play upon a Conflagration with a Syringe, as attempt to make a wise and vertuous

tuous Nation with pleasant Humour and facetious Fancies.

I do not believe that the most celebrated Comedies, how much soever they have entertain'd the Audience, have reduc'd any Libertine, or improv'd any Coxcomb. Let the famous Author of the *Tatlers* and *Spectators* declare his Experience, who, if Wit could have made Men wiser, must certainly have succeeded; that Gentleman says, in one of his Discourses, *I have many Readers, but few Converts*; I believe he might have said none: For it is my Opinion, that all his fine Raillery and Satire, tho admirable in their kind, never reclaim'd one vicious Man, or made one Fool depart from his Folly.

The Preface.

As to the Essay upon False Vertue, when I reflect that loose Principles and diffolute Manners, have spread to Astonishment, their malignant Contagion among the People, and have so far prevail'd, that in a great degree the essential Dissimilitude of good and bad Actions is effac'd in the Minds of Men, and Vertue and Vice begin to look kind and friendly upon one another, as if they had compromis'd their old Disputes, and had brought their Controversy to an amicable Conclusion; while the reputed Atheist and the Christian, the Libertine and the sober Man, the dissolute Woman and one of unblemish'd Reputation, shall caress each other, freely converse together, mutually make and receive Visits with all the Marks of Respect and Friendship, and communicate with one another in the most

sacred

sacred and awful Mysteries of our Religion; while I contemplated, I say, this amazing Degeneracy, I concluded that Vice and Immorality had lost their intrinsick Deformity, and wip'd off their moral Turpitude in the general Opinion of the People; and therefore I cannot but think, that it is a commendable Undertaking to attempt the Correction of a Mistake of such Consequence.

Men of irreligious Principles and loose Behaviour, have sometimes told their Acquaintance in Conversation, that they could not believe they were sincere and in good Earnest, when they profess'd their Belief of the Christian Institution, and have express'd their Reasons in this manner; Were it our stedfast Opinion, that the Doctrines and Precepts, as well as the Sanction of

end

The Preface.

endless Pain and Misery contain'd in the Christian System, were establish'd by the Authority of Divine Revelation, we would feed on Bread and Water, despise Wealth and Power, and renounce the most tempting Enjoyments that gratify our Senses, rather than indulge our selves in the Practice of the most pleasant Sins: And it is so agreeable to the Instincts of Nature and the Dictates of Reason, rather to forbear a transient Satisfaction, than to expose one's self to Divine Wrath and Everlasting Sufferings; that we cannot imagine how it is possible that you should really assent to the Truth of Christianity, and yet live a Life so repugnant to your Creed. This is indeed a smart and cutting Expostulation; and but two Things can be alledg'd in Answer to it; one is this, That many sincerely assent, tho in a low and unprevailing Degree, to the Truth of the Christian Institution; but their Belief is so much born down and over-power'd by the criminal Propensions of corrupt Nature and evil acquir'd Habits, that their Actions bear no Conformity to the Rules of the Religion which they profess. Another is, that many have such crude and erroneous Notions of the Nature of Christian Virtues and their opposite Vices, that tho they really act in contradiction to their Religion, yet they are not conscious of that Inconsistency, and do not know that they are Christians only in Name, and not in Reality; and therefore to convince them of the Absurdity of their Sentiments on a Subject of this Importance, I have endeavour'd in this ESSAY, to set the Matter in a true Light; where I have demonstrated, that the Essence of Moral

ral Goodness and the Divine Simplicity of Religion, consist in the Rectitude of the Intellectual Faculties, and the predominant Purity of the Heart, whence Streams of beautiful and praise-worthy Actions constantly flow, which have no genuine Vertue in themselves, let the Matter of them be ever so shining, but what they derive from their inward Fountain.

I HAVE already laid down this Position, That it is in vain to persuade a bad Person to correct his Life and become a vertuous Man, that is, one who acts from a Principle of Obedience to the Divine Being, and conforms himself to his unwritten and reveal'd Laws, with a Prospect of acquiring his perfect Happiness in the Fruition of his Creator, which is the essential and distinguishing Character of a good Man,

The Preface.

Man, by any other Motives and Arguments than what are drawn from a Future State of Felicity or Misery. It is true, that some Persons are reclaim'd from vicious and destructive Practices, by the Consideration of the Inconveniences and evil Consequences that attend them in respect of themselves and their Families; and many more do the same from a Change of Taste that happens in the different Periods of Life, our Relish of Satisfaction and Pleasure being various in Youth, Manhood, and old Age; but if their better Course of Life and Sobriety of Manners do not spring from that Divine Principle and Regular End above describ'd, they cannot be denominated Good Men. Their degenerate Nature continues the same, and tho the Object is chang'd, their evil Inclinations are unalter'd; and their Actions, tho for the Matter

The Preface.

ter of them, they make a much better Appearance, are no more in reality vertuous than those before. For this Reason I have, in the Essay upon the Immortality of the Soul, endeavour'd to evince the Certainty of a Future State of endless Happiness or Sufferings, as being fully assur'd that no Motives of less Weight will prevail with Men to correct an irregular Life: And I hope I have establish'd this Article by such full and clear Evidence, that it will be acknowledg'd by every impartial Reader who will attentively exercise his Reason upon this matter, in which his Interest is so much concern'd.

In the Dissertation on the Laws of Nature, I have drawn the Discourse into as close a room as so copious a Theme will admit, if the Perspicuity of the Stile, the natural Depen-

Dependance and Connexion of the Conclusions, and the convincing Force of the Evidence are preserv'd : and for that Reason I have forborn to cite Opinions of many celebrated Writers upon that Subject, particularly *Suarez*, *Grotius*, and *Puffendorf*, who tho an Author by many admir'd, is to me often disagreeable and uninstructive, because of his Obscurity and the Confusion of his Ideas. Should I have enter'd into a Dispute with these great Writers, and attempted to lay open their Defects, and confute their erroneous Positions, I should not only have interrupted the Thread of my Discourse, and disappointed my Design of exhibiting in one View, to the Reader, an entire Scheme of my Opinions, but I must likewise have extended it to a greater Length than I thought proper for an ESSAY.

AND

And for the same Reason in the Discourse upon the ORIGIN of CIVIL POWER, I have not mention'd the Notions of many Learned Authors, which are contrary to mine, that I might not embroil my self in Controversy, and grow uneasy to the Reader by numerous Citations.

THE CONTENTS.

I.

AN Essay *on the* Nature *and* Constitution *of* Epick-Poetry.

The Preface.	Pag. iii
——*Of* Probability.	24
——*Of the* Marvellous.	33
——*Of the* Fable.	37
——*Of the* Allegory.	41
——*Of the* Unity.	47
——*Of the* Importance *of the* Action.	48
——*Of the* Episodes.	52
——*Of* Integrity.	59
——*Of the* Duration.	61
——*Of the* Machines.	63
——*Of the* Dignity *of the* Narration.	75

—*Of*

The Contents,

———*Of the* Moral. 76
———*Of the* Characters. 82
A Comparison between Epick Poetry *and* Tragedy. 85

SECTION. II.

———*of the* Sublime Stile. 93
———*Of the* Sublimity *of* Thoughts. 94
———*Of the* Choice *of* Words. 97
———*Of the* Ranging *of the* Words. 108
———*Of the* Versification. 111
———*Of Cool and Sedate* Figures. 120
Of Amplifications, Descriptions, *and* Similitudes. 134
———*Of Pathetick* Figures. 140
An Appendix. 156
An Account of the present Controversy concerning Homer's Iliad. 157

The Contents.

II.

An Essay *upon* Wit.   189
    The Definition *of* Wit.   191
Its Efficient Cause.   193
The End and *Usefulness* of this Ingenious Qualification.   200
Of the *Abuse* of Wit.   203
The *Immorality of the* Stage.   218
A Method propos'd for its Reformation.   229

III.

An Essay *upon* False Vertue.   239
    Instances of False Vertue.   245
Of the Desire of Glory *that most resembles* True Vertue.   261
A closer Enquiry into the Distinction of True *and* False Vertue.   268
Of Vertue *arising from Fear of Punishment.*   281

IV.

The Contents.

IV.

An Essay *upon the* Immortality *of the* Soul. — 293

——*The* Immortality *of the* Soul, *demonstrated from natural Arguments.* — 303

Of Moral Arguments. — 329

Objections against the Soul's Immortality. — 344

Answer'd. — 350

V.

An Essay *upon the* Laws *of* Nature. — 355

The Laws of Nature, *how promulgated.* — 371

Of Moral Obligations *respecting our selves.* — 384

Of Moral Obligations *in respect to our Neighbour.* — 408

Of

The Contents.

of Relative Duties *from one Subject to another.* 410

VI.

An Essay *upon the* Origin *of* Civil Power. 423

Moral Obligations *on Civil Powers.* 438

Of Obedience *due from Subjects.* 441

ERRATA.

PAGE vii. of the Preface, Line 1. for *Cornishes*, read *Cornices*. p. xxii. l. 23. *leave out* Humour. p. 15. l. 21. of the Essays, for *Tast* read *cast*. p. 18. l. 15. for *varius* r. *Varius*. p. 30. l. 26. for *who* r. *and*. p. 72. l. 18. for *their own Religion* r. *his own*. p. 74. l. 18. instead of, *as if*, r. *as it would be if*. p. 110. l. 12. for *as* r. *and*. p. 129. l. 2. for *abuse* r. *amuse*. p. 130. l. 21. for *intending* r. *intended*. p. 133. l. 2. for *been* r. *be*. p. 152. l. 24. leave out *also*. p. 157. l. 14. for *any new Notions* r. *any Notions*. p. 174. l. 4. leave out *in* before *which*. p. 172. l. 8. after *the Sacred Writings*, add, *cited before*. p. 191. l. 11. for *or* r. *of*. p. 297. l. 7. for *Foundation* r. *Foundations*. p. 303. l. 25. for *Conversation* r. *Conservation*. p. 331. l. 16. after *the Philosopher said well*, add, *as is mention'd in another Essay*. p. 334. l. 19. after *Divine Goodness* r. *and Wisdom*. p. 366. l. 14. for *evil Things* r. *evil of Things*. p. 409. l. 22. after *Guilt* r. *and which proceeds*.

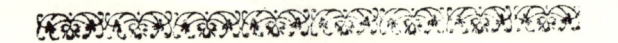

AN ESSAY ON THE NATURE AND *CONSTITUTION* OF EPICK POETRY.

THE
PREFACE.

AFTER the Ruin of the Grecian and Roman Empires, under whose Protection the Arts and Sciences had long flourish'd, Polite Literature soon languish'd, and at length became universally neglected. It continu'd in this State during the unrefined Ages, in which the Colleges of Europe *were entirely taken up in studying* Aristotle's *dry Philosophy, and the uninstructive Speculations of the dark School-men; till in the Reign of Pope* Leo *the Tenth, a generous Patron of Letters and Ingenuity, it began to revive and get ground. About this Time, among other* Greek *Authors, the Springs whence the* Romans *and the* Italians, *their Successors, deriv'd their Learning,* Aristotle's *Book of Poetry publish'd by* Victorius *at* Florence, *stir'd*

PREFACE.

up Men of Genius and Lovers of Science, to enquire, for their own Improvement and the Instruction of others, into the Notions and Rules of that great Master, especially those that related to the sublime manner of Writing. Soon after rose up many Criticks in this Art, of whom the most eminent were, Vida, Castelvetro, *and* Paul Beni. *Nor could this curious and inquisitive Spirit be confin'd to* Italy, *it soon pass'd the* Alps, *and entring* France, *excited the Natives of Poetical Inclinations and Capacity, to imitate their ingenious Neighbours; and these, to their Honour, carry'd on the Critical Knowledge of Epick Poetry to a greater Height, especially the two Fathers* Rapin *and* Boffu; *the last of whom has excell'd all the Masters, who had writ on that Subject before him.*

IT must be acknowledg'd, that till about forty Years ago, Great Britain *was barren of Critical Learning, tho' fertile in excellent Writers; and in particular, had so little Taste of Epick Poetry, and were so unacquainted with the essential Properties and peculiar Beauties of it, that* Paradise Loft, *an admirable Work of that kind, publish'd by Mr.* Milton, *the great Ornament of his Age and Country, lay many Years unspoken of, and entirely disregarded, till at length it happen'd, that some Persons of greater Delicacy and Judgment found*

PREFACE.

found out the Merit of that excellent Poem; and, by communicating their Sentiments to their Friends, propagated the Esteem of the Author, who soon acquir'd universal Applause. This Curiosity spreading among Persons of Poetical Genius and Critical Taste, and animated by the Treatise of Bossu *on Epick Poetry, which about this Time was brought over from* France, *the finer Spirits of the Age began to enquire into the Nature and Qualities of it, and enter'd much farther into this Subject, than the Grammarians and Commentators had done before; who only hover'd on the Surface, but never ventur'd into the Depths of Heroick Poetry. Now it was that Mr.* Dryden *adorn'd several of his Discourses in Prose, by interspersing various useful Observations on this Subject. Mr.* Rymer *at the same time publish'd his judicious Remarks on Epick Compositions, together with his more copious Dissertation on Tragedy. Not long after, the Appearance of Prince* Arthur *increas'd this growing Ferment, by ingaging the Poets and Criticks to exercise their Reflection on this kind of Writing, that they might be qualify'd, as they favour'd the Author and his Design, to sink or support the Reputation of the Poem. In the Preface to that Poem, I have given a Draught of this Species of Poetry in little; which however, I imagine, exhibits the intrinsick Nature and essential Properties of it in a*

B 3 *clear,*

clear, tho not a diffusive Light; and lately a judicious Critick, in his Discourses on Milton, *has deserv'd well of the Polite World, by his curious and rational Observations, which at once have advanc'd the Knowledge of Heroick Poetry, and given an excellent Example of the free Exercise of Reason in Criticism.*

SINCE that, a very laudable Translation of some Books of the Iliad, *with a Promise of the rest, and an accurate Edition of* Spenser's *Works have been publish'd, with Critical Remarks prefix'd by the ingenious Writers.*

BY this it appears, that this great and elevated manner of Writing is now study'd, and that at present the Epick Taste is in Fashion. Our Poets apply to this Subject from a Principle of Emulation; and whoever wishes well to Mankind, and desires the Honour of his Country, will encourage their Labours, and give to each his just share of Applause. Nor will the Contests among Poets themselves about Superiority have any ill Effect, if the Patrons of Polite Learning impartially divide their Favours among them, according to their Degree of Merit. This Race of Men are of a delicate and nice Complexion, full of Suspicion and Caprice, and as liable to be jealous of Competitors in Wit, as others are of Rivals in

Love;

PREFACE. vii

Love; *and therefore should be consider'd as Poets, and be indulg'd in their little private Contentions; for it can never be expected, that while they aim at the Laurel, they should look kindly on others who stand in their way.*

OUR Wits and Beauties, in which this Island does equally abound, will, I imagine, at the same time become Enemies to Envy and Detraction; will caress with sincere Friendship those of the same Rank, propagate the Opinion of their Merit, and take delight in each other's Reputation.

IT is remarkable, that about that Period of Time, when this Nation first express'd a greater Relish of Epick Poetry, they likewise began to taste the sublime Stile in Musick. We had, till now, contented our selves with light Tunes, and low familiar Airs, but now we aspire to higher Strains; we take Pleasure in Corelli's *Compositions for the Instrument, and* Buonancini's *for the Voice; and nothing will now please, but what has something of the great* Italian *Manner: And as these Tastes of elevated Poetry and Musick began together, so they have kept an equal Pace in their Progress.*

TO accommodate my self to the prevailing Inclination of the Times, and promote the generous Design on foot of improving the Criti-

cal *Knowledge of Epick Poetry*, which is a boundless Field of delightful Contemplation, I have given to the Publick the following Essay; in which I have enquir'd into the Nature and Constitution of this sublime kind of Writing; I have lightly touch'd those Subjects which have already been exhausted by other Pens, and have been copious only, where, as I hope, I have improv'd and strengthen'd by new Arguments and Illustrations the common Opinions, which I believe are just; or where I have endeavour'd to confute others, which, tho generally received, I look upon as erroneous.

AN
ESSAY
UPON
EPICK POETRY.

AFTER *Aristotle*'s School, in the eldest Times of Christianity, had prevail'd over *Plato*, and the Colleges of Learning had universally submitted to their new Master, soon was his Authority so well establish'd, that for many Centuries his Doctrines became uncontested, and were receiv'd as first Principles, that needed no Proof or Demonstration. During many succeeding Ages, the Learning of *Europe* consisted in the Knowledge of this Philosopher's Opinions; and those only were applaud-

applauded as eminent Scholars, who were the most laborious and skilful Commentators on his Writings. The voluminous Lucubrations of these idle Students, who only copy'd and expounded their Leader's Sentiments, which they follow'd with a blind Obedience, were esteem'd the only valuable Productions of Philosophy. At length arose some famous Worthies, who, animated by a generous Impulse to deliver *Europe* from the basest Servitude, that of the Understanding, attack'd *Aristotle* and his Adherents with great Vigour, declar'd against all arbitrary Impositions on the Mind, and asserted the Liberty of Reflection, and a Power of examining Evidence, and judging for themselves. These excellent Persons, who deserv'd so well of Mankind, by vindicating the Dignity of Humane Nature, and standing up for its Rights and Prerogatives, against the Usurpation of a particular Sect, having by an impartial Search discover'd that the Peripatetick System had nothing in it for its support, but precarious and unevident Principles, effectually expos'd its Weakness, and soon brought the greatest Authority, that was ever establish'd in the Schools, into general Contempt.

BUT

But when these extraordinary Men, by encouraging the free Exercise of Reason, had infus'd an active Ferment into the Minds of an ignorant and slothful Generation, by the Operation of which they were excited to throw off the Yoke of *Aristotle* in Matters of Philosophy, it is wonderful that the Effect was not more extensive. They had as great Reason to have proceeded to the Examination of his Rules in the Art of Poetry, and to have made Enquiry, if those were settled on better Foundations. But I know not how it came to pass, his Notions and Precepts in this Art have still remain'd unquestion'd and untry'd. The modern Criticks, contemning the Examples of the Philosophers, have still proceeded in the old beaten Track, of believing and admiring whatever *Aristotle* advances on the Subjects, where the Muses are concern'd. They are all like their submissive Predecessors, mere Expositors, scarce excepting *Bossu* himself, of the Writings of that great Man, and have made no Improvements, nor asserted the Liberty of Poetry, as the other freer Spirits have vindicated that of Philosophy. It's clear, that *Aristotle* form'd all his Axioms and Doctrines in Poetry, from the Patterns of *Homer* and other *Greek* Writers;

and,

and, without affigning any Reafon of his Pofitions, relies for the Truth of them on his own, or the Authority of thofe Authors. But it is not the Authority of the greateft Mafters, but folid and convincing Evidence, that muft engage our Belief, and make us fubfcribe to any Maxims in any Art or Science whatfoever.

I look upon *Ariftotle* as a great Genius, and a Perfon of more than common Erudition; but will no more fubmit to him as a Law-giver of the Poets, than of the Philofophers. I fhall always pay Refpect and Deference to his Judgment and Opinions, tho not acquiefce in them as infallible and decifive Decrees. And if Men, from a generous Principle of Liberty, would renounce the unjuft, tho prevailing Power of Authority, and claim their natural Right of entring into the Reafon of Things, and judging for themfelves, it is highly probable that the Art of Poetry might be carry'd on to greater Degrees of Perfection, and be improv'd, as Philofophy has been.

When thus unfetter'd and difingag'd from a flavifh Dependance upon celebrated Writers, Men would foon difregard the crude and unreafonable Affertions, frequently laid down by injudicious Commentators

mentators and superficial Grammarians, whose Attainments consist in a Collection of Examples, and an Ability to explain the *Roman* and *Grecian* Authors: Nor will a modern Heroick Work be any longer acquitted or condemn'd, merely as it bears a Conformity or Dissimilitude to the *Iliad* or the *Æneid*; but when future Criticks shall approve or censure an Epick Performance, they will produce clear Evidence from the Nature and Constitution of that kind of Poetry, to make good their Opinions; and not rely on the single Authority of ancient Writers, tho of the greatest Name, to support them: It will no more be allow'd an undeniable Proof of any Poet's erroneous and absurd Conduct, that he deviates from the Examples of *Homer* and *Virgil*; nor will it justify him in any Instance objected to his Writings, that he has the Practice of those excellent Poets to bear him out.

NEITHER is it sufficient to alledge, that *Aristotle* has express'd greater Judgment and Accuracy in his Discourses on Poetry, than in his Philosophical Productions; and therefore, tho the last, upon a just Tryal, have been exploded, yet the first have been esteem'd in all Ages by the Learned World as masterly Instructions, and continue

tinue undifputed to this Day; for this is ftill to prefs us only with the Authority of *Ariftotle* and his Commentators. If his Rules and Precepts of Poetry ought to be fo highly regarded, it muft be upon this Account, That ftronger Reafons can be produc'd in Defence of thefe, than of his Syftem of Natural Science: But how can this appear, if we take his Writings on the Art of Poetry upon Content, and do not by an impartial Examination make it clear, that the Evidence of Reafon is on their Side; which was wanting to fupport his Philofophy? And this, as far as I know, has not been attempted.

I would not be fo underftood, as if I condemn'd in general *Ariftotle*'s Rules of Poetry, and was about to fet up another Syftem of Opinions and Precepts in their room; my Purpofe is, to give them a fair Hearing, and if upon an impartial Tryal they appear to be built upon good Foundations, to confirm the Authority of the *Greek* Critick by the Force of Reafon. But, on the other hand, I fhall freely reject any Maxims, whether his, or thofe of his Commentators, which cannot be fupported by any Arguments of Weight and Solidity; and I fhall ufe the fame Liberty in adding any new Opinions on this Subject,

ject, which in my Judgment will improve the Art of Poetry. I have not, from a superstitious Veneration of Antiquity, that excessive regard for the Precepts of *Aristotle* and the Practice of *Homer*, as to receive them without Examination; for were they in every Instance just and right, as I believe they are in many, yet I am under no Obligation to submit to them, till they are demonstrated to be so by the Evidence of Reason. I must however acknowledge, that I have so great a Deference and Esteem for the Judgment of *Aristotle*, and the Examples of *Homer* and *Virgil*, that I shall not give them up, but where it is very clear, that they cannot be defended. Some Persons, whether out of a peculiar Curiosity of Taste, or Affectation of Learning, have all modern Productions in Contempt, and can relish nothing but what has an antique Taste and an Air of *Greece*. These would prefer a ruinous Wall, if part of an ancient tho mean Structure, to the most beautiful and magnificent Palace, if newly built. They look on the Fragments of an old Author as an inestimable Treasure, while they allow nothing tolerable that is lately written, unless it bears a Conformity to the Plans of former Ages.

OTHERS, on the contrary, have conceiv'd such a Disgust to the ancient Fathers of Learning, that they pay no respect to the Primitive Ages of Arts and Science; at least, they prefer all modern Productions in their several Kinds, to the most valuable Works of remote Writers. I shall endeavour to steer a middle Course between these Extreams.

I SHALL not enter into a Disquisition of *Aristotle*'s Rules in general, but content my self with a Discussion of those that relate to Epick Poetry; and, according to the Opinions which at present prevail among the *Aristotelian* Criticks, lay down the Definition of a Poem of that Species. To promote the free Exercise of the Understanding on the Subjects of Poetry, I shall examine the several Parts of an Epick Writing, and, setting aside Authority, will endeavour to shew how far the Rules in Fashion are upheld by Reason, and in what they appear by the same Light to be defective, and then frame a Definition more agreeable to Reason. According to the present Rules, an Epick Poem is a feign'd, probable, wonderful and allegorical Story, of a great Atchievement perform'd by some illustrious Person, extended by va-

rious

Epick Poetry.

rious Incidents or Episodes, and related in Verse, of the sublime Stile, to afford Delight and Instruction.

To convey great Ideas and worthy Conceptions to the Understanding, to excite Religious and Moral Passions, and elevate the Mind above low and vulgar Opinions, is a very reasonable Undertaking; and therefore this Species of Poetry, which has these Ends in view, is a laudable and noble Art; for what can be more desireable, than to cultivate the Minds of Men, and make them wiser and better, by correcting their false Maxims, freeing them from groundless Prepossessions, and inspiring them with generous Instincts and exalted Sentiments? Therefore this kind of Poetry, which of all others conduces most to this end, must be look'd on as highly valuable: And as upon this account it is most excellent in its own Nature, being employ'd upon the sublimest and most important Subjects; so by the almost universal and unanimous Suffrages of the ingenious and polite Part of Mankind, it has in all Ages been esteem'd the most difficult, as well as the most excellent Production of the Mind: Of which more hereafter.

This Species of Poetry is stil'd sometimes *Epick*, and sometimes *Heroick*; the first Appellation is deriv'd from the *Greek* Term ἔπος, which is so far appropriated to Poetry, that it is scarce ever, or very seldom us'd by the Writers of Prose; for the Truth of which Assertion I rely on the Authority of *Henry Stephens*, whose consummate Skill in that Language is universally acknowledg'd by the Learned World, and its first and most common signification is a *Word*. Besides this, it is us'd by way of Eminency to signify an Heroick Poem; so *Horace* says, *Fortè Epos acer, ut nemo, varius duxit*; as if the Language of that Poetry was so rich, splendid, and sublime, that no other ought to be call'd *Diction*, or a Scheme of Words. The second Appellation, *Heroick*, ariseth from the Heroes, whose illustrious Actions are related in these Poems: And therefore *Bossu* does, in my Opinion, unjustly reject this distinguishing Epithet as improper; because, as he believes, it took its Rise from that Species of Verse call'd Heroick, that is employ'd in this Poetry. But were his Opinion true, as the contrary is evident, notwithstanding this and his other Objection, that Heroes are the Subjects of more kinds of Poetry besides this; yet Custom, which

settles

EPICK POETRY.

settles the signification of Words, and gives them their Purity and Propriety, has so far obtain'd among Learned Men in all Ages, that I shall not scruple from that Authority to use the Words Heroick and Epick indifferently in this Discourse.

It is stil'd, as I have said, an Heroick Poem, because the principal Action related in it is the great Atchievement of some illustrious Leader. Tho the first Notion of Heroick Vertue had its Rise from any eminent Benefactors, who had deserv'd well of their Country and of Mankind, by laying the Foundations of Cities and Empires, and by inventing useful Arts; such as planting the Vine, sowing Corn, curing Diseases, and freeing their Country from Plagues and wild Beasts; for which they were consecrated after their Decease, and worship'd as Demi-Gods or Heroes: yet at length it became appropriated to those, who with great Valour and Conduct had attack'd or defended a City, or defeated an Enemy in the Field.

The general Idea of Heroick Poetry, is that of Imitation. To imitate, is to express a Resemblance of any Object, either by Action or Imagination; the last of which taken in a larger Sense, may be subdivided into Imitation by the Power of Imagination, where the Ideas of the Mind bear a Similitude to Objects, that really exist or have existed; and that, where the Ideas of the Mind shew a Conformity or Agreement to feign'd Objects, which however are founded in Probability, and are capable of real Existence. In the first Sense, that is by Action, we are said to imitate when we form our Gestures, Habits, and Schemes of Life, by some Pattern or Exemplar, that we set before us. Thus one is said to imitate another in his manner of Walking, Dancing, or Singing; and one Poet, Orator, Architect, or Painter, one General or Statesman imitates another, on whose Model he endeavours to fashion himself. The second way of imitating, is by Imagination; which is nothing else but a Power or Faculty of framing Images, whence it plainly derives its Name; and this is of two sorts.

As to the first, where the Conceptions of the Mind have a Likeness to the real Objects which it conceives, it arises from the native Power of the Understanding to create Ideas that represent any external Object, and to draw, for its own Contemplation, Instruction and Delight, an endless variety of such intellectual Idols or

† Pictures,

Epick Poetry.

Pictures, and to express them in a Scheme of Words; by which this Faculty is distinguish'd from the Arts of Painting and Sculpture, which represent the Archetype by Figures, Lineaments, and Colours. All Imitation, in proper speaking, is the Effect of Art; and 'tis in an equivocal Sense, that we say, when two Things in Nature are alike, as for instance, a Cat and a Tyger, that they imitate one another.

Besides, the Imagination has a Power of drawing Pictures of feign'd Persons, Manners, and Actions, which it does not represent as true and real, but as likely and agreeable to Exemplars actually existing in Nature; and this sort of Imitation is found not only in Epick Poetry, which it has in common with Tragick, Comick, and the upper Lyrick Writings, but likewise in Fables, devis'd Novels, and Romantick Stories writ in Prose.

That in which Imitation essentially consists, and is seen in all the Kinds of it, is the Conformity and Similitude between the imagin'd Representation and the Object represented. Then is a Picture or a Statue just and true, when it bears a Resemblance to the Original; when the Artist, by the Power of Imagination, separates and abstracts the Similitude from the Object, and transfers it to the Canvas or the Marble: and the greater the Likeness and Conformity is between them, the more exquisite and perfect is the Work.

By this it appears wherein the Operations by which the Understanding imitates, are distinguish'd from Symbols, Hieroglyphicks, personal Types, and significant Ceremonies, which do not express any Object by Representation or Resemblance, but only admonish and put us in mind of something. that by Custom and common Consent they stand for, and are us'd to signify.

This is the general Idea of Imitation, the Species of it are various, as diversify'd by their Characteristick Properties. The Poet imitates Nature by Sentiments and a Scheme of Words, the Sculptor and Painter by Lines and Colours: The Poets imitate by Terms and Sentences bounded by Metre; Writers in Prose, which equally aim at a Conformity and Resemblance between the Ideas of the Mind and the Objects represented, imitate by a Train of Words not measur'd and limited by Numbers And by what essential Boundaries Epick Poetry is separated from the other

Epick Poetry.

other Species of that Art, which all agree is imitation of Nature, will afterwards appear.

It is said in the Definition, that an Epick Poem is a Narration of a feign'd Story, and the Reason is, that it may be distinguish'd from History, which is a recital of a Series of true Actions; and tho the chief Event in an Epick Poem may be real, and so the Poem will be founded in a Truth, yet the Plan, the Incidents, the Digressions, and in short, the Means by which that Event is brought about, are invented by the Author; and if any of the Incidents are true and unfeign'd, yet they are not introduc'd as such into the Poem; for they are not recited as Matters of Fact, but only as they are probable, of which more in the next Article. If therefore the Performance is not cast into a Fable devis'd by the Writer, from which artful Contrivance the Poet originally derives his Name, it would by no means be an Epick Writing. If *Livy* or *Thucydides* were turn'd into Verse by the most excellent Pen, let the Numbers be ever so musical, and the Diction ever so splendid and admirable, they would no more become Poems, than a News-Paper would be dignify'd with that Title, tho related in the most correct and beautiful Numbers.

A WELL imagin'd Romance, or such a Writing as the Adventures of *Telemachus*, tho in Profe, approaches nearer to the Nature of an Heroick Poem, than a true History would do, tho exprefs'd in all the Charms of Poetry, that the greateft Genius could give it.

ONE infeparable Quality of Epick Poetry, is Probability. It has been already fhewn, that the general Idea of this kind of Writing, which is common to it with all the other Sorts, is Imitation, as its fpecifick Nature is conftituted and diftinguifh'd by the Properties enumerated in the Definition: But in the firft unreftrain'd Senfe, as it is only a Reprefentation of Nature, it is evident, that nothing unlikely fhould enter into it; for whatever is unlikely is unnatural, and for that Reafon improbable. We look on every thing incredible, which we judge impoffible: Impoffible Things, as implying contradictory Terms, are never the Effects of Nature: Things improbable may fometimes happen by an unufual Concurrence of Caufes, but fince they happen rarely, and when they do, they break the common Courfe of Things and the Chain of ordinary Events, they are reckon'd monftrous strous and unnatural. It is not therefore enough for the Poet to introduce an Incident, becaufe it is poffible, and perhaps has fometimes actually come to pafs; for it may ftill appear incredible to the greateft Part, who never faw fuch a furprizing Fact, and are uncapable of difcerning the Poffibility of it. The Writer therefore fhould act like prudent Travellers, who forbear in Converfation, to relate fome Matters of Fact, which, tho they know them to be true, yet by their furprizing Novelty, and fome extraordinary Circumftances that attend them, they forefee will be look'd on by a vulgar Audience as impracticable, and therefore not to be credited. Nothing therefore fhould be an integral Part of an Epick Poem, but what is eafy, natural, and probable; which will be always fo, if nothing is admitted that does not frequently fall under Obfervation, and is the common Refult of Phyfical and Moral Caufes.

As the Narration ought to be probable, fo it ought to be only probable, and not actually true; for fince Poetry, as in many other refpects, fo in this refembles the Art of Painting, that it always ftrives to exprefs fome Object, it is very evident, that the Imitation muft be form'd by a devis'd devis'd Probability of Actions and Circumstances, and not a relation of real Events; for otherwise it would not be an imitation of Nature, but Nature it self. Poetry being a Picture of feign'd or real Objects, Probability, as before asserted, is every where to be preserv'd; and as it should exhibit nothing inconsistent, monstrous, or unnatural, so it should relate nothing as real; for that would be a Transgression on the other Extream, and utterly destroys the essential Idea of a Poem. I admit, that a true Fact or Event may enter into the Work, but then it must not be introduc'd as it is true, but only as it is likely, and bears a Resemblance to Truth. History receives and recites Things true, tho they have a face of Improbability; and Epick Poetry rejects nothing false, provided it has a probable Appearance. This Property must shine in the general Model, in the Contrivance, Symetry, and Connexion, in the Incidents, Episodes and Digressions, and in all the integral and ornamental Parts of the Structure; and by this the Truth appears of what was above asserted, That a true History, tho compos'd with all the Advantages that the Art of Poetry can give, will not become a Poem; for that would be no Representation of Nature, but the very Things them-

themselves, which is inconsistent with the Notion of such a Writing.

Soon after the Restauration of Polite Literature in *Europe*, the Men of elevated and refin'd Parts unhappily contracted a false Taste, and grew every where fond of extravagant Romantick Fables, the Original of which may be thus accounted for.

The *Egyptians* are generally allow'd to have first cultivated and adorn'd the Understanding with Science and liberal Arts; and that this Nation had made great advances in these intellectual Acquisitions some Ages before that of *Moses*, appears by the Character given to that famous Law-giver in Sacred History, that he was learned in all the Learning of the *Egyptians*. Hither as to the Source of Knowledge, for the Improvement of their Minds, Men of great Genius resorted from foreign Countries, particularly *Homer*, *Pythagoras*, and *Plato*; as afterwards the neighbouring Nations, for the same purpose, frequented *Greece*. These Sages envelop'd their Knowledge of Philosophy in Apologues, Hieroglyphicks, and Symbolical Characters; as they disguis'd their Sentiments of Theology in Allegories and mystical Fables. All Nations, that had any Taste of Learning, either from imitation of of the *Egyptians* or their own native Impulse, which is more probable, affected to convey their Instructions by Ænigmatical Discourses and Allusions. This strong Inclination in Men to express their Sentiments and communicate their Knowledge by Apologues and Fictions, appear'd in the eldest Days of Letters, and spread it self through all the People of the *Eastern* World. Not only the *Egyptians*, but the *Arabians*, *Syrians*, and *Persians*, propagated their Opinions and Instructions in mysterious invented Fables. At length they devis'd Narrations on the Adventures of Lovers; which being agreeable to the most prevailing Passion of the Heart, were receiv'd with Pleasure and much applauded. The *Milesians*, part of the *Ionian* Colony transplanted from *Greece* to *Asia Minor*, a soft and effeminate People, dissolv'd in Luxury and sunk in the Dregs of Vice, were the first that invented, or at least greatly improv'd and encourag'd this kind of Compositions, from them call'd *Milesian* Fables; which, as they sprung from the dissolute Manners of that degenerate People, so by their immodest and obscene Mixtures with which they abounded, they increas'd and heighten'd that general Depravity, from whence they took their Rise.

The *Milesians* therefore seem to be the first Inventors of the Art of writing Romances, of which before the Reign of *Alexander* the Great, there are no Examples. And as these amorous Fictions owe their birth to the most profligate and vicious Nation that ever appear'd on the face of the Earth; so they have a great Influence on all People, where they are generally received and applauded, by corrupting their Manners, dissolving their Minds, and destroying their Taste of useful and solid Learning.

The Art of Writing these light Fables was soon translated from *Asia Minor* to *Greece*, by the Commerce and Correspondence mutually kept up by the *Ionians* of the same Stock, tho in different Countries. The *Grecians* receiv'd them with Pleasure, imitated their *Asian* Colony, and carry'd on this Invention to greater Degrees of Perfection. *Heliodorus* and *Achilles Tatius*, two Christian Bishops, engag'd their Wit on these Subjects: And the Writing of the first is not only chaste and free from the impure and lascivious Blemishes of the *Milesian* Stories; but it is more perfect for its Incidents, Contrivance, and Probability: Whence it became

came the Model on which the numerous Authors of Romances in following Times form'd themselves, as the Poets imitated that of *Homer*.

This Contagion greatly prevail'd, and eminent Men for Wit and Learning became fond of being Authors of such amorous Writings, which Inclination the more useful Improvements and severer Studies of Philosophy and Polite Literature in *Greece* and *Rome* could not extinguish. Persons of a warm Imagination and poetical Genius, apply'd themselves with as much Zeal and Diligence to the compiling of these pleasing Romances, as the Philosophers did to the Advancement of Natural and Moral Science; and as much outrival'd them in the Number of their Admirers, as the Productions of Wit on amorous Subjects are receiv'd with more relish by the greatest part of Mankind, than the dry and difficult Speculations of the Schools of the Sages.

At length, after the Irruptions of the *Goths* and *Vandals* had broke the Power of the *Roman* Empire, who carry'd their Arms and their Ignorance over the politer and more enlighten'd Parts of *Europe*; the Learning of *Greece* and *Rome*, that flou-

Epick Poetry.

rish'd there, was intirely effac'd by the Rudeness and Barbarity of the *Northern* Conquerors. As soon as Knowledge began to break through this total Eclipse, and before Letters, under the Direction and Encouragement of eminent Patrons, rose to a greater height, it made its first publick Entrance into *Europe* by amorous Songs and Fables, like those of the *Milesians*; and these were cultivated and advanced much sooner than Philosophy, Mathematicks, and Classick Learning. They began in *Provence* about the sixth Century, if the *Arabian Moors* did not bring them into *Spain*, from whence these Natives of *Provence*, as some imagine, deriv'd them. This way of Writing having taken the first Possession of the World after the Restauration of exil'd Learning, *Europe* every where was fill'd with these Romantick Stories. The Wits of these Ages were seiz'd with an irregular Poetick Phrenzy, and having Decency and Probability in Contempt, fill'd the World with endless Absurdities; their fertile Imaginations perpetually brought forth some new deform'd and frightful Productions. Phantastick Giants and imaginary Heroes, who made no difficulty of working a thousand Miracles, daily issu'd from the Press. In short, all *Europe* on a sudden saw it self chang'd into *Fairy-Land*, replenish'd plenish'd with Monsters and Necromancers, Castles, Palaces, and delicious Gardens, and many other incredible Effects of Magick Power. Besides this, one every where met with extravagant Knights stroling after Adventures, and unguarded Ladies rambling after their Lovers. And hence it came to pass, that the modern Writers of Epick Poetry, who were train'd up from their Youth in extravagant Romances and improbable and monstrous Narrations, which were the Subjects of all Conversation, and the most fashionable and applauded way of Writing, lay under an invincible Temptation to accommodate themselves to the Relish of the Times, by mingling in their Epick Compositions so great an Allay of Knight-Errantry and extravagant Adventures. While this sort of Writing was in fashion, the Imaginations of the modern Poets, who were the best qualify'd to attempt the sublime Manner, imbib'd a strong Tincture of the Romantick Contagion, which corrupted their Taste, and occasion'd their neglect of Probability. The Age was so far gone in this Delusion, that the best Writers could not free their Minds from the prepossession which they lay under. Hence it came to pass, that there is so great a Mixture of Knight-Errantry, Sorcery, and incredible Atchieve-

Epick Poetry.

Atchievements in the Poems of *Ariosto*, *Tasso*, and our famous *Spenser*; who, notwithstanding they had the Precepts of *Aristotle* and *Horace*, and the Examples of *Homer* and *Virgil* back'd with Reason to direct their Conduct, were caught in the general Infection of the Times, and accommodated their Writings to the prevailing Opinion; by which they transgress'd one essential Rule of Poetry, I mean, Probability: For Poetry being an Imitation of Nature, that can never be a regular Performance, which represents Things that never did or can exist, and therefore are unnatural and not to be imitated.

Of the Marvellous.

Another thing indispensably requir'd to the Constitution of an Epick Poem is, that the Narration be marvellous; and the Reason is, that when the Poet intends to give Delight and convey Instruction, as Admiration engages Attention, so it prepares and opens the Mind to admit the force of the Poet's Sentiments, and receive from them deep Impressions. Hence the beautiful and surprizing Turns, as well in the Diction as the Incidents of a noble Poem, strike the Imagination with resistless Force, break in upon the Soul and excite generous and divine Passions suitable to the Subject. This therefore is a necessary Property, by which the Poet is qualify'd to gain his principal End, which is to afford Pleasure and Instruction; and is a peculiar and inseparable Character, that limits the general Nature of Poetry, and makes the Epick differ from the Tragick, to which however it is more nearly ally'd than to any other Species.

All Things excite Admiration that either transcend the Sphere of finite Activity, or that break the usual Series of Natural Causes and Events. The first sort, which proceed from Almighty Power, are stil'd Miracles: I shall not here by a strict Disquisition, enter into the Nature and Definition of a Miracle, which some look upon as an immediate Effect of unlimited Might, and others as an Action which the Spectators believe the Supream Being to be the Author of, while they are unable to account for any Natural Cause, from whence it should arise. It is enough, that in this Place, I give this Idea of it, That it is a presumptive, immediate Operation of Divine Power. The other sort of Effects that move Admiration, do not surmount the Limits of created Activity,

Epick Poetry. 35

ty, but proceed from second subordinate Causes; yet then they interrupt the ordinary Course of Things, and deviate from the establish'd Custom or Laws of Nature.

Some of these irregular Productions are monstrous and frightful, and strike the Imagination with Disgust and Terror, and others are Sports of Nature, which are often pleasing and beautiful Errors: Other Things raise our Admiration by their singular and extraordinary Perfection; so exquisite and consummate Beauty, extraordinary Strength and Agility of Body, as well as the finish'd Pieces and Inventions of the most excellent Masters in Painting, Building, and Polite Literature, because they surpass their own ordinary Performances and those of other Artists, fill the Mind with agreeable Amazement. Other Objects, tho not irregular, nor more or less perfect than the ordinary Individuals of their Species, are marvellous, because they seldom come to pass. We view a Planet or a Star without Concern or Emotion of Mind, while the sight of a Comet raises our Admiration; not by its being a more excellent Luminary, but by its unfrequent Appearance. Our Wonder is likewise mov'd by common Objects represented in uncommon Circumstances; as for

for Instance, the Sun when eclips'd, Foreigners in a strange Habit, the Shells of Fishes found on the Tops of Mountains, and Trees and Nutshels discover'd in the Bowels of the Earth.

It is in the Novelty of these Appearances, that the essential Idea of Marvellous does consist. Any thing is therefore admirable, because it is surprizing, and therefore surprizing because extraordinary and unexpected. All unusual Occurrences, especially the Excursions and Transgressions of Nature in her Operations, move the Imagination with great Force, agitate the Spirits, and raise in the Soul strong Emotions, which by degrees diminish after long Acquaintance; and as Familiarity wears off our Abhorrence and reconciles us to frightful Objects, so it abates the Pleasure of constant Enjoyments, and by degrees creates Satiety. Exquisite Musick, delicious Gardens, magnificent Buildings, and ravishing Prospects, after long Possession, do not excite that delightful Wonder which it produces in those who are unaccustom'd to them. Novelty, as before asserted, is the Parent of Admiration; and it is for this reason, that the Sentiments in Epick Poetry, which by their Beauty, Strength and Dignity, are rais'd above the

Epick Poetry.

the Level of vulgar Conceptions, and are always new, either in themselves or the uncommon Turn given to them by the Poet, act powerfully upon the Imagination, and surprize the Soul with pleasing Astonishment. And hence likewise it is, that the rich, splendid, and figurative Diction, which is proper to that Species of Poetry, like the Magnificence and Pomp of Princes on solemn Occasions, excites the Wonder of the People not inur'd to such Prospects.

Of the Fable.

TO form a Poem capable of raising Admiration, must conspire a Fable contriv'd with Art and Judgment, a natural Subordination, and a just Proportion of the Parts mutually inlightning and supporting each other, and the Regularity, Beauty, and Importance of the Incidents resulting, without constraint, from the Subject. Besides this, the principal Persons must be of illustrious Blood or high Station, the Action of great Consequence, the Turns strange and surprizing, the Sentiments strong, noble, and elevated; the Stile figurative and lofty, the Diction splendid and magnificent, and the Machines proper and pertinent. Should the Structure of the Poem want Unity or Integrity; fhould the Action be of little Moment, the Characters of mean Rank and Condition, the Expreffion low and poor, the Stile bafe and ruftick, or fwoln into the falfe Sublime; fhould the Incidents be trivial, the Thoughts weak and vulgar, the Turns in the Action obvious and familiar; or fhould the Machines be omitted or ill chofen, or unfeafonable, the Performance would be contemptible, and more apt to move Laughter than Admiration: And if it be defective in any of thefe Qualities, the Beauty and Dignity of the Poem will in proportion be diminifh'd, and become uncapable of raifing Wonder and Delight.

Therefore the Criticks in a peculiar manner require in the Poet, that undertakes this difficult Province, an elevated, inventive and enterprizing Imagination arifing from an inborn Fire, that impels and agitates the Soul with great Vehemence, heightens and inflames the Spirits, and kindles a Heat that approaches to the Nature of Fury and Phrenzy; whence the Ancients affirm'd, That poetical Raptures were the Effects of Infpiration and Divine Impulfe.

Tho

Epick Poetry.

Tho this inbred Endowment is abfolutely, and in the firft place, neceffary to the Poet, a cool and fevere Judgment muft however hold the Reins, and prefide over this warm and hardy Imagination, to guide its Motions, and prevent its Errors, which otherwife would be numerous and unavoidble; and fince this happy Temperament is feldom found, where two contrary Elements, Fire and Phlegm, of which each is demanded in a high Degree, are reconcil'd, and fo blended and united, as to conftitute a Genius capable of this fublime Species of Poetry, it is no wonder that few Perfons have attempted it, and that fewer have fucceeded in their Undertaking.

The Genius's fit for Epick Poetry are conftituted and divided into various forts, as poetick Energy and Imagination, or Judgment and a true Tafte of Propriety and Beauty are predominant in the Mind. From the firft Mixture comes forth a *Homer*, by the fecond is a produc'd a *Virgil*; and if thefe Endowments fhould happen to be equally mix'd and ballanc'd in the original Conftitution of any great Poet, a third Species would be form'd. *Homer* and *Virgil* are two different Genius's of

Nature's own making, abstracting from the Improvements and Advantages that arise from Learning, from Observation of the Works of eminent Writers, from a greater Comprehension of the Properties in an Epick Poem, and an accurate Knowledge of the Rules of Writing. If *Homer*, after he had finish'd his *Iliad*, could have acquir'd the Erudition and Skill of *Virgil*, his Genius would have been still the same, tho more refin'd, better govern'd, and more adorn'd by adventitious Embellishments; as an exquisite Beauty is the same, when at one time she appears in a wild and careless Dress, and at another is set off with the greatest Art and the richest Ornaments. *Virgil* and *Homer* are not therefore two different Genius's, because the Latin Author has more Learning, and is a greater Master of the Rules of Poetry, that is, is a better Critick than the *Grecian*; but their distinct Characters arise from the different Combination of the unacquir'd Qualities and Powers of the Mind, while in one poetical Heat and Inspiration and in the other, Judgment and Discretion evidently prevail.

Of

Epick Poetry.

Of the Allegory.

IT is likewife requir'd of an Epick Poem, that it fhould be Allegorical. By an Allegory is fometimes underftood a Continuation of Metaphors in the Writing, by which it is rais'd above vulgar Expreffion; and this is neceffary to the Species of Poetry, of which we are difcourfing: For tho it ought to abound with all manner of beautiful and moving Figures, yet the Stile chiefly is elevated above ordinary Converfation, and the Diction of Philofophers and Hiftorians, by a Series of metaphorical Words and Sentences through the whole Work, as oft as the Subject will bear it; whence the Expreffion becomes fplendid and admirable. Thefe elegant and furprizing Figures enrich, warm, and animate plain and cold Sentences, till they glow with Life and Spirit, and appear in all the Charms of Eloquence.

But an Allegory is fometimes taken in another Senfe, that is, when Vertues and Vices are reprefented as Perfons either Humane or Divine, and proper Paffions and Manners are afcrib'd to their refpective Characters: Of this are feveral Examples in *Homer*'s *Ulyffes*, and too many in the modern

modern Epick Writers, and there is one Instance of this sort in the sixth Book of King *Arthur*. In the first Sense an Heroick Poem cannot be too Allegorical, that is, too Figurative in those Parts, which require, or at least will endure to be rais'd from a flat and low Manner by the Ornaments of surprizing Metaphors, beautiful Similitudes, and just Allusions. But in the second Sense, the modern Epick Poets, especially *Ariosto* and *Spenser*, have ran too far into Allegory. This sort of allegorical Imaging resembles the emblematical Draughts of great Painters, where Vertues are represented as Goddesses, and Vices as Furies; and where Liberty, Peace, Plenty, Pleasure, and various Qualities of the Mind are exhibited in Humane Forms, with peculiar Properties and Marks of Distinction. An elegant Instance of this kind of Writing is the Representation of Sin and Death in the appearance of two odious and terrible Monsters, by our celebrated *Milton* in his *Paradise Lost*; of which, I imagine, he took the Hint from the famous *Spenser*. This sort of Allegories, tho not strictly Epick, us'd with Temperance and Judgment, affect the Mind with Wonder and Delight, and enliven and beautify the Poem. There is yet a third sort of Allegory, which if it is

not

Epick Poetry.

not essential, is however very agreeable in Epick Writings, and render them more perfect; which is, when the chief Actors, especially the principal Hero, are made the Types of some other illustrious Persons, whose Actions and Manners are shadow'd forth by the Qualities of those that act in the Poem; and in this Case the artful disguise should be drawn so thin, that the real Characters in the View and Intention of the Poet may appear underneath, and be seen with ease through the transparent Veil; as in the first sort of Allegory, which consists in a Train of Metaphors, the Sense is foreign and different from the direct and usual Meaning of the Words; so in this, the Persons really intended are different from the Persons of the Poem, whose Actions and Manners are there exhibited.

Thus the *Roman* Emperor, *Augustus*, is represented under the Character of the *Trojan* Hero, *Æneas*, in the famous Poem of *Virgil*, by which he is said to have paid him the greatest Complement that was ever made to any Prince: And it is not improbable, that *Homer*, in his *Iliad*, design'd to honour some great Persons then flourishing in *Greece*, under the allegorical Characters of *Agamemnon*, *Achilles*, *Diomedes*, and the other principal Actors in that Poem,

Poem, tho by the diftance of Time we cannot trace the Allufion; for it is not likely that *Virgil*, who is fo exact an Imitator of *Homer*, would have attempted to have writ in this way, if *Homer* had not encourag'd and directed him by his Example.

In this Cafe the Poet fhould take care, that the diftinguifhing Accomplifhments and great Exploits of his principal Hero fhould be fo delineated, that in the Series of the Actions and Manners, and the Allufions and Incidents of the Poem, the intended great Man fhould be plainly pointed out. Thus the typical Hero is introduc'd at once to conceal and difcover the real one, who is lightly difguis'd, that he may be fhown to greater Advantage. To bear downright upon an excellent Perfon with Applaufe, is bold and ill-manner'd, and for that Reafon difagreeable and fhocking to Men of Tafte and Judgment. The Epick Poet therefore exhibits the Perfon whofe Praifes he defigns to celebrate under another illuftrious Character, that by this means he may break the Violence, and correct the Rudenefs of bare-fac'd Commendation, and that the Panegyrick thus qualify'd may fhine through the allegorical Cloud with milder and more agreeable Luftre.

Epick Poetry. 45

In this Place I shall assert the Liberty of Reason, and endeavour to shew that in this, which likewise is true in some other Instances, the admirable Poem of *Virgil*, for no Humane Works that are extant are free from blemishes, is defective, which however in the Contrivance, Conduct, and Diction, is the most finish'd of the kind; and perhaps the Time may come, when the learned World may bear an impartial Examination of the Writers of the most establish'd Authority, and not condemn every thing that deviates from the Precepts of *Aristotle*, and the Examples of *Virgil* and *Homer*, as poetical Heresy.

'Tis evident that this excellent Author intended, as before-mention'd, to celebrate the great Prince above-nam'd under his Typical Hero, *Æneas*. But as the general Character of Piety is not, I imagine, perfectly drawn, particularly in his Behaviour to *Dido*, and his interesting the Gods in the dishonourable Usage of that Queen, after her obliging Reception of himself and his shipwreck'd Companions; which never fails to move the Reader's Pity to the injur'd Lady, or to make the ungallant Hero the Object of his Censure and Resentment; so neither is this Character of Piety perhaps

so

so well accommodated to the Qualities of *Augustus Cæsar*, if authentick Historians may be credited. But suppose this general Idea does bear a similitude to the Disposition and Habits of that Monarch, there are very few Particulars in the Poem that carry any Resemblance between *Æneas* and the typify'd Hero, or that put the Reader at any time in mind of such a Person. There are no peculiar Manners of *Augustus*, nor any of his great Actions or Exploits shadow'd forth by those of *Æneas*; none of his Battles, Expeditions, Dangers, or Successes, represented or alluded to in the whole Story of the *Trojan*'s Hazards and martial Atchievements, no, not the famous Sea-Fight at *Actium*, which crown'd all the Labours of *Augustus*, and establish'd him in the Possession of the *Roman* Empire, tho nothing was more memorable and important, and therefore nothing more pertinent or ornamental could have been introduc'd into the Poem, as might have been done with great ease.

The Fights and Adventures in the *Æneid* might have serv'd as well for any other Hero as for *Augustus*: The first seem to be *Homer*'s Battles fought over again in *Italy*, and not appropriated to the *Roman* Emperor. The Army of *Æneas*,
with

Epick Poetry. 47

with which he made his Defcent upon *Latium*, is compos'd of many of the fame Warriors, who were engag'd at the Siege of *Troy*, and thofe too not *Trojans*, which would have made it more excufable, but *Grecians*, their victorious Enemies. This Inadvertency will appear to any, who fhall attentively read the Battels in *Virgil*, and compare them with thofe of *Homer*. The truth is, that while *Virgil* was contemplating *Homer*, after whom he copy'd, he was fo intent on the *Grecian's* Model, and fo careful to follow him in every Part of his Poem, that he forgot his own Hero.

Of the Unity.

IT is requir'd in the Definition of an Epick Poem, that it fhould be the Narration of fome one Action. One principal End muft be defign'd by the Author, and the Contrivance, Difpofition, and Dependence of the Parts muft be fuch, that all the Incidents and inferior Actions may evidently conduce to the compafling of the main Event. From the Order and Connexion of the Parts confpiring in their Places to promote the chief Defign, arifes the Unity of the Action, on which depends the Unity of the Poem : For if any Part is co-ordinate and not fubfervient to the principal

cipal Aim of the Poet, the Unity of the Action is broken, and the Work is no longer one Piece, but becomes as many diftinct Poems or Fragments of Poems, as there are found unconnected and independent Actions. The two laft Books of the *Iliad* are therefore fuperfluous and out of the Poem, becaufe the Celebration of the Funerals of *Patroclus* and *Hector*, which are there recited, came after the main Defign was attain'd, and the principal Action was ended.

Of the IMPORTANCE *of the* Action.

AS the principal Action ought to be one, fo it ought to be important; the Reafon is, that it may excite Admiration, which is effential, as before has been fhown, to this Species of Poetry. By this Property it is likewife diftinguifh'd from Comedy, where the Characters are inferior and the Action of little Confequence. *Boffu* requires no more to render the Action important, than that it fhould be the Action of an illuftrious Perfon, to which I cannot agree; becaufe great Men may fometimes, for their Recreation and Diverfion, or worfe Purpofes, be taken up in mean and trivial Matters. If the Emperor *Commodus* fhould be introduc'd fight-

ing

Epick Poetry.

ing as a Gladiator in the Amphitheater, or *Domitian* as engag'd in his darling Pleafure of chaceing Flies, the Dignity of the Actors would by no means render the Action important; I conceive therefore, that to give Importance to the Action, it is not only neceffary that the Actor fhould be a Perfon of Diftinction for his noble Extraction or high Employment, but that the Action related fhould be of great Confequence in it felf, and fuch as becomes an illuftrious Actor.

The Criticks have univerfally declar'd their Opinion, that the chief Hero of an Epick Poem ought to be engag'd in fome eminent Action; but this, I imagine, is from their following, in a fervile manner, the Dictates of the Stagyrite, and the Examples of the *Iliad* and the *Æneid*. I have, in the Preface to the Paraphrafe on *Job*, advanc'd a contrary Pofition, and endeavour'd to prove, that the principal Character of the Poem may be as well unactive and in a State of Suffering and Calamity. It is evident, that none of thefe Criticks have enquir'd into the Grounds and Foundation of this Maxim, That the Hero muft be always a fighting, or at leaft, an active Perfon: They have, from one Generation to another, taken this Affertion upon content,

tent, and rely'd upon a continu'd Chain and uninterrupted Succession of Authority down from *Aristotle*'s Days to the present Age, without examining the Matter, or offering any Reason to support their Doctrine. Setting then aside the Veneration of great Names and the Authority of the Schools, I appeal to the Tribunal and decisive Decrees of Reason. I have in the Work above-mention'd demonstrated, that the principal End and all the essential Properties of an Epick Writing may be attain'd, tho the chief Person should be an eminent Sufferer, and no Battle should be fought through all the Poem. As much Divine Instruction relating to Providence, to the Encouragements and Rewards of Vertue, and the terrible Consequences of Irreligion and Vice; as great and illustrious Examples of Piety, Fortitude, and Heroick Firmness of Mind; as noble and useful Morals, and as sublime Sentiments, all fit to inspire the Reader with excellent Notions, to excite the most generous Passions, and to produce the most vertuous Resolutions, may be found in such a Poem, as well as in that which is full of Action and martial Atchievements. And where this principal End of an Epick Poem may be attain'd, and the Characteristick and essential Difference, with all the concomitant and inseparable Properties of it may be found, as they may be, where no Camps are form'd, nor any Armies engag'd, why this should not be denominated a genuine Epick Poem, I am not able to imagine; and on this Plan I take *Homer*'s *Ulysses* to be form'd. Besides, let it be consider'd, that many excellent Tragedies have been compos'd by the Ancients, as well as Moderns, where the Hero or Heroine of the Poem has been passive and unhappy; and why Nature in this Instance, may not with equal right be imitated by the Epick Poet, I believe is difficult to assign a Reason.

If this arguing be allow'd, then the Criticks will have no occasion to exercise their Sagacity, in finding out the Hero of *Milton*'s Poem; for then it will be evident, that it must have been *Adam* himself. Nothing could have tempted learned Men to have search'd after any other Hero, but the Prepossession under which they lay, that the chief Person of the Poem ought always to be active, and in the end prosperous: But by what has been alledg'd I imagine, that Prejudice may be remov'd; and under this view that celebrated Poem will appear more regular and perfect than it has hitherto been allow'd to be. Another Reason why they are not willing to allow *Adam* to be the Hero of the Poem is this, That they believe the Idea of a Hero implies illustrious Vertue as well as military Fortitude; but this Error is occasion'd, by confounding the Notions of a Moral and a Poetical Hero; the first is always a Person of regular and vertuous Manners, but the other may be a flagitious, unjust, and cruel Man; nothing being requir'd in his Character, but that he should be pertinent and necessary in the Fable; that is, that he should eminently serve to bring about the principal End, whence some useful and instructive Moral shall arise: But more of this afterwards.

Of the Episodes.

IT is demanded in an Epick Poem, that the Recital of the Action should be extended by Episodes. An Episode at first was nothing but an Action interpos'd to diversify the Pleasure of the Audience, and relieve the Satiety of the Tragedy, which then entirely consisted in Musick; and an Episode had its Name from being something superadded to it. At the beginning only one, afterwards more such Actions, bearing relation however to the Tragedy, were

Epick Poetry. 53

were introduc'd; till by degrees the Episodes, which before were foreign and superfluous, became the whole Poem, and
the Musick was retain'd only in the Cho-
rus. The Episodes then, or Incidents, are
the integral Parts of the Poem, which consider'd as united, make up the Matter
that is essential to the Constitution of the
Work; and if taken singly the Absence of
any one would leave it mutilated and defective.

The Connection and mutual Dependance of the Episodes are so necessary to
make the whole one Action, that where
those are wanting the Poem is imperfect
and vicious, its Unity being broken; and
as oft as this happens the Incident is no
part of the Structure, but stands by it self
as a divided Piece or Outwork, detach'd
and separate from the Building: And
therefore as *Rapin* observes, the Episode
of the Voyage of *Telemachus* in the *Odysses*,
which has no relation to the main Action,
and contributes nothing to the Return of
Ulysses, or the Events that follow'd it, is
superfluous, and no integral part of the
Work. The Poet has scarce enter'd upon
his Subject when he takes his leave of it,
and for four Books together entirely loses
sight of his principal Design. Several o-
ther

ther Instances of this Nature might be cited out of the Poems of that admirable Writer, which, notwithstanding the Authority of his Example, cannot be justify'd; for it is evident, that having no Union or Correspondence with the other Episodes, nor any Influence on the chief Action, they make so many Chasms or Breaks in the Poem, and therefore must be impertinent, Nor can this Practice be vindicated, by alledging, that this loose manner of Writing is agreeable to the Custom and Taste, not only of the *Eastern* World, but of the most eminent Poets of *Greece*, especially *Pindar*, who, not solicitous about Transitions and Connexions, frequently start from their main Design, and without any warning or preparation, abruptly pursue a foreign and unexpected Matter, till tir'd with the long and independent Digression, they sometimes return to their Subject, and sometimes entirely forget it. And in this they are imitated by *Horace* in his *Odes*, who on a sudden springs from his Theme, and follows another Chase, neither very pertinent, nor of a suitable Proportion; tho these Excursions are perhaps less blameable in the great Lyrick, where the Stile is more passionate, rapid, and violent. If the Beauty and Perfection of a poetical Frame, according to the uncontested

Epick Poetry. 55

tested Doctrine of the Criticks, arise from the Regularity, Union, and just Length of the Parts, then I shall always believe that Defect and Deformity will naturally result from Disorder, Incoherence, and Inequality: Nor can I give into the contrary Opinion, tho press'd by the Example of the greatest Writers, while the Dictates of Reason condemn their Practice.

If any Episodes exceed a due Proportion, or if they are extended too far, or are too short, tho the Unity of the Action is preserv'd, yet the Symetry of the Work is blemish'd according to the Degree of such Excess or Defect in the length of the Parts. And here I shall take notice, that the Episode which takes up the second and third Book of Prince *Arthur*, which how necessary soever it is to carry on the main Action, swells to a disproportionate Size, and is therefore obnoxious to Censure. This I well knew when I writ that Poem, but because the Subject was of such Dignity, Usefulness, and Importance, I deliberately suffer'd that Defect to continue, for the sake of a greater Advantage to the Work.

The Criticks allow *Virgil* to annihilate Time, and sink above 200 Years upon his
Reader,

Reader, that *Æneas* and *Dido* may become Contemporaries, and that the Poet by this means might have a Foundation for the Epifode of the fecond Book, which however does not add any Beauty, as before fuggefted, unlefs Ingratitude and the want of Gallantry in *Æneas* to a Queen, to whom in his Diftrefs he had been fo highly oblig'd, and his charging upon Heaven his faulty Behaviour, can adorn a Poem: And if this Maxim be eftablifh'd, that an Author with a Defign to introduce a greater Beauty, may be allow'd to commit fome inferior Error, then much more may a Poet be juftify'd, who, for the fake of a confiderable moral Good, tranfgreffes a Rule of lefs Importance, which he would otherwife have obferv'd; fince that Benefit will better bear him out in doing fo, than the mere Entertainment and Diverfion of his Reader.

BESIDES this fort of Epifodes, which, taken as united integral Parts, conftitute the whole Matter of the Fable, there are other Parts call'd by the fame Name, which for diftinction fake I will ftile Digreffions. Thefe do not neceffarily and immediately grow from the main Action, but refult from fome Incident, by which it is united to the Body of the Fable. Thefe

Epick Poetry.

These Digreſſions, which perhaps beſt deſerve the Appellation of Epiſodes, are not indeed neceſſary to the Being nor the Integrity of the Poem, but they add to it Beauty and Ornament; they reſemble the Hair on a Man's Head and Eye-Brows, and the Leaves and the Bloſſoms of a Tree, which ſpring from the integral Parts of the Individual, tho they are not ſuch themſelves, and without which the Eſſence is preſerv'd intire, tho naked, and in a manner deform'd. If theſe Digreſſions are forc'd and unnatural, that is, if they do not evidently ariſe from ſome Incident or Epiſode of the Action, by the Mediation of which they are connected to the Poem, they are no more a part of it, than a Worm is of an Animal, to which it adheres, or than Ivy or Woodbine are parts of the Tree, to which they cling. If they are very frequent, they call off too much the Attention of the Mind from the principal Buſineſs and Deſign of the Poet, and inſtead of Ornaments they become an Encumbrance, and oppreſs the Fable; and if they ſwell to a great length, by which the main Action is forgotten and left out of Sight, they are ſo many Tumours and large Excreſencies, that deform the Narration and weaken its Force.

THE Action of the Poem is carry'd on as well by Epifodes that contain Confultations, Conferences, Songs and Speeches, as by thofe which are entirely active, efpecially if they are put into the Mouths of the Actors. Some, for want of Judgment, have imagin'd, that the Poem ftands ftill while any of the Perfons are engag'd in fpeaking, and not in Action or the Narration of fome bufy Story; but this is never true, but when the Poet in his own Perfon makes Remarks and moral Reflections. We do not find that the Song of *Jopas* in *Virgil*, is condemn'd by any Criticks for delaying the Action or interrupting its Continuity, tho many have cenfur'd it as not pertinent to his Subject, while they allow to that of *Homer* in his *Ulyffes* greater Propriety. Narrations that are unactive are fometimes neceffary to carry on the Poem; and tho they do not ftrike the Imagination with fuch Vehemence as military Exploits, or other active Objects, yet in Epick Poetry, which is more fedate than Tragedy, they are not only in themfelves beautiful and entertaining, but they temper and reduce the Emotions of the Mind, which would be too violent and unfupportable, if the Vehemence of the Action fhould be conftant, and not interrupted through a Poem of fuch extent. *Of*

Epick Poetry. 59

Of Integrity.

AS the chief Action of the Poem ought to be one and no more, so that one Action ought to be finish'd and compleat, in which the Integrity of it does consist. Should a Painter delineate the Figure of a Man, either without a Head or without Feet, the Picture must be imperfect and deform'd; in like manner, should an Epick Poet so contrive his Fable, that any integral Parts of the Action should be wanting, the Piece would be lame and defective. And this Error is conspicuous in the Plan of the *Iliad*, where, if according to the Judgment of *Horace*, the *Trojan* War is the Action, that Action is not perfect and entire, because it neither begins with that famous Siege which commenc'd many Years before, nor does it end with it, since it continu'd a Year after the Death of *Hector*, and the Conclusion of the Poem. If it be said that the Action began with the Anger of *Achilles*, which *Homer* mentions in his Proposition that introduces the Fable, then *Rapin* thinks there would be two Angers of *Achilles*; one for the Loss of his Mistress detain'd by *Agamemnon*, which occasion'd his departure from the Army; and another quite distinct, which arose upon

upon the Death of *Patroclus*, and brought back the Hero to the Field, that he might revenge the Fall of his Friend upon the *Trojans*: Whence, says the Critick, it will evidently follow, that the Action or Subject of the Poem will be double; which is at least as great a Defect, as the want of Integrity.

Of the Metre.

IT is requir'd in the Definition of an Epick Poem, that the feign'd Story should be recited in Verse; the reason is, that it may be specifically limited and diversify'd from Writings in Prose, which is *Oratio Soluta*; that is, a Speech or Diction free and unbounded by Metre. I do not affirm, that Rhime is necessary; tho in the modern Languages, which cannot imitate the Numbers of the *Greek* and *Latin* Poems, it is a Beauty and a musical Entertainment, and when it is easy, unconstrain'd, and manag'd with Skill, has a good Effect. It is true, as before-mention'd, that a devis'd Story related in Prose, where the Action is important and its Unity is preserv'd, where the Characters are illustrious, the Sentiments great and noble, and the Diction figurative, splendid and spiritful, comes near to the Nature of

Epick Poetry.

of an Epick Poem, and wants nothing but Numbers to make it such; but without this essential Property it cannot claim that Appellation. If an invented Action recited in Sentences not limited by Metre were a Poem, then all the Fables of *Esop*, and of the Romantick Writers, would merit the same Denomination: The Truth is, that the Narration of an imagin'd and contriv'd Action without Numbers, is a counterfeit Poem in Prose; as the recital of real Facts and Incidents in Metre, is a true History in Verse.

Of the Time.

THE Duration of the Action in it self is unsettled, and must be determin'd by the Judgment of the Poet, according to the different Nature and various Circumstances of his Subject: If that be violent and full of Passion, or on the contrary, calm and moderate; if it be simple, or less or more implex, the Narration will be shorten'd or more extended. Besides, it is in the Power of the Writer to invent variety of Episodes and Digressions, and to contract or enlarge them, provided he preserves Order and Proportion, in respect of the Parts one to another: And in this his Liberty is like that of of an Architect, who may act in conformity to the Rules of his Art, whether he gives more or less, larger or narrower Rooms to his Building, so he maintain that Regularity and Symetry of the Parts, which the Perfection of the whole requires.

Hence it is that the Duration of the Action in the *Iliad*, the *Odysses*, and the *Æneis*, is very different; the Extension of the Time, which the Business of the Poem shall take up, being of arbitrary Determination; in fixing, however, of which the Poet is oblig'd to have regard to the Nature of the Action, and the Beauty and Order of the Structure.

The Writer is at liberty to begin his Poem with the first Part of the Action, and to continue the Relation by a regular Succession of Incidents, till the Work is finish'd, which Method is observ'd in the *Iliad*; or else at the Beginning of the Poem he may enter upon any subsequent Part in Order of Time, and reserve the first Part of the Action to be introduc'd by way of Recital, which is practis'd by *Virgil* in his *Æneis:* Both these ways are warrantable, since no Dictate of Reason in this Case, restrains the free Choice of the Poet. It is evident that this Historical Relation, which is made by some proper Actor, is as much an Episode or integral Part of the Poem as the rest, which united, constitute the Matter essential to the Action; since without it the Work will be maim'd and defective. But the Narration of Events that shall happen in Times to come, after the Epick Action is ended, which is sometimes made by way of Prediction, as that of *Anchises* to *Æneas*, that continues the Story down to the Reign of *Augustus*, cannot be esteem'd an Incident or integral Part of the Action, but is to be reckon'd a Digression springing from an Incident or Episode, by the Means of which it is united to the Poem, and the Reason is evident; for if the Prophecy were remov'd, there would be indeed a great Beauty lost, but no Episode or material Part would be missing by its Absence, but the Poem would continue unmaim'd and entire.

Of the Machines.

AS to the Machines, that is, the Celestial and Infernal Powers introduc'd by the Poet, tho they must not be look'd on as necessary and essential, yet when they are interested in the Action, they raise raife the Dignity of the Poem, and make the Narration more illuftrious and important; whence they muft be efteem'd highly expedient and ufeful. This Practice is warranted and encourag'd by the eldeft Example of fublime Poetry, which was long before the Age of *Homer*, I mean, the Book of *Job* compos'd under the Guidance of Divine Infpiration ; in which the Supreme Being and the chief Apoftate Angel are engag'd as Parties concern'd ; whence it appears very probable, that the Ufe of Machines in Heroick and Tragick Poems took its rife.

It is by fome objected, that the introducing of Divine and Angelick Beings to affift the Hero of the Poem, and fight againft his Competitor, muft highly detract from the Glory of his Actions, and diminifh the Opinion of his Bravery and Conduct; for, fay they, What Honour can juftly redound to the Warrior, who has conquer'd his Enemy not fo much by his own Arms, as by the Power of mighty invifible Beings, who aided and protected his Perfon, and difpirited and affrighted his Rival? If *Minerva* fupports *Achilles* againft *Hector*, and *Jupiter* engages on the fide of *Æneas* againft *Turnus*, can it be any Difhonour to the

Van-

Epick Poetry.

Vanquish'd, if they are look'd on as inferiour in Power to the Gods? Had Heaven stood neuter and espous'd neither Cause, who can tell whether *Hector* or *Turnus* might not have triumph'd over their Enemies? If two Champions are engag'd in Combat, and a third superior or equal in Strength to either of them, should step in to assist one to subdue the other, would this be a fair Decision, who of the two did excel his Competitor in Strength and Courage?

To this I answer; That it does by no means derogate from the Glory of the victorious Hero, that in the Fight he was animated and assisted, as his Rival was terrify'd, by supernatural Powers; the Reason is, because the Action is entirely his own, notwithstanding the Assistance of Celestial Beings. But the Case would be quite otherwise did another Champion rush into his Aid, for then the Action would be evidently shar'd between them, and no Honour would redound to either. The Supream Being, as universal Cause, must afford his concurring Power, not only to support the Existence of all his Creatures, but likewise to enable all their Faculties and Powers to exert themselves in Action. Should we suppose a created Being inde-

independent on the Creator in any one natural Operation, let it be the flighteft fenfitive Perception, the firft Formation of a Thought, or the leaft Impulfe or Volition of the Will, that Creature would be independent in all his Actions, there being nothing more requir'd for the Independency of all, than of any one Operation, and then it would follow, that this Being would be endow'd with Divine Perfections, and become a Deity. Befides the Phyfical Neceffity of the Concurrence of the Supream Being to enable his Creatures to act, all Men, who have a juft Idea of him, will allow that he does actually intereft himfelf in the Government of Humane Affairs, and by his Providence difpofes Things in fuch a manner, that thofe Events, which he defigns, fhall certainly come to pafs; that he brings about the Rife and Fall of Empires, promotes or difappoints the Schemes of Statefmen, and as Lord of Armies, beftows Victory on which Leader he pleafes; that he infpires the Heart of his favour'd General with Courage and Wifdom, fhields his Head in the Day of Battle, animates his Troops, and difheartens and confounds the Enemy. Nor is the Hero's Valour or Prudence the lefs his own, becaufe infpir'd and given by Heaven; nor is his Honour
dimi-

Epick Poetry.

diminish'd by the Intervention of Providence, that difpos'd Circumftances in his Favour; for our Faculties and Powers are freely, and without conftraint, exerted in all our Operations; and the Concurrence of Divine Aid does not fufpend, much lefs deftroy, the Liberty and Self-determining Power of the Will; and therefore how much foever we are affifted by the Supream Being, as an univerfal Caufe, our Actions are as much our own, as it is poffible that a Creature's fhould be.

The Poets therefore out of Reverence to the Deities, whom they fuppos'd to be interefted in the Adminiftration of Humane Affairs, efpecially of thofe that are attended with memorable and important Events, by introducing their Machines in all great Actions, defign'd, as I imagine, no more than to give an allegorical Reprefentation of that fupream Providence, which guides and directs the Univerfe, and particularly interpofes in the Concerns of Mankind; and by this means they fuppos'd they fhould make a greater Impreffion on the Minds of Men, and propagate more effectually the pious Notion of God's Government of the World in a Moral Senfe; and perhaps they might likewife have some regard to him as a Physical universal Cause.

A SUPERIOR Critick of our own Nation has affirm'd, that to be thus assisted by the Gods is so far from debasing, that it very much heightens the Character of the Hero, since it is in it self and in the Opinion of the People, a greater Honour to be a Favourite of Heaven, than to perform the greatest Actions without Divine Aid; it being justly look'd on as the strongest Proof of any Man's uncommon Merit, that he is belov'd and supported by the Gods, to whom an ill Man can never be dear or acceptable. This Assertion has, at first sight, a good appearance, but in my Opinion, if examin'd, it will be found more ingenious than solid. In the first place it is not in Fact true, that the principal Hero of the Poem, how great and successful soever he is, and how much soever encourag'd and aided by the Gods, is, or ought to be a good or vertuous Person. An ill Man may be a very good poetical Hero, and this is the Case of the *Iliad*. *Achilles* is not drawn as a Character of a pious and prudent Warrior, but is always furious, cruel, and inexorable, and sometimes unjust and impious: Nor is he favour'd

EPICK POETRY.

vour'd by Heaven for his Piety and Vertue, but for his Caufe, and the fake of his Country, whofe Intereft the prevailing Part of the Deities had efpous'd. And this has been actually the Fate of many other fuccefsful Generals, who by an uninterrupted Series of glorious Actions have acquir'd univerfal Fame, notwithftanding they have been eminent for no Vertue, but Military; for Divine Providence often animates and fupports a valiant, tho a vicious and profane Leader, and enables him to do Wonders, that by his over-ruling Wifdom he may bring about fome great Event that ferves the Ends of his Government, which however were never intended by the Warrior, that promoted them. And this being an evident Truth, it is plain, that to be affifted and favour'd by Heaven is not a Mark of extraordinary Merit in the Hero, and therefore cannot redound to his Honour.

But were it otherwife, and could we fuppofe that the Pagan Deities never took part with any Heroes, but thofe that were eminently Moral and Pious, and that no ill Prince or General was favour'd by Heaven and crown'd with great and wonderful Succeffes; yet if it be allow'd, that the Deities do any thing more than as univerfal Caufes, which concur and co-operate with the Hero, that is, if their Actions are diftinct and feparate from the Hero's, if in Perfon they fight againft, or by their menacing Prefence terrify the Enemy, as in the Cafe of *Turnus*, *Dii me terrent & Jupiter hoftis*: It is clear, that this Action is no more the Hero's than if a third Man had thruft a Firebrand in the *Latian's* Face, to facilitate the *Trojan's* Victory. Let the Hero then be ever fo much a Favourite of Heaven, and ever fo illuftrious for his Vertue and religious Qualities, if it be fuppos'd that the Gods do actually engage in Combat with his Rival, and perfonally help to fubdue him, the Hero can by no means derive any Honour from this Conqueft : But if it be allow'd that the Poet, by interefting Celeftial Powers in the Action intends no more, than in an allegorical Manner, to inculcate on the Minds of the People a juft Notion of Divine Providence, and the Neceffity that we lie under to implore his Favour, and rely on his Affiftance in all important Undertakings : If it be likewife acknowledg'd that the Affiftance, which he gives the Hero, is by infpiring his Mind with intrepid Refolution, and animating him to put forth his utmoft Strength, as well by difpofing of Circumftances fo as to intimidate

midate the Enemy, or to occasion his Confusion and Distraction; this Concurrence will not detract from the Glory of the Conqueror, but augment it; for this does not make his Actions to be less his own, since the Aid he receives from Heaven is by Co-operation, and by enabling him to exert his Faculties and Powers to the highest Degree of which he is capable, but not farther: And if this Explanation be allow'd, the Difficulty arising from the above-mention'd Objection to Machines in Epick Poetry, is remov'd.

The famous *Raphael* in his only Heroick Piece, I mean, the Battle fought by *Constantine* and *Maxentius* for the *Roman* Empire, delineates three arm'd Angels flying over the Head of the first Leader; by which he represents the watchful Care of Heaven, in protecting the Persons and assisting the Troops of favourite Leaders; but he judiciously chuses not to mingle them in the Army, or to exhibit them actually fighting against *Maxentius* or his Soldiers; for had that been done, the Honour of the Victory could not justly have been ascrib'd to his Rival. If therefore *Homer* and *Virgil* by engaging the Deities in the Action, meant any thing more than a figurative Representation of Divine Providence,

vidence, that concerns it self intimately in Humane Affairs, in my Opinion Reason will not bear them out; but that strange Mixture of Gods fighting with Men must be not only harsh and uncouth, but unnatural and absurd.

There are two sorts of Men among us, those who disbelieve invisible Beings of a superior Order to that of Men, and many Christians of the contrary Opinion, who notwithstanding they are pleas'd with the Machines introduc'd by Pagan Writers into their Poems, and think they impart Ornament, Strength and Dignity to the Work, are not satisfy'd that a Christian Poet should engage Celestial or Infernal Powers, agreeable to the Scheme of their own Religion, either in Epick or any other great Poems. They had rather all Things should be represented as manag'd and over-rul'd by Pagan Deities; and therefore the Poets of this Principle do not make use of Christian Machines in their Writings, tho in a Country where that Religion is profess'd and establish'd, but employ the Idols of the ancient Heathens in all their Works, notwithstanding the Practice is so incongruous and absurd. The Reason I suppose, why the first sort, I mean our irreligious Scepticks, act in this

Epick Poetry.

this manner is this, That they know the Heathen Deities, whom they intereft in their Poems, are no more than imaginary Beings, and they can freely concern themfelves with fuch Gods, without difturbing their Minds, by raifing Apprehenfions of Divine Juftice, Remorfe for Guilt, or Fears of Punifhment. They can mention *Mars*, *Apollo* and *Venus* with great Satisfaction and Serenity of Mind; for they are paft doubt that thefe are invented Divinities, that have no Exiftence: But when they name the Creator and fupream Moderator of the World, the Celeftial Hierarchy and Infernal Spirits, as afferted by the Chriftian Revelation, not being certain, that is entirely deliver'd from diftruft, that thefe Beings are the mere Creatures of Fancy and Fiction, they cannot think of them without fome inward Awe and Difturbance; and this is a good Reafon to prove, that tho the Atheift is fully fatisfy'd of the Falfhood of Heathen Schemes, yet he is not fure of the Falfhood of the Chriftian; for if he were, he would equally be inclin'd to the one and the other, and then he would infallibly prefer the Chriftian Religion, and out of Decency and Congruity make ufe of it in his Writings, fince it is the eftablifh'd Religion of his Country.

But

But the Reason why many Christians oppose the Use of Machines agreeable to their own Religion, is of a different Nature. These Gentlemen are of *Boileau's* Judgment, that the Greatness and Majesty of the Christian Religion would be debas'd, by engaging in Epick Poems superior, invisible Beings, according to that System; and Sir *William Temple* is of the same Opinion. But let it be consider'd, that Epick Poetry is indeed the Theology of the Country where the Poet lives, and every Work of this kind is a System of the Religion, and a sort of Confession of the Publick Faith there establish'd; and therefore it is as great an Absurdity for an Epick Writer to employ any other Scheme of Religion in his Poems, as if a Christian Preacher should form his Discourses upon the Plan of *Mahomet*, or in Conformity to the Doctrines of the *Gentiles*. Besides this Objection, that the Christian Religion does not furnish such proper Materials for Heroick Poetry as the Pagan Theology, will fall to the Ground, if it be con der'd, that the Supream Being and the first Apostate Angel have actually been introduc'd in the Book of *Job*, without debasing the Dignity of Religion; that *Milton* has, with Success, employ'd in the

Action

Epick Poetry.

Action of his Poem Machines suitable to the Chriftian Scheme, and that the like is done in Prince *Arthur*, and other Poems that follow'd it, without finking the Sublimity or diminifhing the Majefty of that Divine Inftitution.

Of the Dignity of the Narration.

IN an Epick Poem all Things fhould be great, ferious, and elevated, without any Allay of puerile and light Ideas. The Gravity and Dignity of the fublime Stile will not endure facetious Expreffion, much lefs fuch Strains as have an Air of Raillery and Burlefque. None of thefe low and ludicrous Mixtures, which are inconfiftent with the Height and Importance of an Epick Action, is any where found in *Virgil's Æneis*; fo careful was that judicious Author not to debafe the Greatnefs, corrupt the Purity, or fully the Luftre of the Heroick Stile, by interfperfing gay Conceptions and Sports of Fancy, which can only be agreeable to a falfe Tafte, that cannot judge of the true Sublime. And when *Homer* entertains his Reader with the Pleafantry and Laughter of the Gods, occafion'd by the awkward Behaviour of the limping Deity that fill'd out the *Nectar* at their Feafts, and with the merry Pranks of *Mars* and *Venus* entangled in his artful Net, he offends againſt Propriety of Manners, by repreſenting Celeſtial Beings engag'd in mean and trifling Paſtimes, unbecoming their Divine Character. And as by introducing into Heaven Farce and Buffoonry, an improper Place for ſuch Diverſion, he has broken in upon the Congruity and Decency which ſhould be always preſerv'd in the Characters, ſo he tranſgreſſes the Rule, that baniſhes in general from Heroick Works, all comick Manners, witty Conceits and Ridicule; the reaſon of which Rule is founded on the Nature of Epick Poetry, whoſe Property it is to celebrate the Actions of the Supream Being, Angels, and illuſtrious Men, and therefore is too ſolemn and noble to bear the little Plays of Imagination.

Of the MORAL.

AN Epick Poem muſt be inſtructive, and it is requir'd that it ſhould be agreeable only that it may the more effectually leave vertuous Impreſſions on the Mind; which uſeful end is common to this, with the other Species of Poetry. It is not ſufficient that ſome few moral Sentences are here and there interſpers'd, but a Divine Spirit ſhould reign through the

* whole

Epick Poetry.

whole Compofition. The Incidents and Digreffions fhould every where convey to the Imagination great and elevated Ideas, fill the Breaft with generous Paffions, and produce in the Soul warm Refolutions to follow the Dictates of Reafon, and obey the Precepts of Religion and Vertue; and befides this, fome important Moral fhould arife from the whole Fable.

I CANNOT conceive that *Boffu*'s Affertion, however ingenious it may be, is founded on good Reafon, which is, that the Poet muft in his firft Intention be dogmatical and pitch upon fome confiderable Moral, and then contrive his Fable fuitable to that Defign: If it be well obferv'd it will evidently appear, that no Author can form the Narration of any great and memorable Action but fome Moral will arife from it, whether the Writer intends it or not: And fince *Homer* and *Virgil* do not exprefly draw any Doctrine from their Fables, it is uncertain whether they defign'd any, tho they ought to have done it; and it is ftill more uncertain, whether they intended thofe particular Morals which are generally afcrib'd to them, becaufe many fuch Leffons of Inftruction will refult from the Imitation of any illuftrious and extraordinary Action,

either

either in Epick or in Tragick Poems. As from Pulpit Difcourfes on Divine Subjects, many ufeful Inferences may be deduc'd by the Preacher; fo in thefe fuperior Poems various Doctrines may arife, which the Poet may himfelf mention if he pleafes, or leave them to be drawn by the People for their Improvement.

Tho the Epick Poets feldom name their Moral at the end of the Action, yet the Tragick often do; and when they mention it, they are not to be cenfur'd, becaufe others likewife may be nam'd, fince many, and thofe very different too, may naturally fpring from the fame Subject. But when the Writer mentions thefe inftructive Sentiments at the end of the Poem they are no Parts of it, but are out of the Action, and only refult from the Cataftrophe; which is evident, fince the Action is compleat without it.

That in the end of the Action the chief Perfon fhould be fuccefsful, has been the general Opinion of the Poets and mere Criticks; which Rule they have laid down and propagated without confulting Reafon in the Cafe, being led into it by the *Iliad* and *Odyffes* of *Homer*, and the *Æneid* of *Virgil*; in which the Event is profperous,

and

Epick Poetry.

and the Hero furmounts all his Difficulties. See here another Inftance of the Submiffion which the Poets and Commentators have made to naked Authority, by which they have advanc'd Maxims out of Reverence to great Names, without any difcuffion of the Subject, or entring upon any Enquiry into the Foundation that fupports their Affertion. I fhall therefore reject this Rule, which is unwarrantably impos'd upon Epick Writers, and maintain the contrary Opinion, as more agreeable to Reafon.

There is no Neceffity that the Hero fhould finifh the Action with Victory and Renown, if we reflect, that the end of the Epick Poet may be equally attain'd, tho the Event fhould be unfortunate; various and important Inftructions will arife as well from a calamitous as a happy Iffue, and which perhaps will have a better Effect and leave a more lafting Impreffion on the Mind. If Men would not cut off the Connexion of this Life with the next, but would contemplate this State of Probation and that of Immortality and judicial Retribution to come, as one Duration unbroken by Death, which does not deftroy and extinguifh our Life, but diverfify and change its Circumftances: In

this

this View the Mind of the Reader would become easy, tho he finds at last a wicked Prince or Warrior triumph over distress'd Vertue, or a Person endow'd with Heroick Qualities left in the greatest Misery; for he will please himself with the Prospect of their future State of Life, when Rewards and Punishments shall be impartially distributed, when Persons of Merit and Piety shall be ever happy, and the Irreligious and Immoral be consign'd to endless Sufferings.

Besides, an unhappy Issue of the Action is no less an imitation of Nature, which is essentially requir'd in this Species of Poetry, as well as in Tragedy and Comedy, than a prosperous Catastrophe: We lament every Day the calamitous Fate of excellent Princes and illustrious Worthies, while cruel Tyrants and impious Generals appear like Favourites of Heaven, blest with Success in all their Undertakings. This, by the Permission of Divine Providence, is most usually observ'd in the common Course of Humane Affairs; and therefore the Representation made by the Poet, of unprosperous Events that happen to the Hero, is the nearest imitation of Nature, as being that which most commonly comes to pass. If it be objected,

Epick Poetry.

objected, that this would bring Dishonour upon Providence that suffers Vertue to be ill treated, while Vice and Impiety are not only unpunish'd, but attended with Wealth and Dignity, and raise in the Minds of the People murmuring and discontent, while these Examples of neglected Merit and distress'd Innocence are set before them, which cannot but discourage Men from imitating those generous Qualities, that are like to involve them in Trouble and Ruin. I answer, that there is not the least Weight in this Objection, if Men, as I observ'd before, would look on the Present and the Future State of Life to be one extended Existence, which Death, 'tis true, varies, but does not interrupt or dissolve its Connexion. Take then into one View, those Parts of Life that shall succeed Death, and those that have preceeded it, and regard it as much an entire and undivided Duration, as that of Infancy, Youth and Age, and the Difficulty will soon be remov'd; for then the Reader will see, that Innocence and Vertue, which suffer in one part of Life, will flourish and be rewarded in another of infinitely greater Extent; and Impiety, tho now prosperous and triumphant, will hereafter meet with condign Punishment.

Of the Characters.

AS to the Persons that enter into the Action, they ought to be distinguish'd by their various Characters, either as Princes or Subjects, Wife or Valiant, Pious or Irreligious, Calm or Turbulent, or otherwise diversify'd by different Inclinations and Habits; and when their Characters are mark'd and settled, their Manners should be suitable and becoming those Characters, that is, every Person should speak and act, where-ever he is introduc'd, as it is reasonable and proper that a Man of such Qualities should do, and that likewise according to the Temper and Circumstances in which he is at the Instant, when he acts. If he is calm and sedate, or agitated by any great Emotion of Mind, he must express his Temper in his Language and Deportment. As the whole Poem is an imitation of Nature, so that Imitation should be constantly preserv'd, and appear every where conspicuous in all the Actors. The Poet therefore ought to observe a due regard to Time Place and Persons, which is the Foundation of Propriety, Fitness, and Decency; for whatever is improper and unbecoming, is likewise shocking and offensive. The Poet's Pictures, as well as the

Painter's

Painter's, should bear a just and lively Resemblance of the Original: When Dissimilitude and Disagreement is found between the Representation and the Object represented; this is not to imitate, but to bely Nature, and impose a Fraud upon the Reader. And this want of Justness, Uniformity, and a beautiful Representation of natural Causes and Effects in their various Distinctions will be a great Blemish to the Writing, and discover, that the Author is either careless or injudicious. For Instance, should a Person in deep Distress, overwhelm'd with Sorrow, transported with Rage, or burning with Revenge, make a long and elegant Discourse full of fine Similies, quaint Turns, and surprizing Metaphors, he would offend against the Custom and Rule of Nature, which in such Circumstances never acts in that manner. But I shall not enlarge upon this useful and copious Subject, which has been already exhausted by many eminent Writers. Hence it appears how necessary it is for the Poet to study and make himself well acquainted with the various Temperaments, Inclinations, and Passions of Mankind, to penetrate into the secret Springs of Humane Actions, and follow Nature through her minutest Recesses; that by this he may be qual.fy'd to appropriate

propriate to each different Complexion and inward Principle of Action, their characteriftick Manners and genuine Expreffion.

By what has been faid it will be evident, that the Difference between an Epick Poem and a Tragedy is not fo great, but that they may be mutually converted one into another. Should the Epick Poet retrench his Invocation, Propofition, and Introduction, fhould he fpeak nothing himfelf, but exprefs every Thing by the Mouths of the Actors; fhould he contract his Epifodes and reduce their Number, omit his Digreffions, cut off the length of his Speeches and Similes, and make his Incidents more vehement and paffionate, he would change his Poem to a Tragedy. On the contrary, fhould the Action of the laft be exhibited by Narration, where the Poet fometimes fpeaks himfelf; fhould the Epifodes be multiply'd and extended, and the whole Action grow more calm and moderate, it would plainly become an Epick Poem.

And for this Reafon it farther appears, that the Event in an Heroick Compofition may be unhappy as well as in a Tragick, the Tranfmutation of one to another being fo eafy.

Epick Poetry.

It was affirm'd in the foregoing Discourse, that Epick Poetry was more nearly ally'd to Tragedy, than to any other kind; and therefore to set the Nature of it yet in a clearer Light, it may not be improper to form a Comparison between them.

A Comparison between Epick Poetry *and* Tragedy.

Tragick and Epick Poetry agree in their general Idea, both being equally an imitation of Nature. But the Tragick Poet imitates by Reprefentation, as the Epick by Recital or Narration: The laft tells what Things were done, and in what Order by thofe who are interefted in the Action: But the firft introduces the Actors doing all Things in their own Perfons. The Epick Poet often interpofes Difcourfes of his own, which the Tragick never does; but every Thing is faid and done by the Parties engag'd in the Poem; the Difference is the fame as between two Authors, of whom one relates a Conference held by two or more Perfons, and tells the Reader what was faid, and by whom in the whole Debate; and the other introduces the Parties themfelves difcourfing and anfwering one another in the Dialogue, without any Intervention of the Author himfelf. Thefe Poets likewife agree in their End, which is to improve the Underftanding with Moral and Divine Inftruction, and infpire the Heart with a pious Ardor and a generous Refolution to aim at Heroick Vertue: But they proceed in a different way to attain their Defign. The Tragick Poet to procure his End, reprefents fuch Actions, and introduces fuch Incidents and various Turns, as are moft proper and effectual to raife Terror and Compaffion in the Minds of the Audience; but the Epick Author contrives his Fable, and forms and connects his Epifodes in the fitteft way to create Delight and Admiration.

It is requir'd, that in each, of thefe Species of Poetry the principal Perfons fhould be of illuftrious Birth or high Station, that is, Poetical Heroes and Heroines, and that the Action be great and important. But they difagree in this, that Tragedy is very bufy and vehement, it works the Soul with turbulent Emotions and endlefs Tranfports, and conftantly either melts the tender, or agitates the violent Paffions; while Epick Poetry is more calm

Epick Poetry.

calm and moderate, where the Reader is carry'd on with a lively and pleasant Gale; but not as in the other Case, hurry'd with Violence, and driven by a Tempest. An Epick Poem being more sedate and quiet, the Action is of long Duration, sometimes of many Years; and the Narration, by multiply'd Episodes, Events, and Digressions, is carry'd on to a great Extent. But the Action in Tragedy being more passionate and impetuous, is of far shorter Continuance, being usually finish'd in two or three Days, or yet a shorter Time. An Epick Poem contains as well plenty of Characters, which enliven and enrich the Work, as great variety of Subject Matter in its integral Parts, and frequent Excursions. Tragedy is more close and concise, being straiten'd and confin'd in a narrower compass of Time.

These two Species of Poetry are universally allow'd to surpass all others, but there is some Controversy which of them is superior and to be most esteem'd; *Aristotle* gives the first Rank to Tragedy, but by the unanimous Suffrages of succeeding Criticks, an Epick Poem is the most noble and excellent Production of Humane Understanding; and it is remarkable, that the Criticks deserted their Master in this

Point, when his Authority was at the greatest Height and the learned World servilely submitted to his Judgment in the Arts and Sciences: Nothing can account for this, but that the Evidence was so strong and clear against *Aristotle*'s Opinion, that they were not able, how willing soever they might be, to resist its Conviction. *Rapin*, a Critick of the first Class, affirms, that an Epick Poem is the most admirable and perfect Work of the Mind, and assigns this Reason of his Assertion, That it contains in it self the Perfections of all other kinds of Poetry. To strengthen and support his Assertion, he cites many of the most eminent Masters of Criticism.

Having thus examin'd the Nature and Constitution of an Epick Poem, and shown in what Instances my Notions agree with, or differ from the receiv'd Opinions of the *Aristotelian* Criticks, I am now oblig'd by Promise to give my own Definition of such a Work, which I look upon as more just and reasonable than that laid down in the beginning of this Discourse; *An Epick Poem is a probable, marvellous, and devis'd Story of an important Enterprize, or great Suffering of some illustrious Person, recited in Verse of the sublime Stile, to afford Delight and Instruction.* I have left out of this Definition, the Term Allego-

Allegorical, because it is not necessary that an Epick Poem should be Allegorical in any other Sense, than that the Narration ought to be Metaphorical and Figurative; which Property is fully express'd by requiring, that the Recital be made *in Verse of the sublime Stile*. I have left out the Term *Action*, and have added *Enterprize* or *Suffering*, for the Reasons alledg'd in the foregoing Dissertation; and I have said *Illustrious Person*, to leave the Definition free, and not restrain'd to a Hero; since no Reason, as I believe, can be assign'd, why a Heroine may not be the Principal Person of an Epick, as well as a Tragick Poem, to which it is so nearly ally'd. It is evident, That the essential Properties of an Heroick Work may be all preserv'd, and the principal End of the Poet be as effectually obtain'd, where an illustrious Woman is introduc'd as the chief Character, as well as where a Prince or General sustain that Province.

SECT.

SECTION II.

HAVING in the foregoing Pages inquir'd into the intrinfick Conftitution and effential Properties of an Epick Work, I fhall now proceed to examine the Stile, and other external Qualities neceffary to this elevated Species of Poetry.

When in the eldeft Ages of the World Men perceiv'd a want of Means to communicate their Sentiments to Perfons at a great Diftance, and to many at once, and defir'd a more faithful and lafting Preferver of their Opinions than Oral Tradition, the Art of Printing being yet unknown, they found out various ways of committing their Thoughts to Writing: At firft they infcrib'd them in Bricks and Stones, and afterwards in Tables overfpread with Wax, ufing a piece of Iron call'd a *Stile*, which is a *Greek* Term made *English*. This fmall Inftrument was pointed at one end, and flat at the other. They employ'd the pointed End to raife up the Wax and form the Letters, and with the
flat

Epick Poetry.

flat they effac'd the Writing at Pleasure, by filling up the Furrows and smoothing the Wax, according to that of *Horace*,

Sæpe Stilum vertas iterum qua digna legi sint Scripturus.

Oft turn your Stile, and use th' unpointed Head,
If you would write Things worthy to be read.

By degrees the Term Stile came figuratively to express the Way or Character of Writing in general, and was divided into several sorts that arose from the various Modes of Diction, in Discourses on various Subjects. It was likewise us'd to signify the Manner of Expression peculiar to this or that Author: So we say *Virgil*'s or *Livy*'s Stile. So *Cicero*, in his Book of famous Orators, describes a wonderful Variety of Eloquence in the *Romans*, whose different Stile he delineates with admirable Distinction. The Word is now likewise translated, and becomes Technical in the Arts of Musick and Painting, by which the Artists express the different Manner of writing Musick, or drawing Pictures, proper to different Masters.

Stile

STILE then, in general, is the Character or Fashion of Writing. This to the Method and Symetry of the Compofition adds Complexion, Vivacity and Decoration, and enlivens the Difcourfe, which before was an imperfect Draught, with finifhing Strokes and beautiful Colouring. Here the Writer exerts his Skill, beftows all the Charms and Graces that his Art affords, and adjufts every thing to the utmoft Advantage that he may raife the Admiration of the Reader.

As the Choice of Words, which, in the Opinion of eminent Criticks, is the principal Part of Eloquence, belongs to the Stile; fo does the ranging of them in a beautiful and harmonious Order, as well as all the elegant and moving Turns of Expreffion, whith adorn their proper Places and give Life and Luftre to the Whole. Hither alfo is refer'd the Art of touching the Soul, and agitating the Paffions by bold and warm Images, Interrogations, Apoftrophes, Profopopeia's, Expoftulations, and other pathetick Forms of Diction.

VARIOUS are the Species of Stile, the Smooth or Rough, the Natural or Affected, the Flowing or Stiff, the Clear or Obfcure,

Epick Poetry. 93

Obscure, the Simple or Ornamental, and the Concise or Diffusive; but the principal Division is into Low and Lofty. I shall confine my self to the Last, which is the Stile requir'd in Epick Poetry.

Tho the Mind should be ever so happily turn'd for Epick Eloquence, yet without the Improvements of Art and a well inform'd Judgment to conduct its Motions, it will not be able to avoid many dishonourable Errors, nor will it ever rise to that Perfection of which its native Faculties are capable. It is true, no Discourse is so masterly and prevalent, as that which appears natural and dictated by the present Passion, and it is for this End that Rules are necessary; for the greatest Art is requir'd to make it seem artless and unlabour'd, and the most effectual Directions for this End shall be afterwards taken notice of.

To form the sublime Stile, that it may answer the Dignity of the Subject, which must be always great and important, the Concurrence of these Particulars is necessary; Elevation of Thought, a due Choice of Words, and a proper Disposition of them; as likewise the use of apt Rhetorical Figures, and a right Address to the

† Passions.

Paffions. The Defect of any of thefe abates the Force and Beauty of the Stile, and the want of fome wholly deftroys it.

Of the Sublimity of the Thoughts.

Thoughts are then fublime, when they are conceiv'd in an extraordinary Manner, and are elevated above obvious and familiar Sentiments; and this Sublimity of the Ideas imparts internal Heat, Vigour and Majefty to the Narration, as the judicious and happy Choice of pure, proper and expreffive Words, and fplendid and polite Diction, give outward Richnefs, Elegance, and Magnificence.

That a Poet of this Kind may raife his Thoughts to a juft Sublimity for Matters of fuch Dignity and Excellence as thofe which he is converfant about, it is neceffary he fhould fix his Mind upon them, that by Familiarity and long Acquaintance with them, he may ftock his Imagination with fplendid and beautiful Images. It is the Remark of *Longinus*, That it is impoffible for a Man inur'd only to bafe and vulgar Thoughts, to reach that Elevation

Epick Poetry.

vation of Mind which is neceſſary for an Orator of the firſt Rank; Such a Man, ſays he, will never ſpeak any thing extraordinary, or write any thing worthy of Poſterity; and therefore he adviſes Men to nouriſh in their Minds a generous Temper, that will always incline them to form high and noble Ideas: And if it be ſo neceſſary for an Orator, it is yet much more requir'd of an Epick Poet, whoſe Subject is always Great and Illuſtrious. If it be his Ambition to write extraordinary Things, becoming the Height and Importance of his Subject, worthy of his Character, and fit to be tranſmitted to Future Times, he ſhould not grovel in the Duſt, nor breath in thick impure Air, but keep above, and inure himſelf to lofty Contemplation, till by a conſtant Correſpondence and Intercourſe with ſuperior Objects, he gets a Habit of Thinking in the great and elevated Manner, peculiar to the Heroick Poet. By this he will be enabled to riſe to the Heights of Heaven, and from thence to caſt himſelf down with a generous Freedom and Reſolution, and plunge amidſt the Depths of Nature, to diſcover the ſecret Springs of her wonderful Operations; and by the ſame Principle he will be capable of penetrating the dark Walks and myſterious Labyrinths of Divine Providence, in

the

the Administration of Humane Affairs; by which means he will collect rich Materials, and proper Ornaments to embellish his Work, and make it marvellous.

And this Power of forming great and extraordinary Conceptions, and laying up Hoards of lively and wonderful Ideas, is so necessary to inspire the Narration with Life and Ardor, that it is impossible by any Means to supply its Absence. Where this is wanting, all artificial Decoration is idle and ridiculous; but this alone gives such force and lustre, that without the Additions of Art, it will attract our Esteem and raise our Admiration. This is remarkable not only in Poetical Eloquence, but in that of the Pulpit, where some Preachers, tho not curious in the choice of their Words, nor correct and musical in their Diction, by the Sublimity of their Thoughts and Divine Expression, accompany'd with an awful Gravity, a becoming Zeal, and the serious Air of One in earnest, succeed far better than many who are more polite and regular in their Stile. It is the Majesty, Strength, and Vivacity of the Images, the Solidity and Loftiness of the Sentiments, that chiefly penetrate and melt the Audience; and the various Precepts of Rhetorick, which of themselves have no Force,

Force, can only assist their Operation: Notwithstanding great Poets, as well as Orators, may be defective in some Points that relate to external Embellishments, they abundantly atone for all their Faults by the admirable and excellent Sense which they every where abound with; and as *Longinus* says of *Demosthenes* and *Plato*, one or two of their wonderful Thoughts make amends for all their Errors. Extraordinary Minds, as that Critick remarks, are so taken up with great Objects, that they have no Time or Inclination to attend to the low and minute Affairs of Rhetorick, and therefore their Omissions are not so much to be imputed to want of Skill, as to Inadvertency; not to the Weakness of their Judgments, but to the Strength and Elevation of their Conceptions.

Of the Choice *of* Words.

AFTER the Sublimity of the Thoughts, a due Choice of Words is to be regarded, which being only Marks and admonishing Signs to transmit the Sentiments of the Speaker to the Hearer, those certainly are the best, as most adapted to their End, which most clearly, and with the greatest Facility, represent the Mind of the one, and are moſt eaſily apprehended by the other; and therefore avoiding all odd and uncouth Phraſes, low Language, and vulgar Metaphors on one hand, and the vain Pomp of the falſe Sublime on the other, the Epick Poet ſhould chuſe the middle ſort, that is, proper, clear, and ſignificant Words, that will not by their Baſeneſs, offend the more Judicious, nor by their Unacquaintedneſs be unintelligible to Perſons of good Senſe, tho not of great Learning. As it is a great Miſtake to think the elevated Stile is form'd of ſounding Words and lofty Diction, which conſiſts chiefly in the Greatneſs, Strength, and Majeſty of the Sentiments; ſo on the other hand, the Poet muſt not uſe courſe and familiar Expreſſion, on pretence of conveying his Thoughts with greater eaſe and clearneſs; for that would deſtroy the Sublime another way.

Since a polite and finiſh'd Stile depends ſo much on a judicious Choice and ranging of the Words, I will be more particular on this Subject. Words are the Marks and Repreſentations by which we communicate our Conceptions to others; and there are three ſorts which we uſe for this purpoſe; the Plain, Strange, and Figurative. The Plain and Simple, whoſe
ſigni-

Epick Poetry. 99

signification is by common Custom sufficiently establish'd, when well chosen and well dispos'd, become the Foundation of all Eloquence: The Poet therefore, that he may write justly and correctly, is obllig'd to use none but pure and proper Words, such as are authoriz'd by the most eminent and approv'd Authors, and are generally receiv'd by Men of Condition, Education, and Learning, in the Age in which he lives.

Tho the *English* have not taken so much Pains nor instituted Academies, like some of their Neighbours, to refine and embellish their Language, yet the Genius of the Times, and the great Improvements made in the politer Parts of Learning, have rais'd it to a greater height of Purity than that of past Ages. Abundance of obsolete Words and sordid Phrases are banish'd, not only from the Press and Pulpit, but from Conversation likewise; and if there be any who continue fond of uncouth and antiquated Terms, they have few intelligent Persons among their Admirers. The Language of the present Times is so clean and chaste, and so very different from our Ancestors, that should they return hither, they would want an Interpreter to converse with us. And why

why should any be fond of an old Mode, when the far greater Part are got into another Dress, and especially when the Change is so much more decent and convenient? It is a sordid Disposition of Mind, that makes any Men prefer their rustick and offensive Stile, before those pure and beautiful Forms of Speech which our Tongue abounds with; where none have reason to complain of scarcity of Words, against which there lies no Objection, to express their strongest Sentiments to the greatest Advantage. Should we lay by all base and unbecoming Phrases, and cast off the Rust and Dross of Antiquity, we should still have enough left, not only to put our Thoughts into a bare Habit, but to serve also for Pomp and Ornament.

And as it ought to be the Poet's Care, that in the Choice of Words he always examines their Purity and Propriety, so in the next place, he ought to have great regard to their clearness and aptitude to represent his Thoughts. All Terms are, by Use and Custom, stampt with their distinct Significations, and when many may be employ'd to express the same Thing, yet some bear a more lively Image of it, and convey it with greater Ease and Advantage

vantage than others. Words, like good Pictures, are to be valu'd more for their Likeness and Resemblance, than their Richness and Splendor: For if they are strong and clear they go immediately to the Head, and thence directly to the Heart, and will instruct and excite the Reader more, and with more ease than long obscure Sentences and tedious Circumlocutions; which is the Reason, why *Aristotle* so much condemns those Orators, who affect always a Paraphrastical way of Speaking, when a few proper and plain Words would have done their Work better, and much sooner.

The Temperance likewise and Modesty of the Words, are Qualities that should greatly recommend them to the Poet: And these Vertues are found in them, either in respect of their Sound, or their Signification, or their Number: A judicious Poet seeks the purest and most natural, not the most sounding and splendid Terms. He does not reject these, provided they have the other more desirable Properties: But he is not solicitous to bring into every Line, such as have little else to make them acceptable, but the Pomp of their numerous Syllables. He does not affect always to shine forth in bright Expressions, nor does he foar aloft in ever Period. A decent and mafculine Stile abhors the Vanity of fuch Diction, which, wanting Thoughts and Senfe to fill and animate the Sentences, is fo far from being ftrong and majeftick, that it becomes feeble and ridiculous.

The next Care of the Epick Poet is to preferve the Chaftnefs of the Stile, by reftraining the Luxuriancy of his Words, which in Reafon fhould be no more than will ferve to convey his Thoughts; nor more than are equal and commenfurate to the Senfe, and adapted to the Capacities of the Reader. And if this Rule were obferv'd, many Writers would be oblig'd to cut off great part of their Poems, as altogether ufelefs and impertinent. Some of a poor and fhallow Underftanding, endeavour to fupply their want of Thought, by the redundancy of their Sentences; others who indeed think well, for want of Skill, do often fo over-charge their Works with unneceffary Diction, that they lofe much of the Beauty and Strength of their Performance, while by many fynonimous Terms and a Train of long and founding Epithets, their Thoughts are overwhelm'd, and the Senfe is carry'd off in a Torrent of Words.

Care

CARE and Observation will correct this Fault, which in many Poets arises from the great Fertility of their Genius, and is mostly incident to younger Men, who have warm and active Fancies, and not Judgment enough to restrain their Excesses. These should therefore study a more sober Conduct, and hold the Reins over their Imagination more steady, that it may not run on with that Violence and Impetuosity, to which it is naturally inclin'd. They should consider, that the Words in which we dress our Sentiments, like the Habits of our Bodies, become beautiful and convenient, by their fitness and exact Proportion; and what is more than this, is ordinarily not only superfluous and useless, but inconvenient and burdensome. Our Garments are made for Defence and Decency, and are not so vast and numerous as to load and oppress us; and if we add Jewels and Ornaments, they are neither many nor ponderous: If in proper Places, as in Epick Works it very often happens, the Poet would appear with greater Splendor, as the most modest Persons do on solemn Occasions, he may give his Fancy greater Liberty, and let it shew its Plenty and Magnificence: He may not only cloath his Thoughts in apt and plain Expressions, but may form others richer and wider for Pomp and Dignity, if his good Senfe has Strength and Majefty enough to fupport them; otherwife there will be fuch an Excefs of Words, as a fober Stile will not endure.

As for ftrange and uncommon Words, they are fuch as convey our Thoughts without a Metaphor, but not without Surprize and Novelty; and thefe are either ancient, but not obfolete, or foreign, which are borrow'd from other Languages, or compounded. *Ariftotle* allows the ufe of thefe to Poets, and fays of the firft, That they render the Sentences more majeftick and venerable; and the reft, as unufual and furprizing, raife our Admiration, and give us Pleafure in the hearing: Yet he enjoins the temperate ufe of them, and tells us, that it requires a great deal of Conduct to obferve the Decorum, it being very eafy to abufe the Liberty of employing ftrange and uncommon Words; but he forbids the ufe of them to the Orator; For, fays he, only proper, familiar, and metaphorical, in exclufion of ancient and unufual Terms, are profitable and becoming in Profe.

As to foreign Terms, it muft be obferv'd, that fince the *Englifh* Tongue has

enrich'd

enrich'd it self with many Words borrow'd from other Languages, especially from the *Latin*, these being insensibly introduc'd and naturaliz'd by Custom, are no longer Strangers. And tho the use of these before they are made free and incorporated into our Language by general Consent, discovers the Writer's Vanity and Affectation, yet afterwards he may safely and laudably employ them; only he should observe that it will be ungrateful to the Judicious, if he shews himself always solicitous to bring in Terms but newly admitted and made *English*, when we have a sufficient Plenty besides, altogether as beautiful and significant. But for compounded Words, they never succeeded well in *English*, either in Verse or Prose; and tho some Writers in Imitation of the *Greeks*, whose Tongue is ennobled and adorn'd by them, have attempted to bring in this Custom, yet they have not been able to establish it; our Language will not bear such Compositions, and therefore *Heart-awakening*, *Nation-destroying*, and such like double Words, make but ill Musick to an *English* Ear.

Of the RANGING of the Words.

WHEN the Poet has chosen the most pure, proper, and significant Words, for the Ranging of them in the justest Order, and the forming of the Periods, the following Rules may be useful. Since in turning a beautiful Sentence, there is requir'd a just Proportion of Quantity, the Poet is oblig'd to observe a due Mediocrity between excessive Length and Brevity; which he will do, if his Periods entirely and clearly express his Mind, and are no longer than may be comprehended at the first Reading.

NOTHING is more tedious and uneasy to the Reader, than protracted and indistinct Sentences, by which his Attention is broken, his Memory confounded, and his Patience exhausted. Therefore *Aristotle* condemns the continu'd and uninterrupted Stile of the Ancients as most ungrateful, and gives this Reason for it, That the People can never see it finish'd. The pompous *Asiatick* manner, where the Period was never compleat, till the Sense was ended, which therefore took up an immoderate Compass, must be very difficult to be apprehended. Few are able

to

Epick Poetry. 107

to manage such long and unweildy Sentences with the Success that *Cicero* has done it: We find, when the Language and Judgment of the *Romans* were rais'd with their Empire to the greatest Height, the Delicacy and Severity of the Age would not bear this tedious and diffusive Stile, tho perhaps the Men that endeavour'd to retrench its Exuberance, especially *Seneca*, ran into the other Extream, a Fault very common to Reformers. But tho the Writers in Prose were more careful to avoid this Error in the *Augustan* Age, yet *Horace* in his Lyricks of the sublime Kind, very often by suspending his Sense for a great number of Lines, disgusts and perplexes the Reader; his Excess in the Proportion of his Sentences in his Odes is the more surprizing, because in his other Poems he is so concise and so frugal of Expression, that he becomes obscure by the contrary Extream. To conclude; the Sentences should be so bounded and so distinct in their Parts, that the Thought may at first View be apprehended, without giving any Pain or Confusion to the Mind.

On the other hand, the Periods of the Poem ought not to be too short, for then the Stile will be so close and the Stream of the Narration will flow with such precipitation,

cipitation, that the Readers will not have time to catch the Senfe; they will be always embarafs'd and troubled to find out the Poet's meaning; and the quick and hafty paffing from one Sentence to another will fo diftract them, that they will not be able to keep Company with the Author. Before one Period has finifh'd its Impreffion on their Thoughts, another coming fuddenly on, effaces the imperfect Strokes of the former, which muft needs difturb and difappoint the Reader.

Next to the due Proportion of the Periods, Care muft be taken that the Words be fo united as to render them clear and perfpicuous; and to this two Things are requir'd, that the Connexion of the Terms be eafy and natural, and that the Period confifts of diftinct Members. As to the firft, an *Englifh* Writer is unpardonable, if the Order of his Words is not plain and obvious, for which perhaps no Language in the World affords fuch great Advantages; no other admits and preferves that regular Succeffion of the Words as our own. In the *Greek, Latin, Italian, German,* and *Spanifh* Tongues, efpecially in the two firft, the unnatural Tranfpofition of the Terms extreamly obfcures the Sentiments of the Writer; their Periods are

are inverted from the Order in which the Mind form'd its Conceptions; and if the Words are the Images of our Thoughts, this is to reprefent them in a very irregular and diftorted manner; as if a Man were drawn with his Head between his Feet, or his Heels in the Air: Nothing being more common with thefe Writers, than to begin with the End or the Middle, and to leave off with the Beginning. The Nominative Cafe, which fhould in Reafon, and does certainly in Conftruction, lead the Sentence, and precede the Verb, in thefe Languages fometimes conceals it felf in the Middle, and is often referv'd for the End: And there are many other Tranfpofitions altogether as crofs and troublefome; and tho perhaps by this means the Period may become more harmonious, yet it grows much darker and more perplex'd, and therefore vexes and diftracts the Mind more than it gratifies and delights the Ear: And tho the *French* are more regular in placing their Words, than thofe above-nam'd, yet they range almoft in every Sentence fo many Particles and Relatives before their Verbs, which according to the Dictates of Nature and Reafon ought to follow, that it greatly abates the Eafinefs and Perfpicuity of their Stile. But the *Englifh* exprefs their Thoughts in the fame Train and Method in which the Mind conceives them; at leaft they may do it, if they affect not to be obfcure: When we form our Periods, no hafty Words thruft themfelves in before their Turn, and none linger or are left behind to trouble and interrupt the Current of the Difcourfe, than which nothing can contribute more to render a Stile eafy and intelligible.

What has been faid on this Article, regards our Writers both in Verfe as Profe; and tho the Poet is allow'd greater Liberty in tranfpofing his Words, yet from what has been alledg'd it will appear, that he has great Advantages from our Language, to enable him to exprefs his Thoughts in a regular Train and Succeffion, and by that to impart Perfpicuity to his Diction.

But this will not be enough, unlefs the Period be alfo diftinguifh'd into Parts of fit Proportion, and regularly fucceeding each other. *Ariftotle* requires this when he fays, " A compound Period is a fort of E-
" locution finifh'd, perfect for its Senfe,
" confifting of diftinct Parts, and that can
" eafily be pronounced in a Breath." And *Cicero* tells us, That a Period of more

Members or Articles is most delightful, most perspicuous, and most easily retain'd, giving the Orator and the Audience time to breath and rest.

Of the VERSIFICATION.

BUT that which in a peculiar manner is required of the Epick Poet, is the Art of Versifying, which consists in a free and natural Order and Connexion of the Words in a beautiful Succession, a musical Cadence, and a noble Train of the Periods; the Sentences should be full, but easy and clear. moderately extended, but not drawn out so far, as to keep the Reader too long in suspence; which generally they will do, if they exceed the length of six Lines. To avoid the Error and Deformity of unconnected and independent Couplets, which, in the Writings of some Poets, are so detach'd and unconcern'd with the rest, that the Reader may as well begin with any Two, either in the Middle or the End, as with the first, and quite invert the Order in which they are placed by the Author, without any Injury done to the Poem, by confounding the Sense: To avoid this Error, I say, the Writer must be careful to unite his Lines, and make them, in their Sense and Construction to depend up-

on

on one another, and not always to compleat the Sentence at the End of the second Verse. To avoid Monotony and Uniformity in finishing the Sense, and giving a Rest at the End of every Couplet, which is tedious and ungrateful to the Reader, the Poet should often run the Second Line into the Third, and after the manner of the *Latines*, and *Milton*, make the Stop in the Beginning or Middle of it; this will vary the Sound that before returned to Satiety, relieve the Ear, and give Dignity and Strength to the Narration.

When the Words are thus rang'd in a free and natural Order, and the Period makes all its Pauses and Advances with due leisure, and each Point succeeds in its proper Time and Place, it will appear beautiful, and be fully comprehended; whereas, without this Oeconomy in conducting the Sentence, there will be such a Tumult and Confusion, such a mix'd and disorderly Croud of Words crossing and pressing upon one another, that the Stile must needs be dark and deform'd. As the just Proportion of the Periods hinders the Stream of the Narration from overflowing, so this orderly ranging of the Words and dividing the Sentence into distinct Parts, saves it from being troubled and interrupted,

Epick Poetry.

rupted. As to the harmonious Course and musical Cadence of the Sentences, which some too much neglect, and others insist upon with too much Care, it arises from a grateful Variety of apt and melodious Words happily intermix'd, and regularly succeeding one another; whence the Period, like a peaceful River, flows without Tumult, and supports it self equally in every Part. If the Objects are noble and majestick, and the Terms significant and well sounding; if they are so artificially connected, that the Strength and Firmness of some uphold the Weakness of others, that are apt to sink and creep; and the Softness and flowing Easiness of these smooths the Roughness and tempers the Rigour of those; the Dignity of the Thoughts, and the Splendor of the Phrases being likewise suppos'd, the Narration cannot fail of being admirable and delightful.

Homer and *Virgil* have given us great Examples of Writing in this manner, whence their Diction is very beautiful and sublime. But tho *Horace* in his Odes is admirable, and the happiest Writer imaginable in the choice of his Words, yet it is evident he is defective in the disposition of them; for frequently his Sentences are not only

only too far extended, but by reason of many hard Transpositions, and the irregular ranging of his Words, his Sense is often so involv'd and clouded, that it is difficult to discover his meaning.

Some Poets, out of Negligence or Affectation, have such a harsh and perplex'd Stile; where the Words so croud and justle each other, and the Phrases have such a staring Look and awkward Pace; where the Links of the Discourse are so broken, the Periods being without distinction of Parts or natural Order, here cramp'd with Parentheses, and there disjointed and gaping for want of Connexion, that the Work instead of a beautiful Structure becomes a rude heap of Words. And this was often the Case of our *English* Poets, before *Waller* attempted to cultivate and refine our Diction, and led others, by his Example, to aim at Elegance and Politeness.

And as these Men are justly censur'd for too great Neglect of their Expression, so are others for their too great Concern and Labour about it. As a Man may as well be too finical as too sordid in his Dress, so a Poet may easily exceed the Bounds of Moderation and Decency, and bestow too much

much Time and Pains in turning the Periods, polishing the Stile, and beautifying the Phrases. True Eloquence is not so much solicitous about its Ornaments as its Strength, and tho it loves Decency it despises the Luxury of a wanton Stile.

Longinus observes of *Demosthenes*, that he us'd to embarrass and trouble his Stile on purpose, that the People might believe the Agitation and Disorder of his Mind was the Cause of this Irregularity; since tis not likely a Man mov'd with violent Passions, should be so elegant and correct in his Diction, as a calm and sedate Writer.

Besides the too strict Observation of Rules about the Choice of Words and forming of Periods, will fetter and restrain the Invention of the Writer; he will compose in such Fear, and his Imagination will be so curb'd and check'd in its Attempts, that he will not be able to form any great and surprizing Ideas; which Effect judicious Men observe in the Discourses and Writings of those, who are excessively curious about their Stile. I confess, I am very much pleas'd with elegant Phrase and fine Expression; but then

I would have *Quintilian*'s Advice obferv'd, That this fhining and beautiful Diction be employ'd to reprefent Thoughts that are much greater and more fublime. If the Sentiments are generous and majeftick, it is but fit they fhould appear in a richer and more fplendid Drefs; but when they are mean and common, their Habit fhould be fo too. An intemperate and too anxious Care about the Ornaments is as ungrateful, and as much to be cenfur'd as our Negligence. *Nefcio negligentia in hoc, an follicitudo fit pejor.*

SOME Poets, mifguided by a wrong Notion of Politenefs, cut and prune their Diction fo clofe, as makes it dry and barren, and dwell fo long on correcting and finifhing, that they emaciate and ftarve the Stile, which by this means wants the Spirit, Strength, and florid Afpect of a mafculine Production. While they aim at a clean and elegant manner of Writing, by too fcrupulous exactnefs, they enervate the Expreffion fo much, that it will never rife to the true Sublime; that is, will never become rich, magnificent and admirable. It may pleafe, but will never aftonifh. It may be without Faults, but then it will have few Beauties; and if there be nothing to be cenfur'd, there will be

Epick Poetry.

be little to be admir'd. These Men are not endow'd with a generous, free and daring Genius, which is necessary for elevated Writing, and have too much of the Grammarian and Corrector to attempt lofty Flights. Their Poetry is so bare and spiritless, that it approaches near to Prose; and a prosaick Poet is no more acceptable than a poetical Orator: It proceeds from a false Taste of Elegance and Simplicity, that the Poet is so thrifty and parsimonious in his Diction, and allows so little Expence in Ornaments. For fear of redundance in Words, too daring Figures and immoderate Pomp of Expression, they defraud their Stile of becoming and necessary Graces. They always grovel and creep below; and least they should fall, are afraid to rise. These Poets dress their Thoughts as *Quakers* do their Bodies, whose Garments are fit, clean and modest, but without Ornament. But it is certain, the Habit of a Gentleman, that is richer and more splendid, is more polite and agreeable. Should a Prince, especially on solemn Days, when usually he is clad in Robes of State, appear in the plain and cheap Dress of a frugal Citizen, he may look neat and decent, but by no means August and Majestick. Now it should be consider'd, that in the Epick Stile where the

Persons

Perfons are Illuftrious and the Action of great Importance, Magnificence and Splendor are always requir'd; and indeed Profufion is here fcarce a Fault, or if it be, it is however more pardonable than a niggardly Oeconomy; and for this Reafon *Homer* may in fome meafure be defended againft the Cenfure of thofe, who except againft his Stile as Redundant.

By a too elaborate and correct Stile the Author will difcover his Affectation, and become obnoxious to *Pliny*'s Cenfure, Such an Orator has no Error but this, That he has none. It is the Vertue of a good Speaker and Writer fometimes to commit a Fault, and by a ftudy'd Carelefnefs to leave fome Blemifhes, to avoid the Vice of too great Politenefs, that expofes the Art by making it too vifible. All the Mafters of Eloquence agree, that it is the greateft Regularity fometimes to tranfgrefs the Rule, for which Reafon we fee fo many rough and abrupt Places, and fo many Diforders in Number, Metre and Syntax interfpers'd in the Orations and Poems of the *Greeks* and *Latins*, yet with fo much Beauty and Art, that they pleafe as much with their Negligence as with their Labour, and from their Faults Pofterity has learned to make Figures.

Besides,

Epick Poetry. 119

Besides, it is doubtful whether Epick Poetry demands that exact and polish'd Diction, which the most careful Writers contend for; there is sometimes a Roughness in the true Sublime, like that in the Surface of some stately Buildings, which makes it appear, if not more Beautiful, yet more Majestick. The Epick Stile requires something above Elegance and Neatness, for the greatest Part it should be elevated and marvellous, which it may be, notwithstanding some Neglects and Inaccuracies that the Writer is not solicitous to avoid; and therefore I am apt to think, that the *Æneid* was industriously transmitted to Posterity without that finishing, which the modern Criticks demand. It is evident, that the Author was able to have given as much Correctness to his Epick Poem, as he had done to his *Georgicks*, and he wanted not Time for it, having employ'd many Years to bring it to Perfection: And therefore that he left it as it is, seems to proceed from Deliberation and Choice. But there is yet a stronger Argument to support my suggestion. Suppose that *Virgil*, out of Negligence, or from want of Leisure or Industry, left his Poem unfinish'd; yet let it be consider'd, that after his Death the Emperor submitted

ted it to the Correction of two great Criticks, *Tucca* and *Varius*, the last of whom was *Virgil's* intimate Friend, and, as *Horace* assures us, an excellent Epick Poet; and therefore there is no doubt but these Persons were well qualify'd to execute the Commission they had receiv'd, that they were capable Judges of an Heroick Work, and could soon discern the Beauties and Errors of it: And as they were able to find out the Errors, so if they had any regard to the Trust repos'd in them, and their Duty to their Prince; if they had any Concern for the Honour of their Country, or the Reputation and Fame of a deceas'd Friend, they must likewise have been willing to correct them; but since they have left several Imperfections without Amendment and unexpung'd, it is evident that these Criticks did not censure them as Faults, or at least look'd on them as such, as would not blemish the Beauty or debase the Dignity of an Epick Poem.

Of Cool and Sedate Figures.

AFTER elevated Thoughts and well chosen Terms, the next Thing considerable in the Epick Stile is the Use of Figures, or such Forms of Expression as raise the Discourse above that of common
Conver-

Epick Poetry.

Converſation; which are ſedate and calm, or vehement and paſſionate: Of the firſt ſort, which concern the beautiful Order, muſical Cadence, and acute Signification of the Words, as well as the ſpiritful and ſurprizing Turns of the Diction I look on a Metaphor to be the moſt uſeful, as that which principally ennobles and adorns the Narration of an Heroick Action, by making it Figurative and Allegorical.

A Metaphor is an oratorical Figure, that repreſents one Object by the means of another, and is of all others of the ſedate ſort, the moſt lively and impreſſive; the Ingenuity and Sharpneſs of our Conceptions chiefly conſiſt in joining Notions, that have a great Likeneſs between them, tho found in diſtant and very different Objects, in which while the Mind conceives and compares many diſtinct Qualities and Habitudes, as it obſerves great Diſſimilitude between ſome, ſo it diſcerns certain Relations and Reſpects in which others are alike; and then ſingling out thoſe Ideas that reſemble each other from the reſt, it makes uſe of one to expreſs the other. It requires therefore a metaphyſical Abſtraction to form a Metaphor; and whereas other Figures are employ'd only about the Words and the Order of them, this
pene-

penetrates the Notion of Things, and searches Affinity and Agreement among the moſt oppoſite and diſagreeing Objects. Therefore to form a Metaphor, as *Ariſtotle* obſerves, is requir'd great Activity and Sagacity of Mind, ſince it muſt run through ſuch variety of Subjects, and ſo many different Reſpects and Conſiderations under which they fall, to find out the Similitude of two Notions, from the Union of which the Metaphor reſults. So that while other Figures cloath and adorn our Thoughts with Words, this enlivens and embelliſhes the Words by our Thoughts, whence it becomes the moſt agreeable of all Figures. Others may raiſe the Narration from a flat and low Manner, but this gives it all that it has of ſurprizing and extraordinary. The Strangeneſs and Ingenuity of repreſenting one Object by another, ſtrikes the Reader with agreeable Admiration. We are gratify'd to ſee an unexpected Idea preſented to our Underſtanding, and wonder at the beautiful Conjunction of Notions ſo ſeparate and remote before; and whatever is marvellous is delightful too; as we always feel a Pleaſure at the ſight of Foreigners and their Garments, ſo the Mind rejoices to ſee an Object out of its ordinary Dreſs, and appearing by the help of a Metaphor in the Habit of a Stranger:

At

Epick Poetry. 123

At the fight of fuch unufual and wonderful Images, we are as much pleas'd as with the fudden changing of Scenes, or with the curious and extraordinary Works of Art or Nature, which we never faw before.

If the Acquifition of Knowledge without Pains and Trouble is agreeable to us, this Figure has the Advantage of all others, fince it leads the Mind with great fwiftnefs from one Object to another, and in one Word reprefents more Things: And as this is delightful to the Reader, fo it is exceeding ufeful to the Poet, who by this means will have great Plenty of Ideas in his Imagination, and be always fupply'd with apt and lively Expreffion, which the Poverty of his Language and the Scarcity of Words could never have furnifh'd; for when-ever a proper Term is wanting, which happens very often in the moft copious Tongue, a Metaphorical one is always at hand to make good that defect.

Neither do thefe Figures afford Neceffaries only, they likewife enrich and beautify the Diction, being difpers'd like fo many Stars or fparkling Jewels through the whole Compofition. *Ariftotle* makes all

all that is extraordinary and admirable to confift in thefe foreign Images, than which nothing can more heighten and illuftrate the Sentiments, or give more Force and Dignity to the Stile. Thus as the ufe of Garments, which is *Cicero*'s Remark, was at firft introduc'd by Neceffity, but did foon after ferve for Pomp and Magnificence; fo tranflated and metaphorical Words, which the Sterility of their native Tongue and the want of proper Terms oblig'd Men at firft to ufe, were quickly employ'd as Ornaments to give Splendor and Majefty.

Nor is it lefs certain, that many Difcourfes would not only lofe their Beauty, but their Force and Spirit too, if the metaphorical Words fhould be chang'd: for the Proper are unable to convey the Thoughts of the Poet with fuch Advantage; and this happens chiefly where Intellectual Notions are reprefented by others deriv'd from the Senfes. The Soul, while immers'd in Flefh, is oblig'd to act in a great meafure dependent on the Body; and having been long accuftom'd to receive her Ideas from the Objects that pafs through the Senfes, fhe contracts a great Propenfion to conceive every Thing by that way of Conveyance; and when that

can-

Epick Poetry. 125

cannot be obtain'd, the Mind acts in Pain and seems uneasy and dissatisfy'd. And therefore to assist her, and render her Conceptions more lively, easy, and delightful, we put our Intellectual Ideas into a foreign Dress, borrow'd from the Senses. Hence we say, the Sight or Blindness of the Understanding, the Bent or Biass of the Will, the Sweetness of Knowledge, the Beauty of Vertue, the Deformity of Vice, a muddy or a clear Head, and a thousand other such Modes of Speech may be observ'd; and no proper Word can in these Cases signify our Sentiments so well. Hence in the sacred Scriptures, the supream Being is pleas'd to teach us spiritual and Divine Things by sensible Representations; such as the Kingdom of Heaven, an Incorruptible Crown of Glory, the Breast-plate of Faith, the Sword of the Spirit; and an infinite Number more of the like Expressions might be mention'd.

As to the Rules that concern the Poet's Choice and Conduct of this Figure; in the first place care should be taken, that it be not obscure, which it will be, as often as it is conceiv'd in Terms not easily understood, or when the Notions are search'd and fetch'd too far; the Mind must be surpriz'd at the Novelty of the Image, but

but not put to any Trouble to find out the Similitude, which gives Being to the Metaphor; and therefore it muſt be ſo repreſented, that the Underſtanding may at the firſt View perceive the Agreement. Nor muſt the Analogy be founded on too nice and fine Conſiderations, nor expreſs'd in Terms to which a competent Reader is not accuſtom'd; for either of theſe will darken the Metaphor, as that will deform the Diction, the Beauty of which much conſiſts in its being clear, and eaſy to be underſtood.

A Metaphor muſt alſo be exactly proportion'd, otherwiſe it will be ungrateful or ridiculous. I do not mean, that there ſhould be no Diſſimilitude or Deformity between the Objects, for very lively Figures of this ſort are found in Things very oppoſite; but that there ſhould be a juſt Reſemblance or Conformity between thoſe two Notions or Reſpects, that are abſtracted from the reſt, and united in the Mind of the Poet, when he forms a metaphorical Idea. Therefore he that has the moſt active Imagination, and that can with a quick and ſearching View paſs through Multitudes of Objects, examine their Nature, and penetrate their ſeveral Qualities, that can readily diſcern their A-

† gree-

Epick Poetry.

greement and Differences, feparate the Like from the Unlike, and join thofe together that exactly refemble one another, will be the moft able to form thefe juft and well proportion'd Figures, which the Mafters of poetical Eloquence fo much admire.

Another thing demanded is, that the Metaphor be eafy and natural, which it will be, if in the Tranflation of the Word from its proper Place to that where it ferves as a Figure, it may feem to come willingly and not by conftraint; otherwife it will appear ftudy'd and affected, and inftead of pleafing, will greatly offend the intelligent Reader. But if the two former Rules are obferv'd, this Error will be avoided; for Metaphors are then forc'd and unnatural, when they are either fetch'd from Objects too remote and uncommon, or if from others more familiar and known, yet the Notions are not well proportion'd and adapted one to another. If the Metaphorical Image be too little or too fhort, the Reprefentation will be lame and imperfect; if it be too narrow and ftrait, it will pinch and fit uneafy on the Object to which it is apply'd, and if it be not fufficiently refin'd and feparated from Notions unlike and difagreeing, it will become irregular and deform'd.

It

It is requir'd, that a Metaphor should not be base or sordid; the Writer must not represent one Object by another, whose Image will be justly shocking to sober and modest Readers: For tho the Similitude, which is the Foundation of the Metaphor, may be clear and perfect between the two Notions, which he compares, and tho that Resemblance only is exprest, yet since the Word, which he uses, conveys an associate Idea, which is indecent and offensive, at the reading of it the noxious as well as the innocent Meaning is awaken'd in the Mind, which can scarcely conceive the one without the other. The Gravity and Dignity of the sublime Character will oblige the Epick Poet to forbear such Metaphors, which by their Courseness will be misbecoming his important Subject, and by their Sordidness will disgust the Reader. If Words of a double Signification, of which one is impure, are justly censur'd in Low, Lyrick, and Comick Poetry, then it must be allow'd to be insufferable in Heroick Works, where all Things should be Chaste, Grave, and Great.

In the next place, the Metaphor in Epick Compositions should not be gay and
*
too

Epick Poetry.

too delicate, for that will emafculate the Stile, and inftead of inftructing, abufe the Mind, and draw it off from the folid and marvellous Part of the Narration, to admire a Train of fine Words, and the Ingenuity of the Conceptions. Many Metaphors are fo light and fparkling, and difcover fo much youthful Fancy, that the Dignity of Heroick Poetry will not endure them. As the Ufe of thefe will betray the Levity and Oftentation of the Poet, which extreamly misbecomes his Character; fo it tends to vitiate the Tafte of the Reader, who will be always hearkening after bright Sayings, and defpife the noble Sentiments and moral Inftruction of the Fable.

Another Rule is, that the Metaphor be not pufh'd too far, left it become tedious and ungrateful; this is a Fault for which *Italian* Authors are juftly cenfur'd, their Metaphors are often fo extended that they tire the moft patient Reader; and it is by this means that their Stile grows redundant and obfcure. It is an Error to lengthen a Comparifon till it takes up great room in the Difcourfe, and much more is it fo to continue and amplify a Metaphor, which is a narrower way of Expreffion than by a Similitude; for that

K   afferts

asserts the Things to be the same, but this affirms only that they are alike, and shews wherein they are so. Metaphors, as said before, when well chosen, give great Life and Vigor to the Narration; but if they are excessive, they make it Ænigmatical and turn it all to Allegory. This especially will be the Event, if they are as intemperate in their Number, as their Length: Figures of Eloquence are chiefly chosen to supply the Defect of proper Words; and when they are sought for Delight, and to give a Relish to the Narration, they must not be so many as will make it luscious.

Another Rule is, that the Metaphor be not too bold and lofty; for the Effect of this will be a flatulent and bloated Stile. Such hardy and swelling Figures sit about the Object which they are intending to express, like loose and wide Garments upon a Man that walks against the Wind; it is more desirable to sink and creep than to be always tow'ring amidst the Clouds. It is enough to be now and then in the second Region, the Store-house of Metaphors as well as Meteors; but to be always in this noisy and tempestuous Place, forming strong and daring Figures, will by no means become the Chastness, Gravity,

Epick Poetry.

Gravity, and Elevation of the Epick Diction.

Another Direction to be obferv'd is, that the Metaphors, how acute foever they are, be not chofen and introduc'd purely for their own fakes. As it is impertinent to ftrain the Fancy upon every Occafion for fome ingenious and polite Figure, to gratify the voluptuous Tafte of the Reader, fo nothing more plainly difcovers the Vanity and Oftentation of the Poet, than when he exerts his Genius and fhews the Riches of his Fancy, where there is not the leaft Occafion for it. I allow, that an Epick Poet may, and ought to ufe Art in adorning his Stile; but if the native Luftre and Dignity of his Sentiments does not break through and eclipfe the Splendor of the outward Ornaments, the Narration will be flat and difagreeable. The Beauty of a good Poem refembles that of a healthful Man, which fprings from within, and arifes from the Abundance and Vivacity of his Spirits, from his vital Heat and the regular Motions of the Blood. A Soldier may polifh his Arms till they fhine and glitter, and by that may dazle and terrify his Enemy; but it is their Edge and Strength that he will confide in, and not their Brightnefs.

THOSE Poets who are greatly concern'd to raife and adorn their Narration, fhould remember *Cicero*'s Remark, That as it falls out almoft in all Things, fo it does in Poetical, as well as Oratorical Works, That thofe very Things that are moft ufeful and profitable, have always moft Dignity and Gracefulnefs. In the glorious Fabrick of the World, if we contemplate the regular and harmonious Order of the Parts One would think the Author defign'd only to raife our delightful Admiration; if their Neceffity and Ufefulnefs, that he refpected only our Profit and Advantage. In the Structure of Man, all the Parts are form'd with fo much Wifdom, are fo exactly proportion'd and dependant on each other in fuch admirable Order, where nothing is either defective or fuperfluous, and nothing to be alter'd, either for its Figure, Place, or Connexion, but to the greateft Difadvantage, that all Things appear fhap'd and united intirely for Beauty and Majefty, and yet nothing feems contriv'd but for Ufe and Convenience. When in this manner good Senfe is fet off with the genuine Beauties of Poetry, the Compofure will be both admirable and ufeful, and yet fo eafy and natural, that notwithftanding there is in it the greateft Art imaginable,

Epick Poetry. 133

able, no Labour or Mark of Affectation will been seen.

The last Rule I shall mention about Metaphors or Translated Words is, that they always ought to be vary'd so as to be accommodated to the Subject of the Discourse. Sublime and excellent Things must not be represented by others that are base and vile; nor must a low and humble Matter assume a pompous and magnificent Figure; such a Decorum is to be observ'd in changing these Ornaments, that they may be Magnificent or Modest, Sublime or Humble, Splendid or Plain, Calm or Passionate, as the Subject is to which they are apply'd; and this Variety, as it will render the Diction very Beautiful and Natural, so it will greatly contribute to the Pleasure and Advantage of the Reader. We are soon cloy'd with a Writer that always runs on in one beaten Track, that still entertains us with the same sort of Phrases, and has only the Sun and Clouds, and two or three more stale Topicks to furnish his Discourse with metaphorical Ornaments. An Heroick Poet should have such sagacity of Mind, and such a fertile Imagination, that he need not be oblig'd, whatever his Subject is, to cloath it still in the same Dress; for tho it should be ever so decent and

and proper, and ever fo well adjufted, yet it will be an Argument of the Poet's Poverty, as well as an Offence to the Reader, if he is always feen in the fame Habit.

Having difcours'd at large of Metaphors, which are the principal Figures of the Cool and Sedate Kind, I fhall pafs by the others of that fort, which are not confiderable enough to be fingly difcufs'd.

Of Amplifications, Descriptions, *and* Similitudes.

Amplification is nothing elfe but fuch a juft Diffufion of the Senfe, as is proper to attain the Poet's End, which is to raife Admiration and Joy; and therefore the Stile fhould be fo far enlarg'd, as a juft Impreffion on the Reader's Mind makes it neceffary. In plain Tranfitions and Hiftorical Recitals, the Diction is to be kept in more moderate Bounds; for in fuch Inftances a few proper, well-chofen, and well-plac'd Words will fufficiently fignify the Writer's Mind, where a natural and decent Simplicity is only demanded.

But

Epick Poetry.

But, on the other side, the Poet muft take care, that the Senfe be not fo much diluted and difpers'd as to weaken its Spirit, and hinder its Effect. Words are but the Vehicles of the Thoughts, and therefore muft be in fuch a meafure as the Ideas can well animate; not fo numerous as to enfeeble them fo far, that they will not be able to move the Reader. As a clofe and concife Stile imprifons the Sentiments in too ftrait Limits, fo this contrary Error ftretches them out into fuch a thin Expanfion, that they hover in the Air without Force and Weight.

That the Senfe may not be too poor and weak by fpreading out the Thoughts too much, the Poet fhould take care to draw Matter from the various Circumftances of the Subject fufficient to fupport his Stile, and fecure it from languifhing. Some Perfons have an extraordinary Felicity in this way. *Longinus* obferves it in *Cicero*, and we may take notice of the fame in many others, as well Poets as Orators, who, tho they give themfelves liberty, and take up a great Compafs with their diffufive Diction, yet ftill they find Supplies to maintain their Difcourfe in equal Vigour, which they take from all

Things

Things that nearly refpect and ftand about their Subject, where they always difcover fomething agreeable to their Purpofe, and fit to furnifh them with noble Ideas.

Among all the Ornaments of a fublime Stile, there are none that give it more Beauty and Spirit than well-drawn Images and juft Defcriptions, which are fo many lively and clear Delineations of an Object intellectual or fenfible. This Faculty of forming Poetical Images, feems to excite an Apprehenfion of a diftant Thing, by giving a Reprefentation of it to the Ear, as Painting does to the Eye; but the former has this great Advantage, that it does not only exprefs the outward Lineaments and Complexion, but alfo the internal Principles of Life and Motion, not only of Corporeal Beings, but likewife of the Soul and Immaterial Natures. When the Mind of the Poet has by vigorous and intenfe Contemplation mafter'd the Object, and form'd a true and bright Idea, it ftamps the Impreffion on proper and well-rang'd Words in fo ftrong a manner, that the abfent Object feems in fome fort prefent to the admiring Reader : And as this difcovers the Regularity and Vivacity of the Poet's Sentiments, and the Extenfion and
Force

Force of his Imagination, so it shews likewise his Skill in choosing and disposing of his Words; both which united cannot but meet with great Success, if the Things, whose Images he represents, are truly Great and Sublime.

Hence by an easy and natural Metaphor the Poet is said to paint, and his Descriptions are call'd Pictures, which as oft as they are of a due proportion, pertinent, just, strong, and a lively Expression of the Objects represented, they are not only great Beauties and Ornaments of the Work, but they recreate and relieve the Reader by an agreeable Variety, retard the Rapidity of the Narration, and make it flow with a more gentle and sedate Course, which is necessary to a Writing of such extent, as that of an Epick Poem. If the Descriptions are luxuriant or very frequent, as they incumber the Poem and weaken its Force, so they misbecome the Gravity and Dignity of the true Sublime, and discover a wanton puerile Genius, which is always intemperate in this Article. But when kept in due Limits, the Poetical Images enliven and beautify the Poem, which is obferv'd in *Homer*'s *Ulysses* and *Virgil*'s *Æneid*; in which the Representation of Gardens, Palaces, rich Furniture,
magni-

magnificent Feasts, Rivers, Embassies, Triumphs, and various other great Ideas, add Splendor and Ornament to the Poem.

A Similitude is an Illustration of an Object, by comparing it with another in some Qualities and Respects in which they agree; and this is a great Embellishment of the Writing, when the Resemblance between those two Objects is express'd fully, clearly, and with Strength and Spirit; but if the Comparison is lame and imperfect, or if it runs off into Circumstances remote and foreign to that Quality or Relation in which the Similitude is founded, it will lose its Effect, and not illustrate, but rather obscure the Poet's Sentiments. And this is evidently a Fault in *Homer*, who amplifies and swells his Similitudes by the Recital of Circumstances altogether impertinent to his Business; and even where there is some Resemblance, it is often so dim and defective, that it is not obvious and easily discern'd; which made a great Wit in the last Age say, That he never met with any Things so unlike, as *Homer*'s *Similies*. If the *Similies* are extended to a great Length they grow tedious to a judicious Reader, and if they are very frequent they suspend the Action too much: If they are base and

courſe,

course, which many of *Homer*'s must be allow'd to be, they offend against the Dignity of the Epick Stile. There is no Rule to settle the Length of a Comparison, it must be determin'd by the Nature of the Thing. If it does not fully and clearly exprefs the Resemblance between the Objects compar'd, it is too short; if it does more, it is weak and redundant. It is therefore ridiculous to affirm, that because *Virgil* and *Homer* have never exceeded such a number of Lines in their Similitudes, this Proportion must be a Rule to all other Poets, as if Examples and not the Reason of Things were to guide our Choice. Sometimes the Simile may be difpatch'd in a Line or two, fometimes it will demand a greater number; moft commonly four or fix, fometimes eight or ten Lines, and fometimes yet more will not be redundant. Tho *Homer* has fometimes crouded one Similitude upon another to illuftrate the fame Thing, and *Virgil* has follow'd his Example; yet if one Simile be ftrong and fully expreffive, a fecond, and much more a third, is, in my Opinion, fuperfluous and offenfive. Similitudes, like other Figures, being the Ornaments and Jewels of the Diction fhould therefore be fparing; the Garniture and Trimming fhould be enough to fet off and adorn, not fo profufe as to

cover

cover and hide the Garment; and these Comparisons should be most us'd, where the Subject is dry and uniform, as in Sieges and Battles, where the same Matter often returning, would otherwise grow flat and tedious to the Reader.

Of Vehement and Pathetick Figures.

I Come now to the vehement Figures of Speech, which regard the Passions, and which no Poet will manage with Success, without his own innate Fire; I mean, that warm and active Temper which we mention'd before, as requir'd on Nature's Part; give him the clearest Head and the most fertile Imagination, without this Poetical Fervency he will never be able to do any thing wonderful. It is true, this generous Impulse or Ardor of Spirit, if left at liberty and unguided, is liable to many Miscarriages and dishonourable Errors, and therefore I shall lay down the Rules which concern its due Conduct, after I have spoken of the Usefulness and Necessity of the Pathetick Figures to the Sublime Stile.

A MASTERLY Way of touching the Passions is always demanded in the upper Species of Poetry, and tho it is chiefly requir'd

Epick Poetry. 141

quir'd in Tragedy, which is more active and vehement, yet it is likewise necessary in Epick Works; and therefore what *Aristotle*, *Cicero*, *Longinus*, and *Quintilian* say, of the Necessity and Usefulness of Pathetick Figures in Oratory, is equally applicable to the sublime Poetical Eloquence. *Longinus* says, I dare affirm there is nothing that raises a Discourse more than a Passion discreetly manag'd. It is like a sort of Inspiration, that animates the Diction, and gives it such Force and Vigor, that it seems altogether Divine. *Cicero* says, all the Energy and Strength of Eloquence is to be express'd in exciting or quieting the Passions; and in another place says he, who is ignorant that the greatest Force of an Orator consists either in exciting in the Minds of Men Anger, Hatred, or Grief, or in reducing them from these Emotions to Tenderness and Compassion: And he affirms, that Orator will do nothing that is not acquainted with the Nature of Man, and the Means by which his Passions are mov'd and govern'd.

Quintilian lays so great a Stress upon moving the Passions, that he prefers this Faculty of the Orator even to his Proofs and Reasons. He says, That Men of a narrow Spirit and slender Vein of Wit may,

by

by the Affiftance of Learning and Ufe, come to fome Maturity in the Laft; and of thefe, fays he, there has been always a great Number: But for Orators that can command the Audience, and transform their Minds into what Shape and Appearance they pleafe, thefe have been very few. Let the Orator, fays he, ftudy how to ftorm and impel the Minds of the Audience; this is his Province, this is his Labour, without which all Things will be naked, jejune, feeble, and ungrateful; as if the Spirit and Soul of Eloquence confifted in managing the Affections. *Ariftotle*, who lays the greateft Strefs upon the Proofs and Arguments, yet relies not a little on the paffionate Forms of Expreffion, and fays, That Men of a warm Complexion are of all others the moft fuccefsful in the Art of Eloquence. And therefore he teaches Orators to exprefs themfelves in a pathetick manner; which they will do, fays he, if in treating of an Offence or Injury receiv'd, the Difcourfe feems to come from a Man in Anger; or if they mention any thing impious or bafe, they feem to fpeak of it with Indignation and Averfion; and on the contrary, whilft they treat of any great and laudable Action, they exprefs an extraordinary Joy and Satisfaction; and

*

if

EPICK POETRY. 143

if the Subject is sad and worthy of Compassion, the Discourse be serious and accompany'd with a becoming Sorrow. Thus likewise speaking of the Choice of Words, he says, that greater Liberty is permitted to the Orator, when he has, as it were, transported the Hearers out of themselves, whether by Praises or Invectives, by his Anger or by his Joy, or the Motion of any other vehement Passion.

It is for this Reason that the great Teachers of Eloquence have left so many Rules and Precepts about the Nature of the Passions, and the most effectual Methods to excite them. For this End *Aristotle* has given a very exact Description of them, as well of those that predominate in the different Ages of Life, as in the different Ranks and Condition of Men; that the Orator being acquainted with the particular Tempers and Dispositions of his Audience, and the true Ways of speaking to the Heart, he may manage and govern them with ease, and lead them whereever he pleases. And what Breast will be able to hold out against a Speaker that is well appriz'd of all its weak and indefensible Places, who is not only able to possess himself of all the Passages, but knows how to form and keep an Intelligence with-

within, and to attack it with his utmost Force in the very Season when 'tis prepar'd to surrender? That Orator will make himself Master of any Spirit, that can assault it with such Advantages, that can command the Passions, those Storms and Winds of the Soul, and they obey him.

Longinus tells us, at the latter End of his Treatise, which is come to the Hands of Posterity, that he design'd to write a Tract apart about the *Passions.* And *Cicero*, where above-cited, declares his Opinion, That it is impossible to be an Orator without the Knowledge of their Nature, and the Art of moving them. And as this is their general Doctrine, so we find their Practice was conform'd to it. *Cicero* admires *Demosthenes* for this, That he never spoke a Sentence but in a warm and pathetick way: Such was the Violence of his Figures, such the Majesty of his Thoughts, such the Force of his passionate Complexion, that a Man might as well stand against Flashes of Lightning, or stem a rapid Torrent, as hold out against his Persuasion. And *Cicero*, who was call'd the *Latin Demosthenes*, was like him in nothing more than his artful manner of addressing himself to the Affections. With what Vehemence of Spirit, with what Energy of Expreffion does he affault *Verres*, *Catiline*, and *Anthony*? With what bitter and sharp Invectives does he purfue them? In how lively and tragical Shapes does he reprefent their Crimes? What Sentence does not penetrate and wound the Perfon he accufes? How bold, how ftrong, how irrefiftible are all his Figures? Is it poffible to ftand againft the commanding Force of his Exagerations, Exprobations, Threatnings. and Exhortations? Like a Tempeft, like a Deluge, like a Conflagration, he fcatters, diffolves, fhakes, and overturns all Things in his way. Are not *Quintilian*'s Declamations likewife full of thefe moving and warm Expreffions? Does he not every where force his Entrance by the violent Affaults he makes on this Quarter? And had not *Cæsar*'s Eloquence been accompany'd with the fame Vehemence and Ardor, which he exprefs'd in the Field, he had never been honour'd with fuch Succefs. When *Cicero* gives the diftinct Characters of the feveral famous Orators of his Time, this paffionate way of Addrefs makes a great part. " *Sulpitius*, fays " he, had fuch a vigorous Impulfe of " Mind, fo full and fo loud a Voice, fuch " Agitation of Body, and Dignity of Ge- " fture, and that Gravity and Plenty of " Words, that no Genius feem'd better " turn'd

" by Nature for the Art of Speaking. And afterward, " Do you obferve, fays " he, the Manner of Speaking proper to " *Antonius*, ftrong, vehement, full of Mo- " tion, on every fide fenc'd and guarded, " earneft, acute, clear, fifting every Thing, " purfuing eagerly, terrifying, befeeching, " with the greateft Variety of Oration, " but with no fatiety of our Ears who " hear him."

Thus in the Opinion of thefe great Men, that Orator will not fail of perfuading, who is thus acquainting with the Avenues of the Mind, and knows how, by the force of his Sentiments, the violent, warm, and active Forms of his Expreffion, to lie and prefs like a ftrong Wind upon the Audience, till he drives them this or that way, as he leans upon them.

What thefe Mafters fpeak of pathetick Figures in Rhetorick, may, with parity of Reafon, be apply'd to all the fuperior Kinds of Poetry, where Proofs and clofe Argument are not fo much requir'd, as in Oratorical Performances. Perfuafive Addrefs, Skill and Capacity to work up the Paffions, and touch all the Springs and Movements of the Soul, are fo neceffary to Tragick and Epick Poets, that it is not poffible

Epick Poetry. 147

possible they should succeed without them. For how shall one of these Writers move Terror and Compassion, and the other Admiration and Delight, without the Art of changing the Soul by these various Emotions? The Instances of this kind are endless, which might be produc'd out of the Conferences, Speeches, and Contests of the *Iliad* and the *Æneid*, of which that of *Dido* to *Æneas* is one of the most admirable for its passionate Eloquence: But no Works whatsoever afford more Examples of pathetick Expressions than the Sacred Writings. Is it possible to use more moving Language, and more piercing Figures than those which every where they abound with in the Poetical and Prophetick Parts? How majestick and terrible are the Threats, and how earnest the Exhortations of the *Prophets* ? How sharp and penetrating their Reproofs? How awakening their Admonitions? How passionate their Expostulations? How few Sentences are there in the *Psalms*, that are not cast into some of these lively Forms? Nor in the New Testament are they less frequent. St. *Paul*, the great Apostle of the *Gentiles*, employs every where this vehement Diction; he intreats, beseeches, terrifies, reproves, exhorts, and expostulates with such variety of violent pathe-

L 2　　　　　　　　tick

tick Figures, that the Kingdom of Heaven, by such a Management, seems to invade, and take the Auditors by Force. It is observable too, that we find the Forms of Prayer address'd to God by devout Men recorded in the Scriptures, full of these figurative Expressions, as if they were design'd to persuade the Almighty, by moving some Passion to change his Purpose; which manner of Invocation evidently shews, that this is the most effectual way to prevail with Men, which we chuse to incline the Will of God.

Because I look on the vehement Forms of Speech in the sublime Parts of the Scripture, for their Greatness, Majesty, and Force in moving the Soul, as superior to any in the Pagan Poets, I will select from them some Examples. What more Tender and Compassionate than this; *O Ephraim, what shall I do unto thee? O Israel, what shall I do unto thee? for your Goodness is as a Morning Cloud, and as the early Dew it passes away. How shall I give thee up, Ephraim, how shall I deliver thee, Israel? How shall I make thee as Admah? How shall I set thee as Zeboim? My Heart is turned within me, my Repentings are kindled together.* — *O Israel, thou hast destroyed thy self, but in me is thy help* — *As I live, saith the*

EPICK POETRY. 149

the Lord, I have no Pleasure in the Death of a Sinner, turn ye, turn ye, for why will ye die, O House of Israel. — *O Jerusalem, Jerusalem, thou that killest the Prophets, and stonest them that are sent unto thee, how often would I have gathered thy Children, as a Hen gathereth her Chickens under her Wing, and ye would not?* —

As to Ironical Forms of Speaking, which have great Force to move the Passions, that of *Elijah* to *Baal*'s Prophets, when they had a long time invok'd their God, in vain, to answer them by Fire, is very farcastical and cutting; *Cry aloud, for he is a God, either he is talking, or he is pursuing, or he is in a Journey, or peradventure he sleepeth, and must be awaked.*— And that of the wise King to inconsiderate Youth; *Rejoice, O young Man, and let thy Heart chear thee in the Days of thy Youth, and walk in the Ways of thy Heart, and in the Sight of thy Eyes; but know thou, that for all these things, God will bring thee into Judgment.*

As to the Forms of calling to Witness, which are also very Passionate, we have several Examples of them in St. *Paul*'s Epistles —*God is my Record, how greatly I long after you in the Bowels of Jesus Christ— Wherefore because I love you not, God knoweth.*

Instances of Repetition, which is a more vehement Reflection upon what has been said, to make a stronger Impression of it on the Minds of the Hearers, are such as these; *What thing shall I take to Witness for thee? What thing shall I liken to thee, O Daughter of* Jerusalem? *What shall I equal to thee to comfort thee, O Virgin Daughter of* Zion? — *Woe, Woe to the Inhabitants of the Earth, by reason of the Voices of the three Angels that are yet to sound—Woe unto you* Scribes *and* Pharisees, *Hypocrites, for ye shut the Kingdom of Heaven*, &c.— *Woe unto you* Scribes *and* Pharisees, *Hypocrites, for ye devour Widows Houses*, &c.— *Woe unto you* Scribes *and* Pharisees, *Hypocrites*, &c.

As to Forms of Admiration, what can be greater than that Epiphonema of St. *Paul, O the Depths of the Riches both of the Wisdom and Knowledge of God, how unsearchable are his Judgments, and his Ways past finding out!*—And that, *O Death, where is thy Sting, O Grave where is thy Victory!*

Forms of Exclamation are such as these; *O foolish Galatians, who hath bewitched you, that you should not obey the Truth*. And that of the Prophet against *Jeroboam's* Altar;

tar; *O Altar, Altar, thus faith the Lord, Behold,* &c.

There is nothing more common than Interrogations in Scripture, which some Masters of Eloquence call the Vigorous and Divine Forms of Speaking. All the inspir'd Writings that are not Historical or Genealogical, so abound with them, that we meet with them in every Chapter, and almost in every Verse. That of St. *Paul*, wherein he Questions and Answers himself, is a way extreamly apt to touch the Readers; *Are they* Hebrews? *so am I. Are they Ministers of Christ? I speak as a Fool, I am more.*

That Prosopopeia of *Job* concerning Wisdom, is very noble; *The Depth saith, it is not in me. — Destruction and Death say, we have heard the Fame thereof with our Ears,* &c.

That Apostrophe of *Isaiah* is very moving; *Hear, O Heavens, and give Ear O Earth, for I have nourished and brought up Children, and they have rebelled against me.*— And this that follows, which supposes both Hearing and Speaking in inanimate Things; *Sing, O ye Heavens, for the Lord hath done it: Shout the lower Parts of the Earth,*

Earth, break forth into singing ye Mountains, O Forreſt, and every Tree therein; for the Lord hath redeemed Jacob, *and glorified himſelf in* Iſrael.

The Forms of Exhortation are ſo many and ſo well known, that I need not ſet down any Example.

Those of Commanding are very moving; ſuch is that of St. *Paul, Tell me all ye that deſire to be under the Law,* &c. And the ſame Figure us'd by *Joſhua* to the *Iſraelites,* is very great and impreſſive; *Chooſe you this Day whom ye will ſerve, the Gods whom your Fathers ſerved, that were on the other ſide of the Flood, or the Gods of the* Amorites, *in whoſe Land ye dwell; but as for me and my Houſe, we will ſerve the Lord.*

The Poet ſhould feel thoſe Emotions of the Soul, which he would raiſe in others; and if his Expreſſions are warm and animated with his own Paſſion, they will eaſily transfuſe the ſame Life and Energy into the Breaſt of the Reader, who is alſo always affected as the Poet is; and therefore the Divine Fire muſt be firſt kindled in the Writer, who deſigns to convey his Impulſe and Sentiment to the Minds of others.

Besides

Besides, the strong and lively Impressions of the Poet have this Advantage, That they give Fertility to his Fancy and Facility to his Diction, and the most natural and persuasive Forms to his Expressions. A Man mov'd with Anger, Sorrow, or Pity, never wants proper Words, fit Language, or a successful manner of Elocution. Hence it is that miserable Men have something more persuasive in their Expression and way of Address, than the politest Poets and Orators in the World. And those, who upon other Occasions had very indifferent Rhetorical Faculties, have learn'd that prevailing Eloquence from their Passions, which the greater Masters could never teach them.

Besides, the Passions give acuteness to the Understanding, quicken and enlarge the Fancy, by expanding, and, as it were, inflaming the Spirits, or by fixing the Imagination intensely on its Object, that the Mind may be able to view all the Circumstances of the Thing it contemplates, and to form a clear and powerful Image of it. Thus we find that some Diseases, by rarifying the Blood, and giving quicker Motions to the Spirits, make Men fluent in Words and fruitful in their Thoughts, tho
most

most commonly they want Judgment to conduct them. I conclude therefore with what *Quintilian* says on this Subject, which confirms the Assertion of *Aristotle*, mention'd before; let those things move our selves which we desire should move others, and let us be affected our selves, before we attempt to affect them: By this means the Poet will accomplish his Design, and not only transmit his Words to the Ears, but his Soul into the Breasts of his Readers.

To the true Sublime in one Extream, is oppos'd the swelling and fustian Stile; where weak and trifling Thoughts are set off with all the Ornament that sounding Words and pompous Periods can bestow, while the slender Sense is effac'd with too much Colouring and Decoration. As this often happens on the Theater, when the Tragick Poet, that wants Judgment and Strength of Imagination, would supply the Defect of great and elevated Ideas, by turgid and windy Diction, and attempts to terrify the Audience by the mere Power of raging Words, or melt them into Compassion with tender and gentle Metaphors; so in the other upper kinds of Poetry, this Error is frequently committed by Writers of a low and barren Genius, who incumber

ber and stifle their jejune and vulgar Sentiments by improper and redundant Expression, for which more Authors than *Statius* are justly censur'd. Tho the Words should be well chosen, and ranged with the greatest Exactness; tho the Figures should be just and splendid, and no external Graces should be omitted, this will not pass for sublime Eloquence, if good Sense and lofty Conceptions are wanting, which should warm and enliven the Composition.

THAT which is oppos'd to the true Sublime in the other Extream is the flat Stile; where the Thoughts are low and puerile, the Diction familiar, courle, and sometimes defective in the Art of vulgar Rhetorick, where the Phrases are base and rustick, and the Metaphors dark, poor, or fulsome, and the whole Discourse is a sad variety of Things ill conceiv'd, ill express'd, and huddled together without Order and Contrivance.

APPEN-

AN
APPENDIX.

MANY Years ago, in the Preface to the Paraphrase on *Job*, I declar'd against the decisive Power of Authority, and refus'd Submission to the Examples of ancient Writers, unless they were support- by Reason; and since it is evident, that among the Moderns we have no Originals, their Poets being all Imitators, who form'd themselves on the *Greek* and *Latin* Models, I exprefs'd my Wishes that some great Genius, qualify'd for such an Undertaking, would break the Ice, assert the Liberty of Poetry, and striking off from a servile Imitation of the eldest Plans, would attempt an Epick Poem, in some measure, of a different Cast, but agreeable however to the Nature and Constitution of that Species of Poetry; such as might bear a Conformity to the Taste of the present Times, and to the Customs, Manners, and establish'd Religion of the Author's Country. I was not without Hopes that some Persons

sons of a free Spirit, Learning, and Capacity, would have improv'd the Hint, and by seconding my Attempt, have carry'd on the Design much farther; that by disingaging our Poets from Prepossession, they would have enlarg'd their Freedom, and deliver'd them from blind Obedience to Antiquity, and their Servitude to Opinions, receiv'd only upon the Credit of celebrated Names. But so great was the Prejudice of the polite Part of the Nation in favour of the ancient Poets, that it was look'd on as no less than down-right Heresy in Poetry, to entertain any new Notions, that had not the Example of *Homer*, and the Warrant of *Aristotle* and his Commentators to bear them out; nor would any Man fail of being universally condemn'd as a Person of dangerous Principles, and disaffected to the Interests of Learning, that should write or speak any thing contrary to the Sentiments of Men of such Erudition and sacred Authority; I had therefore no Followers. The Ancients, especially *Homer*, continue in full Possession of their Reputation and Power.

But since the Writing of the foregoing Discourse, I have read two *French* Criticks, who have lately stood up with great Courage in the Defence of the just Exercise cife of Reafon, in examining the Writers of the moft eftablifh'd Credit. I acknowledge it is a Satisfaction, as it confirms me in the Belief of my having pafs'd a right Judgment, to fee two Perfons of fuch a polite Tafte, of fo much Penetration and good Senfe, fall in with my Opinion, and warmly engage in the fame Defign, of vindicating the Rights of Humane Nature, of fetting prepoffefs'd Men at Liberty, and reftoring to them the free Ufe of their Underftandings. Their Adverfaries exclaim againft them, as prefumptuous and pragmatical Innovators, Men that from a proud and petulant Temper have reviv'd the Schifm of *Perrault*; whofe Arrogance, fay they, was fufficiently chaftis'd, while his Notions were abundantly confuted by the able Pen of *Defpreaux*. The other fide, in their Defence, difown all Partiality to the Moderns, and difrefpect to the Ancients; they declare, they have no other Intention, but to feek and difcover the Truth by an impartial Inquiry into the celebrated Poem of *Homer*, and accufe the Criticks that ftand by him, as Perfons blinded with Prejudice and guilty of fuperftitious Adoration of his Writings, arifing from the Applaufes they have receiv'd from fo many learned Men in all Ages. *Perrault*, fay they, was born down by the fuperior Strength

Epick Poetry. 159

Strength and Judgment of his Rival; and notwithstanding his Cause was good, he miscarry'd by an ill Management; that he was unequal to the Undertaking, and by several Errors and Mistakes, gave an occasion of Triumph to his Adversary. But then, say they, tho this Gentleman for want of sufficient Skill and Conduct, fail'd in his Attempt, at which no Man should be surpriz'd, since it was the first of the Kind; yet this does not bar the Right of any Men to resume the Controversy, who hope they can carry it on with a greater Prospect of Success. Thus a critical War is broke out in *France*, and the Muses are engag'd in Civil Contentions, while one Faction is for pulling down the Authority of *Homer*, and the other strenuously opposes, and maintains the Credit of that Poet. In my Opinion, the Disputants on either side are partly in the right, and have divided the Truth between them, tho perhaps the Aggressors have the greatest Share; while the Poets that depreciate and decry *Homer*'s Poem, stand up for the Privilege of Mankind, and the Reasonableness of examining the Evidence brought in favour of any Opinion before they embrace it; while they affirm, that Example and Authority are not Reason and Demonstration, and that every Man has a

Power

Power of deliberating and weighing the Arguments produc'd on each side of the Question, and a natural Right of judging for himself; lastly, while they assert that impartial Criticks may freely sift the Writings of the greatest Name and Authority; and where they believe they are not back'd with evident Reason, to censure and condemn their Practice, thus far their Opinion will bear the Test. For it is certain, that no Man's Understanding was ever design'd as a Standard for mine, any more than mine was intended as one for his. No Example is to be follow'd, but as it is just and reasonable; and how shall it appear so, if we have no Liberty to examine it? Universality and Antiquity are to be look'd on with Respect and Reverence; but since they have been often produc'd to support manifest Errors in Philosophy as well as in Religion, and have therefore been often rejected, why should they be regarded as infallible in Poetry? I shall therefore readily allow, that the Moderns have an undoubted Right to judge of the Works of the Ancients, and to appeal from *Homer* and *Aristotle* themselves, to the Decision of Reason. But then it must be allow'd, that great Care and Caution should be us'd that our Determinations be just and solid, when we

deviate

deviate from the general Practice and Opinion of Men of eminent Learning and Candor through many fucceffive Ages.

As in my Judgment the critical Aggreffors fall too feverely on this famous Poet, and attack various Places, that may well be defended ; fo on the other hand, their Adverfaries engage in too difficult a Province, when they undertake in all things to fupport him. The firft fhew a free Spirit, and have, to their great Honour, difingag'd themfelves from a fervile Submiffion to the Underftandings and Dictates of the greateft Men, and by their Example have encourag'd a difinterefted and unprejudic'd Exercife of our Reafon. Their Adverfaries feem more fetter'd with Prepoffeffion, and by favouring too much the arbitrary Dominion of Authority and Antiquity, would check the generous Efforts of modern Genius's, whofe Aim is to improve the Art of Poetry, and allow them only the Honour of being Imitators and Copyers of the Ancients.

Might I prefume to offer my Mediation to thefe contending Factions, that this Difpute may be brought to an amicable Conclufion, and that for the future angry

Invectives, and the unnecessary Effusion of more critical Learning may be prevented, I would propose that each Party should lay by their Prejudice, make some Concessions, and relinquish some Pretensions that now they insist upon with too great Obstinacy. It is not to be doubted but there are great, if not equal Prejudices on both sides: When a Person has spent many Years in studying the learned Languages, and acquainting himself with the ancient Writers, it will be very difficult for him to part with the Superiority which he thinks he has acquir'd in respect of others, who are comparatively unvers'd in those Studies; he will be apt to look with Contempt on those that cannot pretend to so much Learning, and have little to trust to but Reason, a solid Judgment, and a good Taste. If I yield a controverted Point, will he be apt to say, to the naked Decision of Reason, how much Time have I spent in vain? How many Volumes have I turn'd over, and how many Common Places fill'd to no purpose? What will become of all my Reading? What will all my Citations and Authorities avail, if young petulant Writers, without *Greek* and Antiquity, shall be allow'd to dispute the receiv'd Maxims of Poetry, supported by the general Suffrages of the learned World?

It

Epick Poetry. 163

It is not, I say, reasonable to suppose, that these Persons will easily recede from their suppos'd Advantage of Erudition, tho it is little more than that of a Grammarian and Commentator, to degrade themselves, and level their Character with that of Men of mere Genius and an arguing Head. Whence it comes to pass, that these Persons (tho of all Learning that of the Commentator and Antiquary, which is the sole Effect of Labour and Memory, is the lowest) are the most remarkable for a fastidious Temper, and appear always ready to take the Chair and dictate to Mankind. But to compose these intestine Feuds and prepare Terms of Accommodation, it is necessary that these Persons should shew a more candid and disinterested Spirit, and at least be willing to acknowledge every thing that is plainly prov'd against them.

Nor is it reasonable to suppose, that on the other hand the Champions of the Moderns are always freed from Prepossession; that they are not prejudic'd in the Favour of the present Age, of their own Country, and their own Performances: May they not envy the superior Fame and Reputation of the ancient Writers establish'd by the concurrent Applause of learned Men through so many Ages, and be very well pleas'd to pull down a mighty Power, which has spread so far, and lasted so long, that upon the Ruins of it they may erect an Empire of their own? Some, perhaps, may be willing to sink the Esteem of the eldest Authors, that they themselves may not seem to want any Excellence in not understanding the learned Languages, or to mortify some supercilious Commentators, whose whole Stock of Merit consists in expounding those Authors, and displaying their superficial Beauties. When such Reasons as these have prevail'd with Men of Wit and Letters, to espouse the Interests of the Moderns against the Ancients, their Engagement to a Party, and their Zeal for the Honour of carrying the Cause and triumphing over their Competitors, will still increase their Prejudice, lay a Biass on their Understanding, and prevent an impartial Judgment: We frequently see the greatest Sticklers for a free Exercise of Reason, and the most vehement Exclaimers against the arbitrary Power of Authority, as much enslav'd to their Prejudice against the Ancients, as the other Party is to theirs against the Moderns.

I PROPOSE therefore, that the Leaders of the Moderns should examine and
weigh

weigh the *Iliad* without Prepoffeffion, premeditated Ill-will, and an obftinate Refolution to be pleas'd with nothing in it; that they would not fhut their Eyes to the fhining and excellent Parts, and open them only to the Errors and Imperfections. I allow, that the greateft number of the Advocates for the eldeft Poets, from an Oftentation of Judgment and Penetration, and to raife the Efteem of their Erudition, can find out nothing but admirable Senfe, pure Diction, and inimitable Contrivance in the *Iliad* and the *Æneid*; and employ all their Critical Abilities fometimes to extenuate and excufe their Defects, and fometimes to improve them into Vertues and Perfections, while they look upon the modern Writers with Contempt and Pity; and as they can difcover no Faults in the firft, fo they can fee no Beauties in the laft. But then, on the other fide, let not the Champions of the Moderns fo far refent this Partiality and ill Ufage of the later Poets, as out of Revenge to imitate the Example of their Adverfaries, by cenfuring and condemning the Ancients to an unmerciful extent, and denying them the Praife which is really their due. Let them not enrich and advance the Moderns, by robbing and degrading their Predeceffors and Mafters; but let them weigh their Merit

Merit in impartial Scales, and do Juſtice to one without defrauding the other. If they diſcern Flaws and Errors in the firſt, let them take notice of their Perfections; if in the laſt they obſerve many Beauties, let them not be blind to their Blemiſhes and Defects. Let Candor and Judgment reign through all their Obſervations on either ſide, that the Reader may not be tempted to ſuſpect the Equity and Sincerity of the Critick, while he ſees him tranſported to indecent Exceſſes by an intemperate Zeal in a Party Cauſe.

As to the Conceſſions to be granted by each Party. In the firſt place, I ſhould judge it reaſonable, that the Champions of *Homer* ſhould no longer continue in their Intrenchments of Authority and Antiquity, defend themſelves by Preſcription, and draw about them Legions of Authors of their own Opinion for their Security; but that they ſhould agree to quit their Faſtneſſes and come forth into the open Field; there let them oppoſe Reaſon to Reaſon, Argument to Argument, and let the ſtrongeſt and cleareſt Evidence prevail. For it is no Demonſtration that their Judgment is Right, becauſe a Multitude of others have the ſame Sentiments. *Ariſtotle's* Notions in Philoſophy were, for many Ages, as universally receiv'd by the learned World as *Homer*'s Poetry, and esteem'd as the Dictates of the most profound Judgment and Oracles of Reason; yet, after he had reign'd in the Schools many Centuries with uncontested Authority, upon Examination he was discover'd to have no just Claim to this great Dignity; he was found out to be an Usurper, strip'd of his Titles and Regalia, and not only degraded, but treated with the greatest Contempt. Unless the Admirers of *Homer* will assert and prove their Infallibility, why may they not be deceiv'd as well as the Disciples and Adorers of *Aristotle*? And if so, what Argument can be brought why they should not submit their Poet to an impartial Trial? It is in vain to urge the Suffrages of Antiquity, against clear and solid Argument. In this Case Citations are neither pertinent nor useful, for the Authors of former Ages are disqualify'd from giving their Votes in a Matter of this Nature; no length of Time, no not three Thousand Years, is a sufficient Prescription to bar the Claim of Reason, which has an undoubted Prerogative to seize upon its Rights, when, and wherever they are discover'd.

It is very plain, that the Admirers of *Homer* should give him up in some Instances,

ces, in which it is too difficult to support him; and since it must be acknowledg'd, that no Production of Humane Understanding is faultless, and that the Intellectuals of Mankind are not more perfect than their Morals, it is no dishonour to any Author, that he is not intirely free from Imperfection; and therefore one has reason to suspect the Sincerity of any Critick or Commentator, that shall obstinately defend every thing in a prolix Author, and not allow, through the whole, the least Error or Blemish, especially when in such a Defence he is obliged to make endless Apologies, and many times such as are forc'd and unobvious, and rather ingenious and subtile, than natural and solid; and this is often the Case with the Advocates of the *Iliad*.

They should, in my Opinion, yield to their Competitors, that there are considerable Flaws and Defects in the Contrivance of the Fable, in the Proposition, the Subject, the Connexion and Dependance of the Episodes, which have been detected by *Rapin*, and by two later *French* Writers; the last of whom has examin'd the Plan, as well as all the Qualities of that Poem, with more Penetration, Exactness, and just Observation, than all that have writ

Epick Poetry.

writ before him on that Subject. And when their Adversaries object to them the Indecency and Absurdity in the Actions and Manners of the Gods, who are drawn by *Homer*, not only with Impropriety and Inequality of Character, but with all the Passions and Infirmities, that are the Shame and Reproach of Humane Nature; in this Case they had better, in my Opinion, yield the Point to their Opponents, and demolish all the Works they have cast up for the Security of these paultry Deities, and give them up as defenceless and unworthy of their Care; for it is impossible to make any Apology, that will cover this faulty Conduct of the Poet.

It is but just likewise, that they should withdraw the Protection of the sacred Writings from the frequent Repetitions in *Homer*, and acknowledge that it is an Error that admits no Excuse; for if any other could have been made, I imagine, no Critick would have search'd for one in the inspir'd Books. A Disputant must be hard driven in a Debate about Poetry, that is oblig'd to defend the Practice of *Homer* from the Stile of the Scriptures, which were no more intended to instruct Mankind in the Rules of Poetical or Oratorical Eloquence, than in Architecture, Painting,

ing and Natural Science. It is true, the Sentiments in the Poetical and Prophetick Parts of the Bible are as great and elevated, and the Figures as bold, strong and expreffive as can be found in the moft celebrated Works of the Ancients; but as that Accuracy, Correctnefs and Perfection, which the Rules of Poetry and Eloquence demand in a finifh'd Piece, are sometimes neglected in the Stile of the Sacred Scriptures, fo were they never defign'd to be a Model of indefective Writing. Tho they abound with noble and fublime Ideas, yet they were propos'd to the World as a Rule of Faith and Manners, and not of elegant and polite Diction. When the modern Aftronomers affirm, that the Earth moves and the Sun ftands ftill, fhould they be admonifh'd that this is to affront the Authority of the Bible, where it is faid, that the Sun runs his Race like a Giant, and that it was ftop'd in its Courfe to favour the *Ifraelites*, while they flaughter'd their Enemies? For many things are exprefs'd there, as accommodated to the general Conceptions of the People ; the Scriptures being defign'd by the Divine Infpirer to inftruct Men in Religion, not in Poetry and Philofophy. It is therefore an Indignity to the Sacred Volumes, to produce their Authority in Juftification of any Defects

Epick Poetry. 171

fects in Writing objected to the Ancients; for this is to misapply the Divine Revelation, by interesting it in the little Disputes of Wits and Criticks, in which it was never intended to decide.

It is likewise very reasonable, that the Idolizers of *Homer* should make a farther step towards an Accommodation, by acknowledging Deformity and Inequality in the Manners of his Heroes; who often in their Actions, Speeches, and Passions, say and do many things contrary or improper to their respective Characters, of which their Adversaries produce many evident Instances.

If they likewise condescend to stop the Mouths of the Heroes Horses, and not allow to Rivers the Privilege of making Speeches in an Epick Poem, which is distinguish'd from other Fables by its strict observance of Probability, it may not be look'd on as an unreasonable compliance: For tho *Virgil* has made the Horses of *Pallas* to shed large Tears at his Funeral, the *Latin* Poet's Authority will no more bear down Reason, than *Homer*'s can do; and tho *Virgil*, while he follow'd the *Greek* Master, corrected many of his Defects, yet here it is plain, that to imitate his Model

he

he mifreprefented Nature, and tranfgrefs'd the Bounds of Verifimilitude; and it is in vain to produce the Error of one great Poet, to juftify the fame in another. The Cafe is quite different, when by eloquent Figures a Poet or Orator attributes Speech to Animals or infenfible Creatures. For Inftance, that in the facred Writings, *Hear, O Heavens, and give Ear, O Earth, for I have nourifhed and brought up Children, and they have rebelled againft me*! And that of one of the Perfons in the Book of *Job*, enquiring after the Place where Wifdom makes her Abode: *The Earth and the Sea say, fhe is not here; Death and the Grave fay,* &c. For the Reader immediately apprehending the Figurative manner of Speaking, is in no danger of being deceiv'd; but in the other Cafe, the brute Animal is engag'd as an Actor, and not brought in by a Figurative Expreffion. *Homer*, by this Management, inverts the Order, and confounds the Subordination of Beings. By endowing with Humane Speech and Paffions, Beafts and inanimate Creatures, and introducing them as Parties acting in the Poem, he raifes them to the Dignity of the Humane Species; as by giving to his Gods the Infirmities and Indecencies belonging to Humane Nature, he degrades and finks them from their high Station to

that

that of degenerate Man; and while he bestows on his Heroes incredible Power, gives them Courage and Strength sufficient to ingage in Combate with the Gods, and to inflict terrible Wounds on immortal Beings, he advances them to the Rank and Character of Deities: Thus he makes Men of his Beasts, and Gods of his Men, and Men of his Gods. The Poet, I imagine, was tempted to bring in this Confusion and Disorder by an affectation of raising Wonder and Surprise in every thing he represented, by which means he often blemish'd his Poem with the false Marvellous; for where there is not a just observance of Decency and Probability, a judicious Reader will always be shock'd, not delighted: And notwithstanding *Aristotle*, sway'd by the Authority of *Homer*'s Example, asserts, That in an Epick Poem, for the sake of raising Admiration, one may sometimes strain it to an unreasonable pitch, I cannot submit to his Opinion; for nothing that is unreasonable can please Reason, and nothing that is unnatural and therefore incredible can be acceptable to a discerning Taste.

On the other hand, Prejudice apart, let the Moderns yield to the *Iliad* the great Honour of being the original Work of the most

moſt excellent Kind of Poetry, as far as appears by any Models now extant; and that if it be not abſolutely perfect, it is neverthelefs a wonderful thing, that the firſt Attempt of ſo difficult a nature ſhould ſucceed ſo well, and come ſo near to a finiſh'd Piece. Beſides, a candid Judge will attribute the Failings in ſo long a Work, ſtruck out and labour'd in the Poet's Imagination without the help of a Model, to the Infirmity of Humane Nature, which is never capable of a faultleſs Production.

Nor will they, I imagine, deny that the *Iliad* ſhews a vaſt Imagination, full of noble and admirable Ideas, a fertile and exhauſtleſs Invention, and great Vivacity and Splendor of Expreſſion: That they obſerve a copious Variety of Characters well diſtinguiſh'd, while his Warriors, tho all Valiant, are judiciouſly diverſify'd by mingling their Courage with various Qualities of another Kind, which is the beſt demonſtration of a rich Genius.

Let it be granted, that the *Iliad* has many Defects, and if they pleaſe, that it is far from being a finiſh'd Work; yet it is ſo perfect, that none of the Moderns dare ſet up any of their Performances in Competition with it. The *French* muſt

not

Epick Poetry.

not produce their *Clovis*, nor the *Italians* their *Taſſo* and *Ariaſto*, as Rivals to this Poet, notwithſtanding his Blemiſhes and Defects: And if *Virgil* himſelf be compar'd with him, ſince it muſt be acknowledg'd that this great Poet is not an original Contriver, and no more than an exact Imitator, I had almoſt ſaid a Tranſlator of *Homer*, the firſt Rank of Honour muſt be due to the *Greek* Poet. It is true, that *Virgil* has avoided ſome of the Errors which he obſerv'd in *Homer*'s Model; but that he has retain'd others, and committed many of his own, and a greater number, perhaps, than his Admirers imagine, will, I believe, appear, ſhould any Man with the ſame Penetration and Severity examine that Poem, with which two new *French* Authors have ſearch'd and ſifted the *Iliad*, to diſcover its Faults.

Justice likewiſe demands that the Patrons of the Moderns ſhould concede to their Competitors, that the principal Actors in an Epick Poem may be unjuſt and impious, violent and perfidious Perſons; and therefore *Homer* is by no means to be condemn'd for introducing Warriors of ſuch Qualities and Manners. The Idea of a moral and poetical Hero are very different; the firſt muſt always be repreſented as a

Perſon

Person of eminent Vertues and superior Merit, but the last may often be as much distinguish'd by his enormous Vices; for an Heroick Work being a devis'd Action or Fable, irreligious and wicked Persons may be engag'd in it, as oft as they influence the principal Design, and are necessary to bring about the Moral, which results from the whole. It is true, when the Characters are settled, the Poet must observe Uniformity and Congruity; and whenever those Persons are introduc'd in the Poem, he is oblig'd to make them act and speak in conformity to the Idea under which he represented them at first; and therefore they must every where appear like themselves; for whenever there happens, through Negligence or Defect of Judgment, a Disagreement or Contrariety in their Expressions or Manners to the first establish'd Character, the Conduct of the Writer will be justly condemn'd: And in this Case the Censurers of *Homer* have sometimes too great Reason to complain. But as to the Objection above mention'd, it arises from a false Notion of a Poet's Hero; the generality of Persons think, that the Conception of a Hero denotes, besides the Idea of Courage, some extraordinary Vertues; and 'tis hard to free the Mind from this Complication when that Term is offer'd to it;

and

Epick Poetry.

and therefore I wish that in speaking of Epick Subjects, Men would lay aside the Word Hero, becaufe of its ambiguous Signification, and ufe in its place, either Chief Perfon, Actor, or Warrior, which would not tempt the Reader to expect a Man of uncommon Merit. *Achilles* and *Mezentius*, tho Cruel and Impious, may be as ufeful to promote the Morals of the main Action, as *Neftor* and *Æneas* with all their Piety and Wifdom. To require that all the Men in the Poem fhould be Perfons of Vertue, is as unreafonable, as that all the Women fhould be ill Characters, according to *Ariftotle*'s Maxim; which Affertion, fince no Reafon can be affign'd to fupport it, I reject as Arbitrary and Abfurd.

These Gentlemen, that have attack'd the *Iliad* with fo much Vigor, are to be greatly valu'd for their free and generous Spirit, in afferting the Right of Mankind to judge for themfelves; and that they have detected many Errors and Defects in the *Iliad*, I acknowledge, feems to me very evident: But as it falls out, that many active and fubtile Politicans, who with Vigilance and Art have pull'd down a fettled Frame of Government, want Skill and Ability to erect a better in its place; fo it happens to thefe Criticks; they ftrive to fink the Reputation of *Homer* and demolish the *Iliad*, before they have contriv'd a wiser Scheme.

As to the first of these ingenious Aggressors, he has laid down such a loose and crude Definition of an Epick Poem, that it will take in the whole Story of any Hero's Life; nor does he see, so he says, why a History of such a long Train of Events, should not be comprehended in the essential Idea of such a Work.

I Imagine that this eminent Poet, having a mind to complement the late King of *France*, by writing the great Atchievements of his Reign, and drawing the Character of an excellent Prince at a fuller Length than what has been yet attempted, as he himself suggests in his Discourse upon *Homer*, was willing that such a History in Verse should be called an Epick Poem; and therefore stretches the Definition of it so wide, that it might include an Historical Recital of the Life of any Illustrious Person. But when he shall consider with greater Attention, the Constitution and Essential Properties of an Epick Writing, and reflect that it is but one Fable, I believe he will, without difficulty, allow, that the Unity of the Poem depends

depends upon the Unity of the Action; and therefore that a Poem that recites a long Train of independent Events, is not one Poem, but in the same Sense that a Heap of Grain is one Heap, or a Crowd of People is one Crowd: And there is yet greater reason to believe, that he will quit this as a defenceless Place, when he observes, that the judicious Author that has since embark'd in the same Cause, has declar'd against that Part of his Definition.

Yet that very Author, who has attack'd *Homer* with greater Violence, has given to the World as faulty a Definition of this kind of Poetry; but, as I suppose, upon a different View. The Poets of the *French* Nation, tho ingenious and polite Writers, not having yet attempted an Epick Work with Success, this Gentleman, that the Nation may not want an Heroick Poem, resolv'd to set up one written in Prose, and to make Quantity and Metre unnecessary in the Sentences of such a Narration, by which the Ideas of *Oratio Soluta* and *Metrica* are confounded.

As the first seems to have accommodated his Definition, so as to take in a History in Verse, for the Reason, perhaps, above-mention'd; so on the contrary, the other has given such a dress'd and forc'd Definition, that a Fable in Prose may claim the Title of an Epick Poem; nor do the Precepts of Poetry, laid down by *Aristotle*, bear a greater Conformity to the Example of *Homer*, than the Rules of Poetry which these Criticks advance, are accommodated to the two several Designs, which I imagine, they had in view.

The Adventures of *Telemachus* is the Writing which this Critick affirms is a more perfect Epick Poem, than those of *Homer*, or any other which he ever read. I allow that Book is the Production of a great Genius, that it contains many extraordinary Beauties, and an excellent Moral; but it can by no means claim the Appellation of an Heroick Work. A very great, if not the greatest part of it, tho the Diction is pure and elegant, is however entirely Prosaick, and not elevated above the familiar Didactick Stile; and therefore does not rise to the true Sublime requir'd in an Epick Writing: And tho some Parts contain a great deal of Poetick and splendid Expression, yet the Sentences not being measur'd nor limited by Quantity and Metre, it is no more a Poem than a Novel or Romance are such, in which the Unity of the Action is tolerably

Epick Poetry.

bly preserv'd. It had therefore been reasonable, that the Critick should have made it appear, that this Book was a Poem, before he had affirm'd that it was one of the Epick Kind. It is true, a Comedy is term'd a Poem, notwithstanding it is writ in Profe; the Reason is, becaufe the Actors have vulgar Characters, and the Subject or Action is low and familiar, and therefore not proper to be reprefented in a figurative and lofty Stile: But if the Upper Lyrick and Epick Poetry, as well as Tragedy, where elevated Diction is demanded, is not rais'd above the Comick Dialogue and familiar Profe Expreffion, the effential Idea of the Sublime Stile is loft and confounded with that of the Low.

Another great Objection to the Work above-mention'd is, that the Writer has not acted in Conformity to his Character; for fince in an Epick Poem, the Author often fpeaks in his own Perfon, there is as great reafon why he fhould preferve Uniformity and Congruity of Manners in refpect of himfelf, as in regard to his Actors. If the Actors in *Telemachus*, who are *Grecian* Pagans, fhould be introduc'd with the Manners of *Jews*, *Egyptians*, or other Nations remote from *Greece*, this Conduct would prefently appear abfurd and ridiculous;

culous; nor would it have been lefs in-congruous, had *Homer* when he fpeaks in his own Perfon, always fpoke as a *Jew*, an *Egyptian*, or *Chaldean*, and not as a Pagan *Greek*. Let it then be confider'd, that this celebrated Author evidently deftroys the Congruity of Manners, while he never fpeaks in his own Perfon as a modern Chriftian, but as an ancient Heathen: He employs all their paultry Machines, engages *Jupiter*, *Venus*, and *Cupid* himfelf in the Action, and in the Character of *Mentor*, his Conduct feems as much abfurd and inconfiftent with the Properties of a Divine Nature, as that of *Homer* in the Management of his contemptible Deities. Certainly that Author fhould not be imitated, who has introduc'd Celeftial Beings into his Action in fuch a way, as would tempt one to believe, that he was impious in Principle, and that to avoid the ignominious Character of an Atheift, and the Punifhment of the Magiftrate, as fome of the Philofophers have done, afferted indeed the Exiftence of the Gods, but defcrib'd them in fuch manner, and engag'd them in fuch unworthy and oft immoral Actions, that they might appear ridiculous, and Religion be expos'd to Contempt.

HAD

Epick Poetry.

Had *Homer* or *Virgil* employ'd in their Poems Deities not receiv'd and acknowledg'd in *Greece* and *Rome*, and such as were look'd on as imaginary Beings that had no real Existence, it must have been condemn'd as an unpardonable Error; yet this is the Case of *Telemachus*. The great Archbishop of *Cambray* does not appear in that Writing a better Divine than the Pagan Poet; and tho the Moral contain'd in it is fine, and very useful, is that sufficient without the Concurrence of other essential Properties to constitute an Epick Poem?

A Tragick Poet, tho a Christian, may write a Poem where the Actors are all Pagans with great Propriety, and without offering Violence to his own Character; because the Actors in Tragedy are introduc'd speaking and doing all Things themselves, while the Poet is intirely silent and unactive: But in Epick Poems the Author has a great Part, and speaks often himself; and therefore, as I have said, he ought every where to maintain his proper Manners, and is oblig'd by the Rule that enjoins such Uniformity, always to speak as a Christian, as much as his Actors, if they are Pagans, are bound to act and speak as such Idolaters.

To set this Matter yet in a clearer Light. If this Writing is an Heroick Poem, the Author, no doubt, might have invoak'd, as is usual, the Assistance of some Deity. Now I ask, what Divinity could he have addrefs'd himself to? Not to the Christian, for that would have been inconsistent with his Pagan Plan: And on the other hand, should he have call'd on any Idol or Abomination of the Heathens, how shocking must such a Prayer have been from the Mouth of a Christian Prelate? Whence it is evident, that no Invocation could have been made by the Author. And tho it should be said, that the Invocation is not necessary to an Epick Poem, yet none will affirm that it is impracticable, which plainly it is in the Prose Poem, of which we are discoursing.

Hence it appears that 'tis impossible for a Christian Poet to write upon the System of the Pagan Theology, without commiting the most offensive Absurdities. Should I undertake a fuller and more strict Inquiry into the Defects of that Writing, I mean, as it is produc'd for an Epick Poem, it would swell this Discourse to a greater Extent than is proper in this place; and were it as perfect a Performance of that Kind as some affirm, yet still it is an Imitation or Copy of *Homer*'s Model in his *Ulysses*. Upon the whole Matter, notwithstanding many Things charg'd upon *Homer*'s *Iliad* by the *French* Criticks must be allow'd to be great Defects and Blemishes, the Author must be acknowledg'd as a Person of an extraordinary Genius and a vast Capacity; and that he has laid two Plans of Heroick Writing so happily, that no Poet has yet excell'd them; and which with all their Faults are so just, that perhaps no future Author, that shall attempt a Work of that kind, is likely to succeed, if he deviates far from those Models, and much less if he leaves them quite out of Sight.

AN

AN
ESSAY
UPON
WIT.

AN ESSAY UPON WIT.

THE Inclinations of Men, in this their degenerate State, carry them with great Force to those voluptuous Objects, that please their Appetites and gratify their Senses; and which not only by their early Acquaintance and Familiarity, but as they are adapted to the prevailing Instincts of Nature, are more esteem'd and pursu'd than all other Satisfactions. As those inferior Enjoyments, that only affect the Organs of the Body are chiefly coveted, so next to these,

that

that light and facetious Qualification of the Mind, that diverts the Hearers and is proper to produce Mirth and Alacrity, has, in all Ages, by the greatest Part of Mankind, been admir'd and applauded. No Productions of Human Understanding are receiv'd with such a general Pleasure and Approbation, as those that abound with Wit and Humour, on which the People set a greater Value, than on the wisest and most instructive Discourses. Hence a pleasant Man is always caress'd above a wise one, and Ridicule and Satyr, that entertain the Laughers, often put solid Reason and useful Science out of Countenance. The wanton Temper of the Nation has been gratify'd so long with the high Seasonings of Wit and Raillery in Writing and Conversation, that now almost all Things that are not accommodated to their Relish by a strong Infusion of those Ingredients, are rejected as the heavy and insipid Performances of Men of a plain Understanding and meer Masters of Sense.

Since the Power of Wit is so prevalent, and has obtain'd such Esteem and Popularity, that a Man endow'd with this agreeable Quality, is by many look'd on as a Heavenly Being, if compar'd with others,

others, who have nothing but Learning and a clear arguing Head; it will be worth the while to search into its Nature, and examine its Usefulness, and take a View of those fatal Effects which it produces, when it happens to be misapply'd.

Tho perhaps the Talent which we call Wit, like that of Humour, is as clearly understood by its simple Term, as by the most labour'd Description; an Argument or which is this, That many ingenious Persons, by their unsuccesful Essays to explain it, have rather obscur'd than illustrated its Idea; I will notwithstanding adventure to give the Definition of it, which tho it may fall short of Perfection, yet I imagine, will come nearer to it, than any that has yet appear'd. *Wit is a Qualification of the Mind, that raises and enlivens cold Sentiments and plain Propositions, by giving them an elegant and surprizing Turn.*

It is evident, that Wit cannot essentially consist in the Justness and Propriety of the Thoughts, that is, the Conformity of our Conceptions to the Objects we conceive; for this is the Definition of Truth, when taken in a Physical Sense; nor in the Purity of Words and Expression, for this may be eminent in the Cold, Didactick

ick Stile, and in the correct Writers of Hiftory and Philofophy: But Wit is that which imparts Spirit to our Conceptions and Diction, by giving them a lively and novel, and therefore an agreeable Form: And thus its Nature is limited and diverfify'd from all other intellectual Endowments. Wit therefore is the Accomplifhment of a warm, fprightly, and fertile Imagination, enrich'd with great Variety of proper Ideas; which active Principle is however under the Direction of a regular Judgment, that takes care of the Choice of juft and fuitable Materials, prefcribes to the lighter Faculties the due Bounds of their Sport and Activity, and affifts and guides them, while they imprint on the Conceptions of the Mind their peculiar and delightful Figures. The Addition of Wit to proper Subjects, is like the artful Improvement of the Cook, who by his exquifite Sauce gives to a plain Difh, a pleafant and unufual Relifh. A Man of this Character works on fimple Propofitions a rich Embroidery of Flowers and Figures, and imitates the curious Artift, who ftuds and inlays his prepar'd Steel with Devices of Gold and Silver. But Wit is not only the Improvement of a plain Piece by intellectual Enameling; befides this, it animates and warms a cold

Senti-

upon WIT.

Sentiment, and makes it glow with Life and Vigor; and this it effects, as is express'd in the laft Part of the Definition, by giving it an elegant and furprizing Turn. It always conveys the Thought of the Speaker or Writer cloath'd in a pleafing, but foreign Drefs, in which it never appear'd to the Hearer before, who however had been long acquainted with it; and this Appearance in the Habit of a Stranger muft be admirable, fince Surprize naturally arifes from Novelty, as Delight and Wonder refult from Surprize; which I have more fully explain'd in the former Effay.

As to its efficient Caufe; Wit owes its Production to an extraordinary and peculiar Temperament in the Conftitution of the Poffeffors of it, in which is found a Concurrence of regular and exalted Ferments, and an Affluence of Animal Spirits refin'd and rectify'd to a great degree of Purity; whence being endow'd with Vivacity, Brightnefs and Celerity, as well in their Reflexions as direct Motions, they become proper Inftruments for the fprightly Operations of the Mind: by which means the Imagination can with great Facility range the wide Field of Nature, contemplate an infinite Variety of Objects, and
by

by observing the Similitude and Disagreement of their several Qualities, single out and abstract, and then suit and unite those Ideas, which will best serve its purpose. Hence beautiful Allusions, surprizing Metaphors and admirable Sentiments are always ready at hand: And while the Fancy is full of Images collected from innumerable Objects and their different Qualities, Relations and Habitudes, it can at pleasure dress a common Notion in a strange, but becoming Garb; by which, as before obferv'd, the same Thought will appear a new one, to the great Delight and Wonder of the Hearer. What we call Genius results from this particular happy Complexion in the first Formation of the Person that enjoys it, and is Nature's Gift, but diversify'd by various specifick Characters and Limitations, as its active Fire is blended and allay'd by different Proportions of Phlegm, or reduc'd and regulated by the Contrast of opposite Ferments. Therefore as there happens in the Composition of a facetious Genius a greater or less, tho still an inferior degree of Judgment and Prudence, and different Kinds of Instincts and Passions, one Man of Wit will be vary'd and distinguish'd from another. That Distinction that seems common to Persons of this Denomination, is

an

an inferior Degree of Wifdom and Difcretion; and tho thefe two Qualities, Wit and Difcretion, are almoft incapable of a friendly Agreement, and will not, but with great Difficulty, be work'd together and incorporated in the Conftitution of any Individual; yet this Obfervation is not fo confpicuous in any, as in thofe, whofe native Complexion comes the neareft to a Subverfion and Abfence of Mind, tho it fhould never degenerate into that diftemper'd Elevation of the Spirits: Nothing is more common, than to fee Perfons of this Clafs always Think Right, and always Act Wrong; admirable for the richnefs, delicacy, and brightnefs of their Imaginations, and at the fame Time to be pity'd for their want of Prudence and common Senfe; abounding with excellent Maxims and inftructive Sentiments, which however are not of the leaft Ufe to themfelves in the Conduct of their Lives. And hence it is certain, that tho the Gentlemen of a pleafant and witty Turn of Mind often make the induftrious Merchant, and grave Perfons of all Profeffions, the Subjects of their Raillery, and expofe them as ftupid Creatures, not fupportable in good Company; yet thefe in their Turn believe they have as great a right, as indeed they have, to reproach the others for want of Induftry, good Senſe, and regular Oeconomy, much more valuable Talents than thoſe, which any mere Wit can boaſt of; and therefore wiſe Parents, who from a tender Concern for the Honour and Happineſs of their Children, earneſtly deſire they may excel in intellectual Endowments, ſhould, inſtead of refin'd Parts and a Genius turn'd for pleaſant Converſation, wiſh them a ſolid Underſtanding and a Faculty of cloſe and clear Reaſoning, theſe Qualifications being likely to make them good Men, and the other only good Companions.

And this leads to another Obſervation, namely, That Perſons of facetious Talents and agreeable Humour, in whoſe Temperament, Judgment, and Diſcretion, as before obſerv'd, are uſually found in a diſproportionate Meaſure, are more inclin'd than others to Levity and diſſolute Manners: The ſame ſwiftneſs of Thought, and ſprightlineſs of Imagination, that qualifies them for ingenious Converſation, Sports of Fancy and Comick Writing, do likewiſe give them an exquiſite Taſte of ſenſual Pleaſures, and expoſe them to the prevailing Power of Tempting, tho forbidden Enjoyments. The Paſſions and Appetites of theſe Men, from the ſame Spring from whence they derive their extraorditraordinary Parts, that is, a Redundancy of warm and lively Spirits, are more violent and impatient of Restraint, than those in a cooler and less active Complexion, who however may be more eminent in the superior Faculties of the Mind: Hence it will be no wonder, that while their Propensions to Pleasure are much stronger, and their Reason much weaker than those of other Men, they should be less able than others, to resist the Allurements of criminal Delights; and this Remark is confirm'd by daily Experience. How few of this facetious and comick Species of Men, carefs'd and applauded for their shining Parts and witty Discourses, escape the Snares that encompass them, and preserve their Vertue and Sobriety of Manners? It too often happens, that a Man elevated above the rest by his uncommon Genius, is as much distinguish'd by his extraordinary Immorality: And it would be well if it stop'd here; but by degrees he often grows much worse, by adding Impiety and Profaneness to Looseness of Manners: For being unable, that is, having a moral Impotence of Will to restrain his evil Propensions and govern his vicious Appetites, and finding his guilty Enjoyments, attended with inward Uneasiness and unavoidable Remorse, and being conscious that his irregular Life is inconsistent with Safety and Happiness in a Future State; to remove the troublesome Misgivings of his Mind from the Apprehensions of Guilt here, and rid himself of the Fears of Suffering hereafter, he at length disclaims the Belief of a Supream Being and a Future Existence, and with much ado brings over his Judgment to the side of his Passions: This ingenious Libertine, having too little strength of Reason to subdue his Appetites, and too much Wit to think, that if that be not done, he shall escape at last Divine Punishment, abolishes his Creed for the Quiet of his Mind, and renounces his God to preserve his Vices.

The Objects about which Wit is exercis'd, are the common and less important Actions of Life. It is the Province of the Civil Magistrate to make Laws against enormous Crimes and great Immoralities, and by punishing Offenders, to deter Men from the like Transgressions; but they take no notice of lower Errors, either because they have not such noxious Influence on the State, or because it is impossible to foresee and enumerate their numberless Classes, and prevent their Growth : Where then the Legislator ends, the Comick Genius begins, and presides over the low and

upon WIT.

and ordinary Affairs and Manners of Life. It extends its Power and Jurisdiction over the wide Field of inferior Faults and ridiculous Follies, over the Districts of Indiscretion, Indecency, and Impertinence, and is Visitor of the Regions void of Discipline, Politeness, and Civility.

WIT is employ'd in its own Province, when the Possessor of it exercises his Genius on the ordinary Customs and Manners of Life, either in Conversation, or Comick Writing. It has therefore no place in the Works where severe Knowledge and Judgment are chiefly exercis'd; those superior Productions of the Understanding must be express'd in a clear and strong manner, without intervening Strains of Wit or facetious Fancies, which, were they admitted, would appear incongruous and impertinent, and diminish the Merit of the Writing. Hence Wit has no place in History, Philology, Philosophy, or in the greater Lyrick or Epick Poems; the two last of which containing either the Praises of Deities or Demi-Gods, or treating of lofty and illustrious Subjects; such as the Foundation, Rise, and Revolution of Kingdoms, Commotions of State, Battles, Triumphs, solemn Embassies, and various other important Actions of Princes and Heroes, are exalted above the Sphere of Wit and Humour. The Strength and Dignity of the fublime Stile is debas'd and adulterated by the foreign and improper Mixture of light Sentiments, and pretty Fancies. Thefe Sallies and Sports of the Imagination, will no more advance the Beauty of fuch fuperior Productions, than the Addition of glittering Tinfel and glafs Beads will improve the Imperial Purple, or adorn the Crowns of great Monarchs. And therefore we fee, with what judicious Care *Virgil* has avoided this Error; how clear are his celebrated Writings from the leaft fprinkling of Wit and pleafant Conceits, which corrupt the Purity, debafe the Majefty, and fully the Luftre of the greater Species of Poetry? And as the Gravity and Chaftnefs of the fublime Stile, in the Works laft mention'd, will not endure the gay Ornaments of Fancy; fo does that light Drefs more misbecome the pious and wife Difcourfes, that come either from the Pulpit or the Prefs. Wit is fo far from being a Grace or Improvement of Divine Eloquence, that on the contrary, it deftroys its Dignity, breaks its Force, and renders it bafe and puerile.

The End and Ufefulnefs of this ingenious Qualification, is to delight and inftruct, struct. It animates and sweetens Conversation, by raising innocent Mirth and good Humour; and by this Effect it relieves Domestick Cares, revives Men of Busineſs and studious Professions, and softens the Asperity of morose Dispositions. It suspends uneasy and anxious Thoughts, dispels cloudy and sullen Melancholy, and by unbending and exhilerating the Minds of the Assembly, gives them new Life and Spirit to resume the Labour of their respective Employments. The Exercise of Wit and a pleasant Genius, excels all other Recreations. What is the Satisfaction that arises from Country Sports, or the politer Diversions of Balls and Operas, compar'd with the delightful Conversation of Men of Parts and facetious Talents? Other Amusements, how agreeable soever, only please the Body and gratify the Senses, but this strikes the Imagination, touches the Passions, and recreates the Intellectual Faculties. And as the Taste of the Soul is more delicate and exquisite than that of the Body, so much superior are the Pleasures of one to those of the other: It is no wonder then, that the Assemblies of Friends are dull and heavy, that Feasts and Wine are flat Entertainments, unleſs some ingenious Persons are present to improve their Taste, and enliven the Company by agreeable Discourses. Ano-

ANOTHER part of the Province in which Wit is properly exercis'd, are ingenious Writings, intended to pleafe and improve the People; and this is more various and extenfive than Comick Poetry, tho of the fame Kind; for it takes in not only the Subjects of Prudence and Decency, regular Behaviour and vertuous Actions, but likewife the juftnefs of Human Sentiments and Opinions in Points of Controverfy; of the laft, the Dialogue of Dr. *Eachard* againft Mr. *Hobbes* is a famous Example, where, by great Strength and Solidity of Reafon, mixt with agreeable Wit and Raillery, he entertains and informs the Reader, and at once expofes and confutes the conceited Philofopher. An Inftance of the firft is, the celebrated Hiftory of *Don Quixote*, compil'd by the *Spanifh* Wit *Michael de Cervantes*; a Book fo well imagin'd, and writ with fo much Spirit and fine Raillery, that it effectually procur'd the End of the admirable Author; for by turning into Mirth and Ridicule the reigning Folly of Romantick Chivalry, and freeing the Minds of the People from that fafhionable Delufion, he broke the Force of as ftrong an Enchantment, and deftroy'd as great a Monfter as was ever pretended to be vanquifh'd by their

their imaginary Heroes. And many more Books on other moral Subjects have been compos'd with much Wit and Vivacity in our own and foreign Countries, to expose Vice and Folly, and promote Decency and Sobriety of Manners. But the Productions of this Nature, which have of late appear'd in this Nation, whether we regard the juft and generous Sentiments, the fertile Invention, the Variety of Subjects, the furprizing Turns of Wit and facetious Imagination, the genteel Satire, the Purity and Propriety of the Words, and the Beauty and Dignity of the Diction, have furpafs'd all the Productions of this kind, that have been publifh'd in any Age or Country. The Reader no doubt is before-hand with me, and concludes, that I mean the *Tatler* and *Spectator*, which for the greateft Part, have all the Perfection of Writing, and all the Advantages of Wit and Humour, that are requir'd to entertain and inftruct the People: And it muft chiefly be owing to the great Depravity of Manners in thefe loofe and degenerate Times, that fuch worthy Performances have produc'd no better Effects.

But this excellent and amiable Qualification of the Mind is too apt to be abus'd and perverted to ill purpofes. Inftead

stead of being ingag'd on the Side of Vertue, and us'd to promote juſt Notions and Regularity of Life, it is frequently employ'd to expofe the moſt Sacred Things, to turn Gravity and referv'd Behaviour into Ridicule, to keep in Countenance Vice and Irreligion, and with a petulant and unreſtrain'd Liberty, to deride the Principles and Practices of the wifeſt and beſt of Men. The Converfation of ingenious Libertines generally turns upon Reveal'd Religion and the venerable Teachers of it; or on thofe of the Laity, who feem moſt fincere in the Belief of Chriſtianity, and exprefs the greateſt Conformity in their Actions to the Precepts of it. Nothing gives fo high a Seafoning to their Raillery, and more improves the Taſte of their Jeſts, than fome ſharp and pointed Ingredients, that wound Religion and the Profeſſors of it; whereof fome are made the Entertainment of the Company by thefe facetious Scoffers, and expos'd as Perfons fetter'd with Prepoſſeſſions, and biafs'd by Notions of Vertue, deriv'd from Education and the early Inſtructions of canting Parents. Others are reprefented as indebted for their Piety to the Prevalency of the Spleen, and an immoderate mixture of Melancholy in their Complexion, which, fay they, give to the Mind a
fuper-

upon WIT.

superstitious Turn, and fill the Head with religious Chimeras, frightful Phantomes of Guilt, and idle Fears of imaginary Punishments; while others are ridicul'd as Men of a cold and phlegmatick Complexion, without Spirit and native Fire; who derive, say they, their Vertue, not from Choice or Restraint of Appetite, but from their deadness and indisposition to Pleasure; not from the Power of their Reason, but the Weakness of their Passions. It would be endless to enumerate the various Ways which the atheistical Wit and merry Libertine employ, to take off all Veneration of Religion, and expose its Adherents to publick Derision. This is certainly the greatest Abuse of Wit imaginable. In all the Errors and monstrous Productions of Nature, can any appear more deform'd than a Man of Parts, who employs his admirable Qualities in bringing Piety into Contempt, putting Vertue to the Blush, and making Sobriety of Manners the common Subject of his Mirth; while with Zeal and Industry, he propagates the malignant Contagion of Vice and Irreligion, poisons his Friends and Admirers, and promotes the Destruction of his native Country? And if these foolish Wits and ingenious Madmen could reflect, they would soon be

con-

convinc'd, that while they are engag'd against Religion they hurt themselves; and that Wit and Humour thus mifapply'd, will prove but a wretched Compenfation for their want of Vertue.

In this Place I crave leave to tranfcribe fome Paffages relating to this Subject, from the Writings of a good Judge of Wit, and as great a Mafter of it as perhaps any Nation ever bred, I mean Archbifhop *Tillotfon*; " I know not how it comes to pafs, " *fays he*, that fome Men have the Fortune to be efteem'd Wits, only for jefting out of the common Road, and for making bold to fcoff at thofe things, which the greateft Part of Mankind reverence —. If Men did truly confult the Intereft, either of their Safety or Reputation, they would never exercife their Wit in fuch dangerous Matters. Wit is a very commendable Quality, but then a wife Man fhould have the keeping of it. It is a fharp Weapon, as apt for Mifchief as for good Purpofes, if it be not well manag'd: The proper ufe of it is to feafon Converfation, to reprefent what is Praife-worthy to the greateft Advantage, and to expofe the Vices and Follies of Men, fuch things as are in themfelves truly ridiculous:

" But

"But if it be apply'd to the Abuse of the
"gravest and most serious Matters, it
"then loses its Commendation. If any
"Man thinks he abounds in this Quality,
"and hath Wit to spare, there is scope
"enough for it within the Bounds of Re-
"ligion and Decency; and when it transl-
"gresseth these, it degenerates into Inso-
"lence and Impiety — And afterwards: A
"sharp Wit may find something in the
"wisest Man, whereby to expose him to
"the Contempt of injudicious People. The
"gravest Book that ever was written,
"may be made ridiculous, by applying
"the Sayings of it to a foolish purpose,
"for a Jest may be obtruded upon any
"thing; and therefore no Man ought to
"have the less Reverence for the Prin-
"ciples of Religion, or for the Holy Scrip-
"tures, because idle and profane Wits can
"break Jests upon them. Nothing is so
"easy, as to take particular Phrases and
"Expressions out of the best Book in the
"World, and to abuse them, by forcing
"an odd and ridiculous Sense upon them."
And in another place, having mention'd
the most proper Objects of Wit, he thus
expresses himself, —— " This I say on
"purpose to recommend to Men a nobler
"Exercise for their Wits, and if it be
"possible, to put them out of Conceit
"with

"with that scoffing Humour, which is so
"easy and so ill-natur'd, and is not only
"an Enemy to Religion, but to every
"thing else that is wise and worthy; and
"I am very much mistaken, if the State
"as well as the Church, the Civil Go-
"vernment as well as Religion, do not
"in a short space find the intolerable In-
"convenience of this Humour."

Tho the Persons addicted to this impious Folly, expose the sacred Mysteries of Christianity, and make its Votaries the common Topick of their Raillery, it cannot thence be concluded, that they are certain that those whom they thus deride, as whimsical, stupid, and deluded Men, have not the least Reason to support their Religious Principles and Practice; for if they were sure of this, they would treat such unhappy Persons as Men rob'd of their Senses, with Tenderness and Compassion; for none will allow such distemper'd Minds to be proper Subjects of Ridicule and Derision: But those who attentively observe the Manner and Air of these jesting Libertines, when they laugh at Vertue, will see plainly their licentious Mirth springs from other Principles; either from this, That the Example of many Persons, who in earnest embrace and profess

the

the Articles of Religion, continually di-
sturbs their Opinion of themselves, and
creates severe Misgivings and Distrust in
their Minds, lest their Notions about Religion should not be true, when they observe, that many Persons of eminent Parts,
superior Reason and Erudition, maintain
with Zeal qu'te contrary Sentiments: or
else it proceeds from their Hatred of Men
of Vertue, founded in the Diffimilitude of
Difpositions and Manners, and Difagreement in Interest, Employments and Designs; or from an Envy of their great Merit, innocent Life, and worthy Actions,
which from the prevailing Power of their
own vicious Inclinations, they are unable
to imitate; for after all their Raillery and
Expressions of Contempt, Vertue has that
native Lustre and amiable Appearance,
that will compel Men secretly to esteem
it, even while they deride the Possessors
of it. Such is the Pride and Vanity of
degenerate Nature, that loose Men will
always endeavour to level the eminent
Characters of religious and sober Persons,
and reduce them to the inferior Degree of
their own: And for that end, they will
labour to sink the Opinion and Esteem of
any Excellence or Merit, to which themselves can make no Pretence. While they
cannot equal the bright Example of Ver-

P   tue

tue in others, they ſtrive to ſully or efface it, and by turning it into Ridicule, make it ſeem rather the Diſhonour and Deformity, than the Beauty and Perfection of the Mind: And if they can diſgrace Religion and ſubvert all moral Diſtinction, Men will be valu'd only for their intellectual Endowments, and then they imagine they have gain'd their Point, ſince the Superiority of Wit, as they ſuppoſe, is on their Side. Theſe ſeem to me the genuine and natural Cauſes, why Men of great Parts and extraordinary Wit, but of looſe Principles and immoral Lives, who above all others affect Popularity and gaſp after Applauſe, take ſo much Pleaſure, without the leaſt regard to Modeſty and Decency, in a Chriſtian Country to mock Religion and jerk with ſpiteful Satire Men of Vertue and inoffenſive Behaviour.

Wit is likewiſe miſapply'd, when exercis'd to ridicule any unavoidable Defects and Deformities of Body or Mind; for ſince nothing is a moral Blemiſh, but as it is the Effect of our own Choice, nothing can be diſgraceful but what is voluntary, and brought freely upon our ſelves; and ſince nothing is the proper Object of Raillery and Ridicule, but what is ſhameful, it muſt be a Violence to Reaſon

son and Humanity, to reproach and expose another for any thing that was not in his Power to escape. And therefore to make a Man contemptible, and the Jest of the Company, by deriding him for his mishapen Body, ill figur'd Face, stammering Speech, or low Degree of Understanding, is a great Abuse of ingenious Faculties.

Nor is it a less criminal Use of this Talent, when it is exercis'd in lascivious and obscene Discourses. The Venom is not less, but more infectious and destructive, when convey'd by artful Insinuation and a delicate Turn of Wit; when impure Sentiments are express'd by Men of a heavy and gross Imagination, in direct and open Terms, the Company are put out of Countenance, and nauseate the Coarseness of the Conversation: but a Man of Wit gilds the Poison, dresses his wanton Thoughts in a beautiful Habit, and by slanting and side Approaches, possesses the Imagination of the Hearers, before his Design is well discover'd; by which means he more effectually gains Admission to the Mind, and fills the Fancy with immodest Ideas.

Nothing can be more ill-manner'd, or disagreeable to Persons of Vertue and
Sobriety

Sobriety of Manners, than wanton and obscene Expreffions; on which Subject the excellent Archbifhop *Tillotfon* has the following Paragraph: " Nothing that tref-
" paffes upon the Modefty of the Compa-
" ny, and the Decency of Converfation,
" can become the Mouth of a wife and
" vertuous Perfon. This kind of Con-
" verfation would fain pafs for Wit among
" fome fort of Perfons, to whom it is ac-
" ceptable; but whatever favours of Rude-
" nefs and Immodefty, and Ill-Manners, is
" very far from deferving that Name; and
" they that are fober and vertuous cannot
" entertain any Difcourfe of this kind,
" with Approbation and Acceptance. A
" well bred Perfon will never offend in
" this way. And therefore it cannot but
" be efteem'd as an Affront to modeft
" Company, and a rude prefuming upon
" their Approbation, impudently taking it
" for granted, that all others are as lewd
" and diffolute as themfelves."

Men of finer Spirits do likewife abufe their Parts, as well as mifapply their Time, when to gain Applaufe and increafe their Popularity, they run, without Diftinction, into Company, and by too great Condefcention and falfe Humanity, mingle in inferior and unworthy Affemblies; where
delight-

delighted with the silly Approbation of ignorant Laughers, they shine forth in a great Effusion of Wit and Humour; by which they make themselves cheap, if not contemptible in the Opinion of wise and discerning Persons. Men of singular Wit, like Women of great Beauty, should never be unguarded; for if not endow'd with a decent Reservedness, a modest Air, and a discreet Behaviour, they sink in their Value, and by appearing in all Places, and becoming common and familiar, lose, in a great measure, their Honour, and the Opinion of their Merit. It is a meretricious Prostitution of Wit, when the Possessors of it can deny no Addresses, and refuse no Invitations and Appointments, but suffer themselves to be shown at every Entertainment: Besides the gratifying of their Vanity, by a constant pursuit of Approbation and Praise, which is the Spring whence this Prodigality of Parts and waste of facetious Humour chiefly arise; it is evident, they spend a great deal of Time, of which a wise Man can give no Account, while Wit, which should in its proper place, renew and revive the Spirits for useful Employment, becomes a continu'd Diversion, and makes everlasting Idleness the Business of Life.

It is pity that a Man of fine Spirit and a fertile, as well as delicate Imagination, should think himself engag'd in high Conversation, when he is only employ'd in the lowest Affairs that concern Mankind. His Post is of the same Kind, and but the next in Order above that of Players on Instruments, admirable Voices, excellent Actors on the Stage, and famous Dancers; whose Province is only to amuse and recreate; and is therefore far below theirs, who are either busied in governing the State, defending their Country, improving the Minds, or relieving the Bodies of other Men.

Hence the Labours of the meanest Persons, that conduce to the Welfare and Benefit of the Publick, are more valuable, because more useful, than the Employments of those, who apply themselves only, or principally, to divert and entertain the Fancy; and therefore must be as much preferable to the Occupation or Profession of a Wit, as the Improvement and Happiness of Men is to be regarded above their Mirth and Recreation. I allow, that the Talents of these ingenious Men are very much to be esteem'd in their proper place; that is, as they unbend the Mind, relieve

the

upon WIT.

the Satiety of Contemplation and Labour, and by the Delight which they give, refresh the Spirits and fit them for the Returns of Study and Employment: But then it muft be granted, that, as I have faid, this is the meaneft, as being the leaft beneficial Province in which our intellectual Faculties can be engag'd; and therefore thefe facetious Men can only claim the higheft Rank among thofe, who are Inventors or Minifters of Pleafure, and provide Amufements and Recreations for the Bufy and the Wife.

I WOULD illuftrate what I have afferted by the following Reflection. Domeftick Fowls, the Hen, the Turkey, and Goofe are preferable, as more ufeful, to the finging Bird, and the Parrot. The Ox, that ploughs the Field and brings home the Harveft, the Horfe, the Mule, and even the ftupid Afs, that carry their Owners, or their Goods and Merchandize, are more to be regarded than the Hound, the Lap-Dog, and various other Animals that feem to have been created only for our Pleafure and Amufement: And the Reafon of this is very evident, Mankind may be very happy, and States and Kingdoms may remain in a flourifhiug Condition, tho there were no fuch diverting Creatures in the World:

World: And from the same Consideration, Men, tho of a lower Station, who are not only beneficial, but neceſſary to the Well-being of Human Societies, are of far greater Importance, and therefore deſerve more Eſteem than thoſe, who only are ſubſervient to our Recreation; for the World may ſtill ſubſiſt, and continue in very comfortable Circumſtances without one, but not without the other: And 'tis eaſy to name ſome learned and powerful Communities, the Envy and Terror of their Neighbours, who tho they abound in Men of good Senſe and diligent Application to Buſineſs, yet have few Wits and Jeſters among them to make them merry.

The Truth of what I have aſſerted will farther appear, if we reflect that generally Men of a plain Underſtanding and good Senſe, but of great Induſtry and Capacity for Buſineſs, are in all Governments advanc'd to Poſts of Truſt and great Employments in the State, while meer Wits are regarded as Men of the loweſt Merit, and accordingly are promoted to the meaner and leſs profitable Places, being look'd on, by reaſon of their Inapplication and volatile Temper, as unfit for a higher Station.

ANOTHER pernicious Abuse of Wit is that which appears in the Writings of some ingenious Men, who are so hardy as to expose from the Press the most venerable Subjects, and treat Vertue and Sobriety of Manners with Raillery and Ridicule. Several, in their Books, have many sarcastical and spiteful Strokes at Religion in general, while others make themselves pleasant with the Principles of the Christian. Of the last kind this Age has seen a most audacious Example in the Book intitul'd, *A Tale of a Tub.* Had this Writing been publish'd in a Pagan or Popish Nation, who are justly impatient of all Indignity offer'd to the Establish'd Religion of their Country, no doubt but the Author would have receiv'd the Punishment he deserv'd. But the Fate of this impious Buffoon is very different; for in a Protestant Kingdom, zealous of their Civil and Religious Immunities, he has not only escap'd Affronts and the Effects of publick Resentment, but has been caress'd and patroniz'd by Persons of great Figure and of all Denominations. Violent Party Men, who differ'd in all Things besides, agreed, in their Turn, to shew particular Respect and Friendship to this insolent Derider of the Worship of his Country,

Country, till at last the reputed Writer is not only gone off with Impunity, but triumphs in his Dignity and Preferment. I do not know, that any Inquiry or Search was ever made after this Writing, or that any Reward was ever offer'd for the Discovery of the Author, or that the infamous Book was ever condemn'd to be burnt in Publick: Whether this proceeds from the excessive Esteem and Love that Men in Power, during the late Reign, had for Wit, or their defect of Zeal and Concern for the Christian Religion, will be determin'd best by those, who are best acquainted with their Character.

But the most extensive Abuse of Parts and Ingenuity, appears in the loose Productions of our Writers to the Stage. It was the Complaint of the celebrated Wit of *Spain*, *Michael de Cervantes*, before-cited, that the Comedies in his Time were not only extravagant and monstrous in their Contrivance, but likewise the Exemplars of Vice and Representations of Lewdness: But had the Plays in *Spain*, at that Time, been as Immoral and Unchaste as the daily Entertainments of the *British* Theatre, which have a manifest Tendency to vitiate the Taste of the People, fill their Imaginations with obscene Ideas, and their Lives

* with

upon WIT. 219

with Levity, Idleness and Luxury; I say, if that great Man, whose Judgment was equal to his admirable Genius, had seen Religion and Vertue so derided, and Modesty, Reservedness, and Decency so insulted and expos'd, his Zeal for the Honour of his Country, and his Love of Mankind, would have animated him to have attack'd the Comick Poets with the same Spirit, with which he assaulted the prevailing Folly of his Age, the Romantick Atchievements of Knights Errant; his Wit and good Sense would have made those merry Authors as odious for poisoning the People with their loose and immoral Writings, as he made the others ridiculous for their extravagant and idle Tales.

No doubt a Comedy may be so contriv'd, that it may at once become delightful, and promote Prudence and Sobriety of Manners; that is, when the Characters are well chosen, justly delineated, and every where distinguish'd; When the various Manners are exactly imitated and carry'd on with Propriety and Uniformity; when the principal Action contains an instructive Moral, and all the Parts in a regular Connexion, Dependance and Proportion, illustrate and support each other, and have a manifest Influence on the main Event;

Event; When the Incidents are well imagin'd, and result from the Manners of the Dramatick Persons, when the Turns are surprizing, the Knots or Obstructions natural and unconstrain'd, and the unraveling of them, tho unforeseen, yet free and easy; and when the Diction is pure, proper and elegant, as well as chaste and inoffensive to the modest and vertuous Hearers. So regular and beautiful a Piece as this cannot but greatly please and divert, as well as instruct the Audience. Nor is it, I imagine, from want of Knowledge of the Rules of Writing, nor of sufficient Genius, in which this Nation abounds, that so few Comedies, distinguish'd by these Perfections, have been produc'd: But this Defect arises partly from this, that the Comick Poets are often Men of loose Manners, and therefore unlikely Persons to undertake the Promotion and Encouragement of Vertue, of which they have no Taste, and to discountenance Imprudence and Immorality, when by doing so, they must expose their own Character to derision; tho sometimes it may happen, that a loose Poet as well as Preacher, merely from his just Manner of Thinking, and his Sense of Decency in forming Discourses becoming his Character, may entertain the Audience with laudable Performances.

† Ano-

ANOTHER, and the chief Cause of the Immorality of the Theatre, is the ill Taste of the People, who, notwithstanding they have applauded several clean and regular Tragedies, such as those which have of late appear'd that are worthy of the greatest Commendation, especially *Cato* and the Plays for the most part of Mr. *Row*, as great a Genius for Tragedy as any Nation in any Age has produc'd, yet still frequent and encourage the loosest Comedies. It happens, that the greatest part of Men of Wit and Humour, who not being easy in their Fortunes, work for the Stage, and are Day-Labourers to the Muses, lie under a Necessity of bringing those Productions to Market, which are in Fashion, and therefore vendible; while others, tho of ever so much greater Value, would be turn'd back upon their Hands; nor would the Actors, who live by their Employment, as the Comick Writers do by theirs, undertake to represent an Innocent, and much less a Comedy of yet higher Merit.

THO several Assaults have been made upon the Comick Poets in Fashion, and many Batteries have been rais'd against the Theatre, yet hitherto they have prov'd
unsuc-

unsuccefsful; the Stage is become Impregnable, where loofe Poets, fupported by Numbers, Power, and Intereft, in Defiance of all Rules of Decency and Vertue, ftill provide new Snares and Temptations to feduce the People, and corrupt their Manners. Notwithftanding the earneft Cries of this great City, that importune thefe Writers to reform the Theatre, and no longer to infect her Youth, and draw their Inclinations from their Profeffions and Employments; notwithftanding the Sighs and Tears of many once flourifhing, but now difconfolate Families, ruin'd by the diffolute Lives of their chief Branches, who loft their Vertue by frequenting the fatal Entertainments of the Theatre; notwithftanding the wife and fober part of the Kingdom earneftly follicit them to fpare the People, to ftop the fpreading Plague and ftay the deftroying Pen, they perfevere with intrepid Refolution and inexorable Cruelty, to poifon the Minds, and ruin the Morals of the Nation.

The great Archbifhop *Tillotfon* has fet our prefent Theatre in a true Light in his Difcourfe upon *Corrupt Communication:* " I fhall only fpeak a few words concern-
" ing Plays, which as they are now or-
" der'd among us, are a mighty Reproach
" to the Age and Nation.

"To speak against them in general, may be thought too severe, and that which the present Age cannot so well brook, and would not perhaps be so just and reasonable; becaufe it is very possible they might be so fram'd and govern'd by such Rules, as not only to be innocently diverting, but inftructing and ufeful, to put some Vices and Follies out of Countenance, which cannot perhaps be so decently reprov'd, nor so effectually expos'd and corrected any other way. But as the Stage now is, they are intollerable. and not fit to be permitted in a civiliz'd, much less a Chriftian Nation. They do moft notorioufly minifter both to Infidelity and Vice. By the Profanenefs of them, they are apt to inftil bad Principles into the Minds of Men, and to leffen that awe and reverence which all Men ought to have for God and Religion: and by their Lewdnefs they teach Vice, and are apt to infect the Minds of Men, and difpofe them to lewd and diffolute Practices.

"And therefore I do not fee how any Perfons pretending to Sobriety and Vertue, and efpecially to the pure and holy Religion of our Bleffed Saviour, can,
"with-

"without great Guilt, and open Contra-
"diction to his holy Profession, be present
"at such lewd and immodest Plays, much
"less frequent them, as too many do, who
"yet would take it very ill to be shut out
"of the Communion of Christians, as
"they would most certainly have been in
"the first and purest Ages of Christia-
"nity."

AND not only wise and sober Men have declar'd their detestation of the Immorality of the Stage, but eminent Poets themselves, who have written the most applauded Comedies, have own'd, that the Theatre stands in great need of Restraints and Regulation, and wish'd that Plays were compil'd in such an inoffensive Manner, that not only discreet and vertuous Persons of the Laity, but a Bishop himself, without being shock'd, might be present while they were acted. Mr. *Dryden* has, up and down in his Prefatory Discourses and Dedications, freely acknowledg'd the Loosness of our Dramatick Entertainments, which sometimes he charges upon the Countenance given to it by the dissolute Court of King *Charles* the Second, and sometimes upon the vitiated Taste of the People. In his Dedication of *Juvenal*, made *English*, to the late famous Earl of *Dorset*,

upon WIT.

Dorfet, he thus befpeaks him; "As a Counfellor bred up in the Knowledge of the Municipal and Statute Laws may honeftly inform a juft Prince how far his Prerogative extends, fo I may be allow'd to tell your Lordfhip, who by an indifputed Title are the King of Poets, what an Extent of Power you have, and how lawfully you may exercife it over the petulant Scriblers of the Age. As Lord Chamberlain, you are abfolute by your Office, in all that belongs to the Decency and good Manners of the Stage; You can banifh thence Scurrility and Profanenefs, and reftrain the licentious Infolence of the Poets and their Actors, in all things that fhock the publick Quiet or the Reputation of private Perfons, under the Notion of *Humour*." Hence it evidently appears, that Mr. *Dryden* look'd on the Decency of the Stage to be violated in his Time, by licentious and infolent Poets; and I wifh I could fay, that there is lefs Reafon of Complaint in ours. In a Copy of Verfes, publifh'd in one of the Volumes of the Mifcellany Poems, the fame celebrated Author inveighs againft the Lewdnefs and Pollutions of the Stage in the ftrongeft Expreffions that can be conceiv'd; and in his latter days, when his Judgment was more Mature, he condemns

demns all his loofe and profane Writings to the Flames, which, he fays, they juftly deferve: Which is not only a free and ingenious Confeffion of his Fault, but a confiderable Mark of Repentance, and worthy to be imitated by his Succeffors, who have broken in upon the Rules of Vertue and Modefty in the like manner.

Tho all Men of Vertue, who wifh well to Mankind, and are zealous for the Happinels of their Country, cannot but obferve the mifchievous Effects of thefe licentious Dramatick Compofitions, yet they will find it very difficult to fuggeft an effectual Remedy for the Cure of fo obftinate an Evil. The ingenious *Spaniard* mention'd before, for ftopping the Progrefs of this contagious Lewdnefs in his Country, propos'd to the Government, that an Officer or Infpector might be eftablifh'd, with Authority to perufe and correct the Poet's Writings, and that no Comedies fhould be prefented to the Publick without his Licence and Approbation.

But if this would have been fufficient to have prevented or remov'd this Hurtful Practice, the *Britifh* Nation would long fince have had no reafon to complain on this Subject. We have Officers intrufted with

with this useful and important Power, and are able, if they pleafe, to hinder the fpreading of the Infection, by not permitting fuch noxious Productions to appear in Publick: But whether thofe Infpectors have had a true Tafte and Judgment themfelves, or have diligently apply'd themfelves to the Reading and Amending the Comedies put into their Hands for their Approbation, or whether they comply with the Importunity of the Actors, who tell them, that fuch is the Difpofition of the Audience, that no Plays of that kind will appear beautiful, if they are ftrip'd of thofe Embellifhments and Ornaments of Wit, which fome morofe and unfafhionable People ftile impure and obfcene, and that to leave out thofe ingenious Strokes and Heightnings of Fancy, and put into the Mouths of the Actors only good Senfe and modeft and clean Expreffions, is to clear and refine our Comedies from the moft entertaining and delightful Parts: Perhaps they affure them, that the Audience will endure no Reformation of the Stage, and that it were altogether as advifeable to fhut up the Doors of the PlayHoufe, as to attempt a Regulation of the Pleafures and Diverfions of it.

An Essay

But tho Men who love their Country, born down with a Torrent of profane Libertines, Persons without Taste and Distinction of Vertue and Vice, have almost despair'd of seeing the Comick Poets reform'd, and the exorbitant Liberties of the Stage restrain'd within the Limits of modest Language and decent Behaviour; yet now their Hopes revive, and they promise to themselves a sudden and effectual Reformation of these Abuses, since the Government has plac'd so worthy a Person at the Head of the Actors, and given him ample Authority to rectify their Errors : What a happy Revolution, what a regular and clean Stage may justly be now expected? How free from all sordid and impure Mixtures how innocent, as well as diverting, will our Comedies appear, when they have been corrected and refin'd by such an accomplish'd Director of the Dramatick Poets? One that has a true and delicate Taste, and who is sensible of the Indecencies and hurtful Nature of our Plays ; who has engag'd his celebrated Pen, in defiance of sneering Wits and powerful Libertines, on the Side of Vertue, and has propagated the Esteem of Morals, Humanity, Decorum and Sobriety of Manners; who with great Spirit, Genius, and Courage, to his lasting Honour,

upon WIT.

Honour, has publickly expos'd the Abfurdities, Vices, and Follies, that ftain and difgrace the Theatre; in which Cenfure he has not fpar'd his own Performances: One who has exprefs'd a warm Zeal on this Subject, and declar'd his generous Intention, if it were in his Power, to cleanfe thefe polluted Places, and not to fuffer a Comedy to be prefented but what had paft a fevere Examination, and where all things which might fhock a modeft Ear, or be look'd on as repugnant to good Manners, might be expung'd.

But if thefe fair Expectations fhould be blafted in the Bloom, and notwithftanding the vigorous Efforts which will be made by this Reformer, Immorality fhall maintain its ground and keep Poffeffion of the Theatre, fome other Expedients may be fuggefted to procure a Regulation. It might, perhaps be defirable, that a few Perfons of Importance, Men of Learning, Gravity, and good Tafte, might be commiffion'd by Authority, as a Check upon the Actors, to cenfure and fupprefs any Dramatick Entertainments that fhall offend againft Religion, Sobriety of Manners, or the Publick Peace; and all Perfons fhould be encourag'd to fend them fuch loofe or profane Paffages which they hear from the
Stage,

Stage, or read in the printed Plays: Nor will it be lefs expedient, that they fhould be inftructed to perufe the Plays already publifh'd, and which are now publickly acted, and to expunge all offenfive and criminal Mixtures, that hereafter they may become a clean and innocent Diverfion. Befides, this End would the more effectually be accomplifh'd, if the Writers of Comedy, Farce, and Interludes, were rewarded and fupported by Means independent on the Actors: For while the Poets, who write for a Maintenance, are paid by the Theatre, they will be under a great Temptation to write as defir'd and directed by the Actors, which was the Complaint of *Cervantes* above-cited, concerning the Comick Poets of *Spain*. The Actors, we may fafely conclude, are not reftrain'd by fuch rigorous Precepts of Vertue, but that they will always be inclin'd to prefent thofe Performances which will beft fill the Houfe and promote their Intereft; and therefore they will readily humour the vitiated Tafte of the Audience, by acting the moft immoral Plays, while they find their account in doing fo: And that which confirms this Obfervation is, that they never, as far as I have heard, rejected any Comedy merely for its Loofenefs, tho I believe they have refus'd many

for

for want of that entertaining Quality. Now were the Comick Writers provided of a Subsistence some other way, they would be deliver'd from the Necessity of complying with their Actors, by writing such Plays as they shall bespeak, or at least approve, as the most likely to invite a profitable Audience.

It would prove an effectual Remedy for this Evil, if the Ladies would discountenance these loose Comedies, by expressing their dislike, and refusing to be present when they are acted: And this no doubt they would do, were they inform'd, that the Comedies which they encourage by their Appearance at the Theatre, are full of wanton Sentiments, obscene Allusions, and immodest Ideas, contain'd in Expressions of a double Meaning: for it cannot be imagin'd they would bear with Unconcernedness, much less with Pleasure, Discourses in Publick, which they detest as unsufferable in private Conversation, if they knew them to be unchast. And should the Ladies assert their Esteem of Vertue, and declare openly on the Side of Modesty, the most attractive Beauty of the fair Sex, as certainly they would do, if they understood how much those amiable Qualities have been expos'd and affront-

ed by our most eminent Comick Poets;
this would lay the Ax to the Root,
and at one Blow destroy this pernicious
Practice; for after this, what Writer
would transgress the Rules of Decency
and Purity of Expression, when he knows,
that by his immodest Mixtures he shall
fright the Ladies from the House?

It would be another effectual Means
to redress the Grievance of the Stage, if
the Clergy could be prevail'd upon to
condemn from the Pulpit and the Press,
as well as in their Conversation, the un-
justifiable Entertainments of the Theatre;
would they insist upon it, and urge it as
a necessary Duty of the People to avoid
these Occasions, and at least Appearances of Evil; would they shew them,
that by frequenting these unwarrantable
Diversions, they rush into Snares, court
Temptation, and invite others to follow
their criminal Example: would they set
before them the Hazard of playing on
the nice and dubious Limits of Innocence, and adventuring to the utmost Extent of Vertue and the Frontier of Vice,
there would be great hopes of stemming
this strong Tide of Iniquity. And this
is no more than the indispensable Obligation, which our Divines are under,
whose

upon WIT.

whose proper Province it is to warn the People of their Danger, and to press them earnestly to fly from it. This venerable Order have, by solemn Engagements, set themselves apart, as spiritual Guides, to point out the fatal Rocks and treacherous Sands to their Neighbours, that they may not make Shipwreck of Modesty and Innocence, and plunge into the Depths of Irreligion and Vice: Nor is it obvious, why these Reverend Teachers, by their Silence and Neutrality, should give Profaneness and Immorality such fair Play, as if the Controversy between the Stage and the Pulpit were compremis'd, and the Poets and the Priests were engag'd, as indeed they ought to be, in the same good Designs, Interests, and Pursuits. It is certain, that this Mildness, and friendly Behaviour of the Clergy to the Comick Writers, cannot arise from any Respect or handsome Usage which that sacred Order has met with on the Theatre, where they have been so often jerk'd and expos'd in such a manner, that their Divine Function has been wounded through their Sides.

The Clergy lie under such manifest Obligations to attack publick Immorality, wherever it is found, and by whatsoever

soever Patrons of Power, Dignity, and Intereſt it is ſhelter'd and ſupported, that, as I have ſuggeſted, it is not eaſy to imagine whence their Lenity and Tenderneſs for the Theatre can proceed. But if the true Reaſon of it, whatever it is, and which is ſo hard to be accounted for, were remov'd, and our Divines would intereſt themſelves with Zeal in the Cauſe of Vertue, in reſpect to our Dramatick Entertainments, as they eſpouſe and defend it in all other Inſtances, I cannot believe that the Stage, without a Regulation, would be able to ſtand, when batter'd with Vigor from the Pulpit. The Poets and Players would ſoon find themſelves oblig'd to reſtrain their licentious Conduct, reform the Theatre, and preſent to the Town, if not inſtructive, at leaſt inoffenſive and unſhocking Diverſions. And it is very deſirable, that this Expedient were ſet on foot, that the Honour of the *Engliſh* Theatre may be retriev'd; that while we juſtly boaſt of our Priority in Wit and Humour to our Neighbours, we may not be oblig'd to acknowledge the great Inferiority of our Comedies, in reſpect of Cleanneſs and moral Beauty; that we may not be reproach'd, that while we profeſs a Reform'd and pure Religion, we encourage

an

an immodeft and unreform'd Theatre, and that we are very defective in the Practice of Vertue and Regularity of Manners, while thefe Abominations are indulg'd, and thefe unhallow'd Groves and High Places of Immorality are frequented without Difturbance.

AN ESSAY

UPON

FALSE VERTUE.

AN ESSAY UPON FALSE VERTUE.

THE Propensions inherent in the Faculties, and interwoven with the Constitution of deprav'd Man, carry the Will with so strong a Bias to sensual Pleasure, that the greatest Part of the World have always disrelish'd those religious Dictates of Reason, which laid them under Obligations to restrain their inordinate Appetites; but at the same time believing the Existence of a Deity, the Moderator and Judge of the World, at whose

whose Tribunal they look'd on Man as an accountable Being, and finding in themselves that the Consequence of Guilt was unavoidable Remorse, as well as terrible Apprehensions of Divine Displeasure, they thought it necessary, for removing the Disquiet of their Minds, to atone the supream Being, and procure his Favour; and therefore instituted such Forms of Religion and Modes of Adoration, as they judg'd most effectual for this purpose. But not being willing to undergo the severe and difficult Task of subduing their irregular Passions, and denying their Senses, they design'd such Schemes of Religion, as might, in their Opinion, at once be acceptable to Heaven, and easy to their criminal Inclinations. In order to this, instead of Purity of Mind and the Practice of Vertue, they contriv'd an external Worship of the Deity, consisting of various Rites and Ceremonies, which only affected their Bodies or diminish'd their Treasure: They erected stately Temples, consecrated Priests to officiate at their Altars, and appointed numerous Festivals, solemn Processions, and various Plays and Exercises, in Honour of their Gods, hoping they would be appeas'd and reconcil'd by this pompous and costly Devotion. Nor did they forbear the Severities and Pains

of

of Fasting, Scourging, and performing Pilgrimages; by which they endeavour'd to revenge the Guilt of their Minds on their suffering Bodies. They likewise profusely presented their Gods with rich Offerings, and beautify'd their Temples and Images with expensive Ornaments: They were willing to commute for inward Piety and essential Goodness at any Price, and could part with their Ease and Wealth, and sometimes with Life it self, rather than renounce the Principles of Religion; from the Practice of which they desir'd however to be excus'd; and were contented to sacrifice their Children, tho not their Vices, to their imaginary Deities.

The greatest part of the Heathen World satisfy'd their Minds with such religious Institutions as I have mention'd, tho it must be allow'd that a small number of more reasonable Persons plainly discern'd the insufficiency of these outward Expressions of Respect and Veneration paid to the Gods, not accompany'd with a vertuous Life, to denominate a good Man, and make him acceptable to Heaven. And notwithstanding the Redeemer of Mankind, when he publish'd his System of Religion to the World, acquainted his Followers in the fullest and clearest Terms, that the Soul and Spirit of Religion consisted in the pious Inclinations of their Minds, and the Innocence and Integrity of their Manners, and not in external Splendor, nor any corporeal Austerities; yet how soon did the Simplicity and spiritual Nature of his Institution degenerate into outward Ceremony and a mechanical Devotion of the Body? All Mankind express an equal deadness and indisposition to the extirpation of vicious Propensions, and the sincere Practice of Vertue, from whatever Sect of Religion they take their Denomination. And tho the Christian Institution, by affording clearer Light and greater Encouragements and Assistance to Obedience than the Pagans ever enjoy'd, is far more prevalent to conquer that Reluctance and Aversion that is found in the Minds of Men to true Piety; yet it must be confess'd, that the far greatest part of Christians have, in common with the Heathen World, a strong Inclination to compremise the Matter with Heaven; and instead of internal Purity and a regular Life, to put off the Deity with superstitious Rites, magnificent Decorations, and bodily Worship, while they flatter themselves that he will rest satisfy'd with this splendid Devotion, tho he expresly declares the contrary.

False Vertue.

In the mean time, a number of more judicious Persons not being able to reconcile the Precepts of Christianity to a meer Ceremonial Religion, abstracting from intrinsick Piety and the moral Goodness of their Actions, to ease their Remorse and unquiet Reflections, and secure their future Happiness, set up spurious and false Vertues in the place of the genuine and sincere; while others yet more inlighten'd bid higher for the Favour of Heaven, by embracing and cultivating some real Vertues; which, however, being in a weaker degree, and over-balanc'd by stronger evil Inclinations in their Hearts, and Immorality in their Lives, are insufficient to denominate them good Men, and to give them a Title to future Felicity.

As to the first of these, to convince them of their Error in this important Case, and subvert their ill-grounded and presumptuous Opinion of their being Men of Vertue, the following Observation may have some Weight and Influence.

The necessary intrinsick Principle which constitutes a moral Action, is an End design'd; and that which confines its general Nature, and distinguishes a good Action from an evil one is a right End, which excites the Will to chuse it, and to which it is directed in the Intention of the Agent. It is not possible that the Author and Lord of Nature should have any other Design in creating an intelligent Being, and endowing him with Faculties to know, obey, and adore his Maker, than to manifest his own Perfections in the Happiness of such a Creature: His own Honour in producing a Being of so high a Rank, by which he express'd his Power and Wisdom, as well as his Delight in communicating his immense Goodness, must be first intended by him. And unless Men may be allow'd to endeavour to disappoint the supream Cause, and oppose the Design of their coming into Being, then the End which the Creator propos'd to himself in creating, ought likewise to be the End which his Creature should chuse and pursue.

Besides, he evidently declares the End for which such a Being is design'd by the Faculties, which he imparted to him in his Formation. Whence it plainly will appear, that it is the Duty of Man to act according to the Capacities, Powers, and Endowments of his Nature, and through all his Schemes of Life, to aim at

the

the only End of his Being; that is, the Glory of his Creator, and his own Perfection and Felicity. The choice of this principal End and the Reference and Subordination to it in the Mind of the Agent, is the fpecifick Qualification of every Action morally Good; and where the Direction of the Mind is wanting to promote this ultimate End by a due Connexion of the Action with it, that Action is morally Evil. And tho it is moft certain, that the Moderator of the World, by his wife and over-ruling Providence, will attain the great and glorious Ends of his Government, and make thofe who have no fuch Defign, his Inftruments to bring them about; yet if any Man does not in his Intention and Choice endeavour to advance thofe Ends, his Pretences to Vertue will be fruitlefs and impertinent.

Inftances of False Vertue.

Suppose a Patriot of eminent Abilities fhould, in bad Times, with great Sagacity, Courage, and Diligence, oppofe and 'efeat the mifchievous Defigns of evil Minifters, and detect the Frauds and Corruptions of Under-Officers employ'd in the Government; if all his Clamour againft the ill Management of Publick Affairs,

fairs, and his great Industry and Zeal for the common Good terminate in private Aims: If his Vigilance and Labour to pull down Men in Power, springs from an ambitious View to raise himself in a new Scheme of Administration, to some great Place of Profit or Honour, let him be ever so much valu'd and applauded by the People, as one that has deserv'd well of his Country, yet his Actions taking their Rise from the irregular Motive of Self-Interest, he has no manner of Claim to the Character of a vertuous Man.

If a Person of Power and Wealth, who designs the Improvement of Mens intellectual Faculties, by advancing Arts and Sciences, and embellishing the Language of his Country, should encourage Philosophy and polite Literature, should caress the Authors of distinguish'd Merit, and reward their Labours with Gifts and Preferment, such a Patron of Learning discovers eminent Marks of a great and generous Mind. But if this Respect paid to Men of Letters proceeds from a Prospect and Expectation, that Persons of Erudition should every where mention his Name with Honour, and that all the fine Pens of the Age should celebrate his Praises, and propagate the Esteem of their bountiful

The Subject therefore for the publick Good and Tranquility muſt bear Hardſhips with Patience, and acquieſce in Male-Adminiſtration, unleſs the Conſtitution of the Community, and the univerſal Welfare of the People are expos'd to apparent Danger. But in Caſe the Civil Magiſtrate ſhall, in a notorious degree, violate his ſolemn Compact, by which he conſented to be reſtrain'd and limited in the Execution of his Power; if he breaks in upon the Rights and Liberties of the People by violent Encroachments, and ſhakes the eſſential Foundations of the State, the Subject then is no longer oblig'd to ſubmit, becauſe now his Patience and Compliance will be more hurtful than beneficial, and will evidently contribute to the Deſtruction of the Community, which he is bound to preſerve and not betray. And even in Abſolute and Deſpotick Monarchies, tho the Soveraign is not reſtrain'd or check'd by any Contract or Stipulation with the People, yet is he under the Limitations preſcrib'd by the Law of Nature, which are altogether as obligatory, not to exerciſe his Authority for the Detriment and Ruin, but for the Good and Benefit of the Society. And where his Commands apparently contradict the Ends of Government, and ſo are

repug-

accomplish'd Person, by his amiable Expressions of Humanity and fine Nature, principally aims at procuring Applause to gratify his own Vanity and Self-Admiration: If he says kind Things to others, that they in their Turn may speak well of him, and strives to oblige every Man, that every Man may applaud his Character and spread the Opinion of his excellent Qualities; it is certain, that while his Intention in all this splendid Train of Actions is chiefly that a plentiful Harvest of Praise and Popularity may come home to himself, this fine Gentleman can never be a Man of Vertue, being mov'd by such an irregular Principle; no, tho he should with the utmost Modesty and outward signs of Dissatisfaction decline the Encomiums of his Admirers, whilst at the same time he thinks, that by so doing he shall acquire yet greater Honour, and make himself more considerable in the Opinion of the World, by adding the Character of Modesty to the rest of his eminent Endowments; for this is still by more subtile, but more effectual Ways, to accomplish his main Design: And therefore while he sets himself up in the place of the Deity, adores his own Perfections, and offers Praise and Admiration to himself, he is a deform'd Being in the most charming

ing and beautiful Dress, and resembles an impure Spirit cloath'd like an Angel of Light.

No Vertue in a Person of high Rank and Fortune, is more amiable or more applauded than Generosity, which is a ready disposition of shewing Kindness, and doing Good to Mankind. A compassionate Heart and an open Hand, above all other excellent Qualities, attract Esteem and create Affection and Popularity; tho we praise and admire Men for their Fortitude and Temperance, their Capacity and Application to Business; yet Love and Gratitude are produc'd only by Bounty and Munificence. It was well said by the Philosopher, That those most resemble the Gods, who need least for themselves, and do most Good to others. To relieve the Wants and Necessities of the Indigent, solace the Disconsolate, and to find out and advance modest Merit and neglected Vertue; to defend the Oppress'd, encourage the Industrious, and lay hold on all Occasions of promoting the Ease and Happiness of others, plainly demonstrates a great and excellent Disposition, as oft as these amiable Actions arise from a good Principle, and are directed to a right End. But if it happens that this liberal

liberal and generous Person aims chiefly at Popularity; if that is the charming Idea that sooths his Imagination, unlocks his Coffers, and dissipates his Treasure; if by the Profusion of his Wealth, he labours to gain the Hearts of the People to carry on his own private Interest, and like *Julius Cæsar*, lavishes out his whole Fortune, that by this means he may engage a sufficient number of Creatures and Adherents to raise him to Dignity and Dominion; it will plainly appear, that this Person is only liberal and generous to himself, and that by all his good Offices and endless Expence, he is purchasing Esteem and Power, and by his Munificence and Bounty, designs no more than to bribe the People, to gratify his Ambition.

Should a General be eminent in all military Qualities, vigilant, wise, and active in disappointing the Projects of an Enemy, and in taking all Advantages to surprize and defeat him; tho he is perfectly capable of governing a War, and forming Schemes of Action with the greatest Judgment, is cool and sedate in Council, and as warm and brave in Battle; tho he thinks justly, determines with Deliberation, and executes his Designs with the utmost Celerity;
tho

False Vertue.

tho by repeated Victories and a long Series of great and fuccefsful Campaigns, he fhould reduce the Power of afpiring Monarchs, and by procuring Safety to his Country, and Peace and Liberty to his injur'd Neighbours, he fhould acquire immortal Honour to himfelf: if this applauded Hero fhould, in his memorable Undertakings, be chiefly mov'd and animated by a paffionate Defire of enjoying the Shouts and Acclamations of the People, and the Triumph of a publick Entry: Or fuppofe this celebrated Warrior fhould be excited by a Principle of Avarice, to engage in Enterprizes full of Difficulty and Danger; fhould he difcharge the Duties of his high Station and Truft with admirable Conduct, and perform ever fo great Wonders, chiefly with a Profpect of heaping up Riches, and procuring an immenfe Fortune to his Family: or if to gratify his Pride and afpiring Ambition, he has chiefly at Heart the Acquifition of Power and Dominion, by which he may be enabled to revenge himfelf upon his Enemies, difpoffefs his Rivals, and advance his Creatures to Pofts of Profit and Honour, it is evident, that this Perfon's great Actions arifing from an irregular Spring, and directed by perfonal Views, can by no means be accounted morally Good: They plainly
pro-

proceed from a falfe Fortitude, nor has the Author any genuine Vertue but Military.

Notwithstanding a Counfellor at Law fhould be ever fo much applauded for his great Abilities and indefatigable Application, and efteem'd for his Probity and faithful Performance of his Duty in the Bufinefs of his Profeffion, by which eminent Qualities he becomes very ufeful to his Country; yet if the Spring of his Induftry is an immoderate love of Mony; if his Soul moves and gravitates to Riches, as it were by a natural and an irrefiftible Inftinct, which exerts it felf without waiting for the Approbation of Reafon, while no Acquifitions can abate his Defire, but his Luft of Riches ftill rages and continues to burn with unextinguifh'd uterine Fury: if he is illiberal, ungenerous, and fordid; if the touching of his Purfe goes immediately to his Heart, and notwithftanding his great Wealth, he fenfibly feels his parting with a Shilling; if the fight of a Dinner at his Table, more expenfive than ordinary, puts him into a cold Sweat, and the News of a trivial Lofs draws Tears from his Eyes; this Perfon has not the leaft Title to the Appellation of a good Man, whofe Aims thus terminate in his worldly Intereft.

False Vertue.

Let an able Physician apply himself with the utmost Diligence to the Duty of his Profession, and express the greatest Tenderness, Care, and Skill, in restoring Health to the Sick, and Ease to Men in Pain; let him, with incredible Industry, weary himself by Day and deny himself Rest by Night; let him, with a sedate and unruffled Temper, bear the Pride and Peevishness of some, the Weakness, Impertinence, and Moroseness of others; let him, with invincible Patience, hear the Reproaches and injurious Reflections cast upon him by angry Families, where notwithstanding his utmost Art and Vigilance, he has miss'd Success; let him be ever so charitable to the Indigent, bestowing upon them, without Reward, Advice, Physick, and Food, and treat all Mankind with Humanity, Condescention and respectful Behaviour; yet should it be suppos'd that this Person is acted by a wrong Spring, and that his chief Aim is to gain general Esteem and the name of a great Man in his Profession, or to make his Credit subservient to his covetous Desires; while from his superior Reputation he hopes to be universally consulted; and by this means be able not only to support, but enrich his Family, purchase great Possessions, and

leave

leave behind him a plentiful Fortune: If this, I say, be suppos'd, the Doctor's applauded Vertue is nothing else but sordid Self-Interest and odious Avarice, conceal'd under the fair Appearance and hypocritical Disguise of those bright Qualities that conspire in his Character. A good Physician he may be, but it is impossible for him to be a good Man, while the Intention of a right End, which is absolutely necessary to give that Appellation, is plainly wanting.

Nor is the Case different with one of the sacred Profession; for should a Divine discover the Marks of the highest Zeal imaginable to instruct and reform the World, to fill the Minds of the People with great and just Ideas of Religious and Celestial Objects, and wife and worthy Sentiments, and raise in their Breasts devout and generous Passions, as well as vigorous Resolutions to correct their Errors; should he exhaust his Strength, sometimes by excessive Reading, and sometimes by intense Contemplation, in composing excellent Discourses for the Press and the Pulpit; should he employ the Vehemence of St *Paul* to convince and terrify, and the Benevolence and Bowels of St. *John*, to entreat and persuade a stupid and degenerate

generate People to take Care of their Intereſt in the future World, by reforming their criminal Life in this: If all the Hours that can be ſpar'd from his Study, his Pulpit and Domeſtick Affairs are employ'd in going about doing Good, in exhorting his People to Acts of Vertue and Devotion, in reconciling the Differences of his Neighbours, viſiting the Sick, and ſolliciting the Rich to relieve the Poor; till by his watchful Care and unwearied Labours, he has exhauſted his Strength and emaciated his Body, and ſeems a venerable Spectacle of Mortification and Sanctity: If, I ſay, the main Deſign of this Reverend Perſon is to acquire Praiſe and Popularity, and the principal Impulſe that moves him is a deſire to be admir'd and applauded as a Man of refin'd Parts and ſtrong Reaſon, of charming Eloquence and conſummate Erudition: Or ſuppoſe, that in the Courſe of his Life his principal End is to gain Preferment, and to riſe by Degrees to the higheſt Order of the Church; that he may acquire great Revenues to gratify his Avarice, and Dignity, and Power to ſooth his Ambition, it will follow that his brighteſt Actions are no more than artful Impoſtures, and have nothing in them but counterfeit Vertue and perſonated Piety.

SHOULD a Magistrate use the greatest Industry, and exert all his Authority to propagate Religion and sober Manners, and suppress the prevailing Power of Immorality; and to this end should, with impartial Justice, punish the Guilty; and to encourage Obedience and Regularity of Life, shew to good Men repeated Marks of his Charity, Respect, and Favour. Besides, should he write Books on the Side of Vertue, expose Vice and Folly by the most pointed and elegant Satire, and in the most pathetick and polite Stile, urge the People to reform their loose Behaviour. Or should he disperse among his Neighbours, at his own Expence, the excellent Writings of other Men adapted to the same laudable Purpose; that is, the reclaiming the Vicious, and confirming the Good in the Ways of Vertue. If these shining Actions flow from an impure Fountain; if this singular Zeal and Concern about mending the World, is to atone for some secret Guilt; or if the Person so employ'd intends to procure the Character of a religious and sober Man, that under that Disguise he may carry on some secret Interest, and principally aims at Profit or Applause, his beautiful Deeds are no more than empty Clouds and gaudy Phantomes,
that

that have indeed the Face and outward Appearance of valuable Performances, but wanting the Effential Part that conftitutes moral Goodnefs, I mean, the Intention of a right End, which is to pleafe the Divine Being, and obtain Future Happinefs in his Favour, they have only the Name, without the Nature of Vertue; nor can they adminifter any folid Satisfaction here, or any juft Expectations of Felicity hereafter. But if any Perfons who endeavour to reform the Manners of other Men, are in the fame or other Inftances, as great Criminals themfelves : If a Libertine, that plunges himfelf in Vice, wallows in Pollution, and gives the Reins to his inordinate Appetites, becomes a great Stickler in the Caufe of Vertue and Religion : If one that defrauds his Neighbour, fhould expofe Falfhood, and difplay the Beauties of Integrity and Juftice; if a profane Swearer, or loofe intemperate Companion, fhould inveigh againft morofe Humour, Cruelty, and Hypocrify ; nothing would be more evident than that the Attempts of fuch unqualify'd Perfons to correct and reform the Errors and Faults of the People, cannot arife from a regular Principle, nor can they be directed to a pious End; the Reafon is, becaufe Vertue is an even and uniform Habit, and where it is genuine and prevalent, it difpofes the Mind to an equal Obfervance of all moral Obligations; and when it is unoperative and ineffectual in any one Inftance, that is, when it leaves any one vicious Habit unfubdu'd, all the other fine Qualities muft be pronounc'd fpurious Vertues; for did they fpring from a right Caufe, and were they guided by a juft Intention, the fame Principle and End would direct and influence all the reft of their Actions, and make their Lives regular and of a piece.

IF this were adverted to, Men would not be fo abfurd and unreafonable as to attempt a compremifing of the Difference between inconfiftent Ideas, by mingling diffolute Manners and flagrant Vices, in the Character of a good Man; and then, if Men will adhere to their criminal Courfes, they may at leaft be fet right in a Matter of this Importance, and not be abus'd by unmerited Panegyrick, flatter'd with Titles of Men of Vertue, and cry'd up as Objects of Applaufe and Admiration. It is obferv'd by learned Men, that nothing perplexes and confounds the Underftanding more, or is a greater Hindrance to right Conceptions and Improvement in Science, than the indiftinct and confus'd Application of Words to Things.

Nor

Nor is it less true, that nothing more perverts the Mind, and obstructs the Growth of Religion and Morality, than the Appellation of a Person of Vertue attributed to those, who have not the least Claim to it. Tho it is a sad Truth, that there are infinite Numbers of loose and bad Men in the World, yet it is as certain that very few, if any, of this vast Body will acknowledge they are so, and take to themselves the Denomination they deserve; which must needs arise from the false Notions they have entertain'd of Vertue and Vice. But if Flatterers would suffer Men to go by their right Names, and were the People appriz'd of the essential Difference between moral Good and Evil, it would be impossible that any should be so grossly impos'd upon. For if a Person may at once be allow'd to be remarkable for Heroick Vertue and Impiety, insatiable Avarice and Love to his Country, Fraud and Humanity, Honour and Injustice, or flagitious Manners and Zeal for Religion; if one that is plung'd in the Dregs of Vice may deserve the Name of a good Man, and the Libertine may expect in a Future State the Reward of a Saint; if these Ideas, I say, are not granted to be destructive of one another, then Light and Darkness are become Friends, the grossest

Abfurdities will be made eafy to our Apprehenfion, nor fhould Contradictions any longer be look'd on as inconfiftent.

Thus I have given many Inftances of fuch Qualities as have the exterior Refemblance and fplendid Appearance of Vertue; but not being animated by a right Principle and End, which are the Life and informing Spirit of moral Goodnefs, are only beautiful Illufions and empty Shadows, and are no more genuine Vertue, than a painted Tree is a real Vegetable, or a Statue is a Man. It is true, that in feveral of thefe Examples, the irregular but hidden Spring of Mens Actions not being difcernable to others, in the Judgment of Charity they ought to be efteem'd vertuous Perfons; but he that obferves the inmoft Receffes of the Heart, and infpects the Biafs and fecret Motions of the Soul, cannot be impos'd on, but will pafs a contrary Sentence, and condemn the Infincerity of thefe pretended Vertues.

Of the Desire of Glory *that most resembles* True Vertue.

BUT there is yet another Passion that approaches nearer to the essential Idea of Moral Goodness, and is therefore with greater Difficulty distinguish'd from it, I mean, the Love of Fame; which has here and there been touch'd upon in some of the foregoing Instances of False Vertue, and shall here be separately set in a fuller Light. The Desire of Glory, that is to be highly esteem'd by others and spoken of with Honour, has been look'd upon and recommended by the best Heathen Moralists, as the Instinct of a great and generous Mind, and a Mark of Sublime and Heroick Merit in Persons of every Denomination; and not a few Christians seem to agree in this Sentiment. But if Applause and a great Name are valu'd and pursu'd for their own sakes, and not as a Means subservient to some nobler End, whatever Encomiums have been given to this Passion, it cannot be admitted to the Rank of vertuous Qualities. To illustrate this, I shall crave leave to transcribe from a Writing, which I believe has fallen into few Hands, a short Discourse, tho perhaps too long for this place, that seems very pertinent to my Subject.

'Fame, which is the Opinion the
' World expresses of any Man's excellent
' Endowments, is the Idol to which the
' finest Spirits have, in all Ages, burnt
' their Incense; and the more generous
' and elevated any Genius is, the more ve-
' hement is his Thirst, and the more eager
' are his Pursuits after this alluring Ob-
' ject. Whatever Power is invok'd, this
' is the real one that infpires the Poet,
' flocks his Imagination with beautiful
' Ideas, and kindles in his Breast the Di-
' vine Rapture. This glorious Prize at
' once dazzles and animates the Warrior;
' 'tis the Applaufe, the Triumph, the Plea-
' fure of being deafen'd with Acclamati-
' ons, and diftinguifh'd and pointed at by
' the People, that makes him fo patient
' of Toil, and pufhes him amidft a thou-
' fand Dangers. As the powerful Inftincts
' of Renown excite an ambitious Monarch
' to repeat his Conquefts and enlarge his
' Empire, fo they raife up Heroes to op-
' pofe his Arms and check his Encroach-
' ments. Thus from the fame Spring and
' Principle of Action, Nations are fome-
' times enflav'd, and fometimes deliver'd.

' This

'This warms the Patriot with Zeal, and makes him think he is only serving his Country, while he is pleasing himself with Pursuits of Popularity. This smooths the Tongue of the Senator, and makes it flow with Eloquence; and it were to be wish'd that none of the venerable Men, who dispence from the Pulpit Divine Instruction, had their Lips touch'd by a Coal from this foreign Altar. Man is naturally a proud Animal, and is fond of nothing more than the Breath of Fame to sooth his Vanity, and flatter his Self-Admiration.

'Tho most of the celebrated Authors among the Ancients wrote by the Impulse of Vain-Glory, and Praise was the chief Reward they panted after; yet none so frankly own this Passion to be the Principle that inspir'd them, as *Horace* and *Cicero*. What Exultation and Rapture does the former express upon the Prospect of imaginary Immortality? How has *Tully* blemish'd his Character and obscur'd his excellent Qualities by Self-Admiration, and an open acknowledgment, that he look'd on Praise and Honour as the chief Reward of Vertue and of Illustrious Actions? I blush for

'this great Man, as oft as I read the in-
'temperate Expressions of his Thirst of
'Glory, which so frequently dishonour his
'admirable Writings.

' 'T is surprizing and painful to think,
' that a Person of his extraordinary Fa-
' culties, Learning, and Wit, should be so
' extravagantly transported with this Paf-
' sion. When he spoke his Invective a-
' gainst *Anthony*, who would have thought
' he was only flattering himself, and pro-
' nouncing a Panegyrick upon his own
' Eloquence and Zeal for his Country?
' That when he defended *Roscius*, he took
' upon him a Theatrical Person, as much
' as his Client had ever done, and only
' acted the Friend in great Perfection; and
' that when he accus'd *Cataline*, he only
' applauded the vigilant Consul, magni-
' fy'd the Patriot, and entertain'd the Se-
' nate with his own Praise? And yet 'tis
' evident, that such was his insatiable De-
' sire of Applause, that whether he assum'd
' the Character of a Patriot, or an Orator,
' whether he arraign'd the Criminal, or
' vindicated the Innocent, he had always
' the same thing in view, and intended
' chiefly, by various Means, to procure
' Glory to himself.

A

'A Writer in love with himself, is
'so puff'd up with Commendation and
'Popularity, that the Miser does not en-
'joy more Satisfaction in surveying his
'Heaps of Treasure, than the Author,
'who ecchoes to himself the Encomiums
'of the People, gives into the general
'Opinion of his own Merit, and approves
'the Taste and Judgment of his Admirers:
'Hence he draws, in his Imagination, his
'own Picture, with such amiable Fea-
'tures, and sets it off with such beautiful
'Colours, that he is ravish'd with the
'Reflection; and no Sycophant can sooth
'an aspiring Prince with more artful Touch-
'es of Adulation, than those with which
'an Author feeds his own Vanity, no
'Man being so hearty and finish'd a Flat-
'terer, as he that is making his Court to
'himself.

'Nor is the Merit of a great Warri-
'or in the Pursuit of Glory, unlike to
'that of a Self-admiring Author: Fame,
'however thin and airy, is the Food of
'great Minds, that are not endow'd with
'a more sublime and generous Principle,
'and to the Desire of this inferior Immor-
'tality, however empty and imaginary,
'are owing, for the most part, the At-
'chieve-

'chievements of Heroes and Patriots;
'These flatter themselves, that after Death
'they shall live by the Breath of Fame,
'and be carry'd up and down the World
'like the airy Phantoms and Apparitions
'of *Epicurus*. It is true, in this they con-
'fess the Belief of a Future State; for it
'cannot be imagin'd why they should de-
'sire to be spoken of with Honour, after
'their Decease, if they did not believe
'they should exist and enjoy the Enco-
'miums bestow'd by Posterity on their
'Names; yet this will not deserve the
'Appellation of Vertue: For if the fine
'Writer or brave Warrior terminate all
'their Views upon themselves; if the Au-
'thor only contemplates the bright E-
'manations of his Mind as reflected and
'coming back to himself in Glory and
'Praise, and the Soldier takes the Field
'and performs Wonders, chiefly for Lau-
'rels and Admiration, tho this approaches
'the nearest to true Merit of any thing
'that is short of it, yet their Actions
'springing from a wrong Principle, and
'being directed to an unwarrantable End,
'are but splendid Illusions and Faults,
'disguis'd under the beautiful Appearance
'of Vertue.

'It

'It is the incommunicable Preroga-
'tive of the supream Being, to search the
'secret Thoughts and discern the Bent and
'Inclination of the Mind, and therefore
'no Man by immediate Inspection into
'the Recesses of the Soul, can charge up-
'on another the Guilt of acting upon the
'Principle of Vain-Glory; but there is
'one distinguishing Mark that discovers
'this irregular Spring to one's self, and
'to others, and that is, if the Hero or
'Patriot, the Philosopher or Poet, who
'pretend to the good of their City, their
'Country, and of Mankind, should, in
'other Instances, express a Contempt of
'Moral Obligations, and become Practisers
'of Vice and Patrons of Impiety; 'tis
'impossible such Men should be govern'd
'by a genuine Principle of Vertue, which
'never fails to produce an equal and uni-
'form Series of good and generous Actions.

'These Reflections cannot but ele-
'vate our Conceptions, and engage the
'Mind in the Contemplation of the ad-
'mirable Conduct of Providence, which
'makes use of culpable Passions and ir-
'regular Principles, substituted by Men
'in the place of sincere Merit, to bring a-
'bout Ends of the greatest Importance

'and

' and Benefit to Mankind. If no great or
' illuſtrious Actions, in which the com-
' mon Good and the Happineſs of Socie-
' ties are concern'd, were to be perform'd
' by any but diſintereſted Men, who act
' from a Motive of real Vertue; how
' often would States and Kingdoms be in-
' volv'd in Confuſion and Ruin, while no
' Warriors would be found to defend,
' nor Stateſmen to direct and rule them.
' But when Principles of Vertue are want-
' ing, as apparently they are in the Maſs
' of Mankind, the Deſire of Popularity
' and Falſe Glory, by the wiſe Admini-
' ſtration of the Moderator of the World,
' in a great Meaſure ſupplies their Ab-
' ſence."

A cloſer Enquiry into the Diſtinction of
TRUE *and* FALSE VERTUE.

IT is very deſirable that Men ſhould be fully inform'd in a Caſe of ſuch Conſequence as this; for while the greateſt part of the People think they are already Men of Vertue, it is no wonder they believe they need no Reformation. But were this Confuſion and Obſcurity of their Ideas remov'd, and the Diſtinction of a Good and Bad Man ſet in a clear Light before them,

False Vertue.

them, they would soon discern their want of Piety and Goodness, as said before, and the next Step would be to seek after these Divine Endowments, on which their Peace and Satisfaction in this World, and their Happiness in the next do absolutely depend.

This being a Point of the greatest Importance, I will enter yet farther into the Discussion of it. Since no Men in this State of Mortality are so compleatly wicked as to be intirely unconscious of Remorse from Guilt, and free from all Esteem and Love of Vertue; and none arrive at that perfection in Piety of Mind and Purity of Manners, as to have no Blemish from the least Mixture of Evil: it is evident, that the Moral Difference, by which Mankind is essentially divided into the two Species Good and Bad, must result from the superior Degree of Vertue and Vice in the Minds of either sort. As good or evil Habits are predominant in the Heart and Life, they denominate and distinguish a vertuous or a wicked Man. But in this Case there is reason to believe, that great Numbers are guilty of a fatal Mistake, while they conclude themselves good Men, because upon the Comparison they find that their Vertues are superior to their Vices, and that more good than bad

bad Actions appear in their Lives. Thus one Man notwithstanding his sordid Avarice, believes himself a Man of Vertue, because he is just, sober, and regular in the Government of his Passions and Appetites: Another is as well satisfy'd with his Goodness, who, tho he is loose in his Behaviour, intemperate, and profane, yet he is liberal, generous, a Man of Honour, and a great Lover of his Country.

SINCE every Man by his native Complexion, by Custom or Interest, is more powerfully sway'd by some vicious Habits and Inclinations, than by others, and is therefore less able to resist Temptations, that address themselves to those predominant Propensions, the just and impartial Trial of any Man's Integrity will be to examine and weigh whether the Degrees of his Vertue are evidently more prevalent than those of the opposite Vice to which he is most inclin'd. For Instance; if a Man is prone by Nature or Custom to Intemperance or other forbidden Pleasures, to discover his moral Goodness, he is not to set his Liberality, Charity, Humanity, Patience, and other laudable Qualities against his Intemperance, and conclude, that by his possession of so many Vertues while he is blemish'd but with one Fault, he he is from the predominancy of good Habits to be denominated a good Man; nor should a covetous Person weigh his Humility, Veracity, and Sobriety of Manners against his Avarice, and then decide the Question in his own Favour, and pronounce himself innocent because he has many eminent Vertues and but one Vice; but the Person often overcome by Temptations to excess in Wine, or other unlawful Pleasures, must compare the Degree of his Temperance and Chastity with those of the contrary Vices, and if he has reason to infer from his frequent criminal Compliances, that his vicious Propensions are the strongest, and that therefore he must be pronounc'd an impure or intemperate Person, this Man is from that single prevalent Habit to be judg'd a flagitious and wicked Person, notwithstanding his specious Pretences to Vertues of another kind, which are all demonstrated to be false and counterfeit by the predominant Power of any one Vice, as said before; so if a Man by a diligent and strict Examination should discover that his Love of Mony is so inordinate and insatiable, that he must needs merit the Appellation of Avaricious, whatever other shining Qualities he may possess, they are no better than splendid Vices, and from the superiority of his covetous Habit he he muft be pronounc'd, what certainly he is, an ill Man: and this Rule is inviolably true in all other Inftances of the like Nature. When a Man enters upon an Examination of his Integrity he fhould know, that if the Superiority of his Vertue is but in a low and weak Degree; if he often breaks his good Refolutions, complies with Temptations, and relapfes into Guilt, he will not be able to determine his Condition, or conclude on which Side the Ballance defcends; and notwithftanding his Goodnefs fhould be predominant, yet while it is unevident to him that it is fo, he will reap no Satiffaction from his Reflections on it, but muft be often obnoxious to frightful Apprehenfions, and live in a doubtful, uncomfortable State.

It will be poffible only to thofe more excellent Minds, that in an eminent Meafure have learn'd to conquer all evil Propenfions, govern their Paffions, and fubdue their inordinate Appetites, that perfevere with Conftancy in an uninterrupted Practice of Vertue and Devotion, to review their Lives with Pleafure and Satiffaction, and to difcern the Superiority of their Vertue, and, in that their Title to future Happinefs.

False Vertue.

If therefore any Man would know, and who would continue ignorant and unconcern'd in a Matter that so nearly concerns him, to what Division of Men he belongs, the Just or the Unjust, and consequently what he must expect in the next Life, eternal Misery or unutterable Bliss; let him strictly observe the Course of his Life, and search his Heart to the bottom, and when he finds he has made a successful Opposition to that particular criminal Inclination which he is most apt to gratify; and tho by Surprize and Violence of Temptation in unguarded Seasons, he is sometimes guilty of Compliances, yet that this rarely happens; while for the general Course and Tenor of his Actions he lives a vertuous and innocent Life, denies his most favour'd forbidden Pleasures, governs his Passions and restrains his Appetites, he may come to a determination of his Condition, and rest satisfy'd that he is a Man of Vertue.

It must here be observ'd, that Vertue which is so denominated from the Superiority of its Degree, that over-ballances the contrary Vice, in which its Essence does consist, is not such in a strict Philosophical Sense; but it is such as is requir'd

by

by the Christian Institution to denominate a Man Upright and Righteous, and to qualify him for the Divine Favour and Acceptance; and this is frequently call'd Integrity and Sincerity of Heart, which overpowers the Opposition of every Vice, tho it never intirely subdues it. It is therefore certain, that when a Man would know himself, he must not believe that he is a good Man, merely because he is conscious to himself that he is sincere and in good earnest in his Resolutions and many vertuous Actions; for tho those Resolutions and Actions are real, yet if they are oppos'd and overcome by contrary Inclinations, which have a greater Interest in his Heart and Power in his Life, they are but false Vertues, not having attain'd that Superiority of Degree that constitutes the Being of Vertue in a Christian Sense. Hence when many good Men question their Sincerity, and are afraid they are Hypocrites, they mean they are in doubt, whether they have attain'd a prevailing Habit of Piety, for all Degrees under that they esteem Insincerity and Hypocrisy; because they are not sufficient to denominate a good Man, or give a Title to Future Happiness; tho in the mean time they are satisfy'd they have some inferior Degrees of Vertue, which they know are sincere, that is, real,

tho

tho fruitlefs and ineffectual to the Purpofes before-mention'd.

It is cuftomary for Men, when they fpeak of others, to exprefs themfelves in this manner; Such a Perfon is a ftrange Mixture, a Man of Pleafure, and too much addicted to Wine and good Company; but he has abundance of excellent Qualities to over-ballance his Faults, and I cannot but look upon him as a very good Man. But this is a deftructive Delufion, and the Error will be foon detected, if we reflect, that the Superiority of Vertue and Vice, that conftitutes the Good or Bad Man, does not arife from the Inequality in Number of their Good or Evil Qualities, for then there would be no Scarcity of good Men in the World. It has been demonftrated above, that one prevailing and predominant evil Habit is fufficient to denominate an ill Man, tho we fhould fuppofe him to be in all other refpects Juft and Innocent. When we would therefore enter upon an impartial and fevere Trial of our felves, that we may determine to which Clafs of Men we belong, the Calculation by which we are to be guided, muft not be between our good and bad Habits and Actions of a different Kind; nor muft the Scales be caft by the greater Num-

Number of either sort, for then perhaps a common Liar, a Swearer, a Drunkard, or Betrayer of his Country, might claim the Appellation of a Man of Probity; but the Decision must arise from a Comparison of a Man's strongest vicious Habits, and the contrary vertuous Inclinations, as before has been obferv'd.

If Persons would converse with themselves, and observe with Attention the Motions of their Hearts, and the Entertainments of their Imaginations, the greatest Part might soon discover what it so much concerns them to know, whether they are good or bad Men. It it clear, that according to the natural Method of the Soul's exerting her Powers, that Object which is most valu'd, and therefore has the greatest Interest in the Mind, must excite the strongest Desires and engage the most ardent Love; whence it will necessarily follow, that the Object that attracts the Soul with a superior Force, must begin and guide her Motions to gain the Possession of it: What we chiefly esteem for its Goodness, we chiefly desire to enjoy, and what we chiefly desire to enjoy, from an invincible Impulse we endeavour to attain, by all the probable Means in our Power; and during this Attempt to acquire the principal Idol

False Vertue.

Idol of our Hearts, we fufpend the Purfuits after thofe Satisfactions that have but an inferior Share of our Efteem and Affection, or at leaft we do not follow them with the fame Diligence and Ardor; and this is the eftablifh'd and unalterable Order of the Operations of the Mind, founded in the original Conftitution of our Faculties.

Upon this Reflection it fhould not, methinks, be difficult to find out what Objects principally attract the Soul, kindle her Defires, and govern her active Powers. Whatever appears to the Mind moft lovely and defirable, muft unavoidably influence and engage the Will with the greateft Force; and what has the fuperior Poffeffion of the Will, is therefore moft earneftly purfu'd. Now thefe Tranfactions cannot pafs fo fecretly in the Mind, but the Perfon muft be confcious of them, and cannot but be fenfible, what it is that he chiefly values, defires, and ftrives to enjoy. And therefore if any Man will reflect with Attention on the Operations of his Mind, he cannot avoid perceiving the principal Object of his Affections, fince he muft certainly feel the ftrongeft Emotions and Inclinations of his own Heart.

To be more particular; fince no Objects can move the Will and excite Defire,

fire, but thofe that are reprefented by the Underftanding under an amiable Idea, it is very evident, that as what we make our firft and principal Choice muft be fo reprefented in the intellectual Faculties, to attract our Wills and command our Affection at the firft, fo, to preferve and to perpetuate its Superiority in our Efteem and Love, that amiable Idea muft conftantly abide in our Minds; and fince in this Cafe, there muft concur various Actions of the Soul, which muft confider, ballance, compare, determine, and at laft chufe the propereft Means for the Attainment of it, it is very plain, that the Imagination and Faculty of Thinking muft of Neceffity be more employ'd about this Object, than upon any others of inferior Confideration.

This being premis'd, whoever would difcover whether Vertue or Vice has the chief Poffeffion of his Soul, and to what Enjoyments, whether Criminal or Innocent, the Bent and ftrongeft Propenfions of his Heart carry him, he will be able to decide the Doubt, by obferving what Things principally engage his Thoughts and dwell in his Imagination, and what Ideas meet with the beft Reception and afford moft Delight, remain longeft there, and

False Vertue.

and return the fooneft. Can it be fuppos'd that a Libertine will feldom think of Scenes of Pleafure and forbiddden Enjoyments; that an ambitious and afpiring Perfon will difmifs the Thoughts of Power and Greatnefs, or the Avaricious fill their Minds with all other Images, excepting thofe of Wealth and great Poffeffions? No more is it poffible for a Man of Vertue, who chufes as his principal End the Fruition of the Divine Being, in a State of perfect Purity and immortal Blifs, to divert his Imagination from dwelling upon that ineffable Felicity, and the vertuous Means of procuring the Poffeffion of it. It is inconfiftent with Reafon and the Nature and Order of the Soul's Operations, that he fhould aim at, and purfue the Enjoyment of his Creator in Heaven as his greateft Happinefs, while at the fame time neither God nor Heaven are in all his Thoughts, or at the leaft are feldom and coldly confider'd. The habitual Difpofition and Biafs of the Will, like a native Inftinct, carries a good Man to Celeftial Objects, and engages him in the Contemplation of his future Perfection and Felicity. If his Thoughts are left to themfelves by a fpontaneous Principle, they move to Heaven and adhere to fuperior Objects; and if his Mind is in a State of Compreffion, and engag'd engag'd by Force in the low Affairs of this Life, when that Violence is remov'd, it recovers by its own inward Spring its Divine Temper, and rises with Delight to the things Above: Neither the Ambitious, nor Covetous, nor Men of voluptuous Disposition, use any Arguments and Persuasions to prevail upon themselves to consider the amiable Nature of Power, Riches, and Pleasure, to entertain these Objects in their Minds, or to deliberate on the Means of acquiring the Enjoyment of them. In the same manner, when Piety has the greatest Power and Interest in the Will, it will as certainly engage the Mind in the Contemplation of Divine Things, and in constant Acts of Piety and Devotion: where a Man's Treasure is, there will his Heart be also; and if it be Above, thither will his Inclinations, his Desires and Thoughts follow it. He will dwell with Pleasure, like a Merchant in a foreign Realm, on the Thoughts of his native Country, anticipate the Raptures of happy Minds, and by the Fore-tastes of his expected Felicity, sweeten and augment his present Enjoyments, as well as solace and mitigate his present Sufferings.

Of

Of Vertue *arising from Fear of* Punishment.

THE Minds of many Persons of a sober and regular Life have been much disquieted, when upon Examination of their Hearts and Actions it has appear'd to them, that they have often paid Obedience to the Divine Laws from Motives of Fear and Apprehension of Punishment; for it is their Opinion, that genuine Piety cannot result from such a mean and ungenerous Principle, and therefore hang in perplexing Doubt, whether their Vertue is sincere and will abide the Test. They believe, that Piety ought to be esteem'd and embrac'd for its own heavenly Charms and beatifick Qualities; That a true Lover of Vertue pursues it for its intrinsick Beauty and amiable Nature, and does not court it under foreign and mercenary Considerations. But this Opinion is founded in a Mistake of the Nature of Man, and the Moral Government of the Supream Being. Man is constituted with such intellectual Faculties, as make it necessary to move him to Obedience by the Objects of Hope and Fear, otherwise those Passions had been in vain implanted in his Soul; and as God has

has made the Mind of Man capable of being influenc'd by Menaces and Promises, so to procure Submission to his Laws he enforces them with the Sanctions of the highest Rewards and the greatest Sufferings. In the same manner that Parents rule their Children, Masters their Servants, and Princes their Subjects, does God govern the intelligent World. What more dreadful Punishments can be threaten'd to deter Men from Disobedience, than those denounc'd in the Sacred Writings. *By the Terrors of the Lord*, says the great Apostle, *we persuade Men*. But certainly those terrible Threats had been useless, were they not design'd to act on human Fears; and therefore that Obedience must be approv'd in Heaven, that springs at first from this Source.

I ACKNOWLEDGE it is a more sublime and refin'd Principle of Piety, by which a Creature endow'd with Reason loves, admires, and adores the Supream Being for his essential Goodness, and absolute Perfections, and that those are mov'd by a more generous and excellent Spring, who embrace Vertue from its own attractive Beauty and intrinsick Excellence, without an Eye to other Motives. But this pure and exalted Piety is perhaps only to be attain'd in

a

a Future State of Happiness, where perfect Love casts out Fear: For tho some elevated Minds may make near approaches to it in this Life, yet I cannot think that these are entirely excited by the native Charms of Vertue, and act without any Impulse of Hopes and Fears, and regard to Reward and Punishment. However, the most eminent Vertue of the best of Men in this State of Mortality, is only rais'd to a superior Degree, and differs not in Kind from that of others, who are chiefly govern'd by the instincts of Fear and Hope. Men at first engage in the Practice of Vertue, to avoid the terrible Consequences of a bad Life, and this is a just and laudable Principle; tho after long Practice and continu'd Diligence, they acquire confirm'd Habits of Goodness, taste the Sweetness and Pleasure of Vertue, and begin to love it for its own moral Beauty and agreeable Nature; and then they act much more from regard to the supream Being and a filial Obedience to his Authority, than from Fear of Punishment. In this more vigorous and adult State of Goodness, when evil Inclinations, tho not extirpated, yet are so far subdu'd, that they now can make but a feeble Opposition, the Practice of Vertue becomes habitual, easy, and natural, and is carry'd on to

greater

greater Perfection; not so much from a Principle of Fear, as from its conformity and suitable Nature to the regular and well-dispos'd Faculties of a good Mind.

All Propensions and Habits of the same Degree, tho of a contrary Nature, carry the Soul with equal Force to their proper Objects; and therefore, as Libertines want no Arguments to persuade them to gratify their vicious Inclinations with sensual Enjoyments, so neither would the Vertuous, if their Habits were equal, require any Motives or vehement Intreaties to do good Actions, and engage them in Works of Piety and Devotion. It would be idle and impertinent to use Reasons to prevail with hungry and thirsty Persons, to accept of Food and refreshing Liquors, with a weary Labourer to enjoy Repose, or a fetter'd Prisoner to receive Liberty. In the same manner were vertuous Dispositions thoroughly confirm'd and predominant in a high Degree, their Operations would be spontaneous and easy, and the Instincts of the Mind would exert themselves in good Actions, without any other Motive than the Pleasure and Satisfaction of doing well, with the same Readiness and Force as the evil Propensions of others incline them to forbidden Objects.

It

False Vertue.

It is true, as I have said, this is the Felicity and Perfection but of a few excellent Minds, for the greatest part of good Men are in a much inferior State: Their Habits of Vertue are so weak and unconfirm'd, that they want Vigilance, Mortifition, and Self-Denial, as well as the lively Apprehensions of the Divine Displeasure that attends criminal Actions, to prevail with them to continue in the Practice of Vertue: whence it appears, that Fastings and bodily Austerities, that some imagine are the Expressions of the highest Degrees of Piety, must be contented with the lowest Rank ; for were the vertuous Inclinations of Men so powerful and confirm'd as to become natural, those Severities would be unnecessary : For 'tis an evident Argument, that their sensual Appetites and vicious Dispositions must be strong, when such Hardships and Mortifications are requir'd to restrain them. I would not be understood as if I condemn'd these Expressions of Self-Denial ; I only assert, that the Vertue which requires their Assistance, is generally that of Persons new enter'd upon a religious Life ; for when Vertue is full grown and establish'd in the Mind, it becomes a new Nature, and draws it in proportion with as forceable a Biass to Good,

Good, as it did before to Evil. Nor would I be so understood, as if I did not look on the Vertue of thofe to be fincere, who ufe fuch Affiftance and frequently confider the terrible Confequences of Guilt to deter them from it; but this is what I affert, that the higheft and ftrongeft Habits of Piety do not demand thefe Motives and Helps, tho the loweft do. Thofe of the moft inferior Clafs of good Men, act partly from a regard to the Authority of the Supream Being, and a Love to moral Goodnefs, and partly from Fear of Divine Difpleafure and threaten'd Punifhment, but the laft Motive is the ftrongeft and moft prevalent in their Minds; but as they continue in the Practice of Vertue, and acquire more powerful Habits by degrees, they act more from their Love to Vertue and the Pleafure of Obedience, than from the other Principle; and when their good Habits are more predominant, and they arrive at the higheft State of Perfection attainable here, they are ftill mov'd in a far lefs meafure by terrible Apprehenfions of Suffering for Difobedience. In fhort, to determine their State whether they are good or bad Perfons, Men fhould not be fo folicitous whether they are obedient to the Divine Laws, chiefly from a Principle of Fear, or chiefly from their Love of
Vertue;

False Vertue.

Vertue; but the important Queftion will be, whether their good Habits and Inclinations do, upon an impartial Examination, in the general Courfe of their Lives prevail, in every Inftance, over their oppofite Vices; for if they do, it is moft certain that their Vertue, tho it is not of the moft eminent degree, yet it is fincere in its Kind, and will abide the Teft.

To fum up the laft Article; deprav'd Man is a furprizing Mixture of inconfiftent Ingredients and contrary Principles of Operation, endow'd with Angelick intellectual Faculties, but debas'd and diftracted by vicious Inclinations and irregular Appetites, which, during his degenerate State, exercife a predominant Power over his Mind, maintain with eafe their Ufurpation, and in a prevalent Degree govern his Heart and Actions. The Dictates of his natural Light are too faint and dim, and the Authority and Efforts of Reafon too feeble to make any confiderable Oppofition. It is true, at Seafons the Underftanding exerts it felf, and protefts againft his unwarrantable and criminal Behaviour, while the Judge within, provok'd by Guilt, ftings the Offender with Terror and Remorfe; yet thefe Struggles are ineffectual, Reafon is overborn, Confcience ftifled, and the Tenor of the

the Man's Life is vicious and immoral. And tho some Men in this State of Depravity may, in the Management of worldly Affairs, be justly applauded for their Wisdom, Vigilance, and Sagacity; yet in respect of Vertue and Vice and the Consequences of each, it is plain the Exercise of their Reason is suspended, and they may properly be call'd moral Lunaticks.

If in such unhappy Circumstances rous'd and awaken'd by some sharp Affliction, dreadful Apprehensions of Death and Future Punishment, or convincing Discourses and importunate Persuasions, a Man begins to reflect, and upon serious deliberation, effectually and in good earnest resolves to reform his Life to escape the frightful Consequences of Guilt; since a vertuous Frame and Disposition of Mind, like other Habits, is acquir'd, at least improv'd and confirm'd by great Diligence and repeated Practice, his first Entrance upon a new Course must be attended with Labour, Trouble, and Self-Denial. And now Fears, Apprehension of Divine Displeasure and Future Sufferings, are necessary Motives to aid and support his unsettled Vertue, and break the Power of evil Propensions; but afterward, the Difficulties, by degrees, abate, and a regular Life becomes less painful

ful and uneasy, till at length after Acquaintance and Familiarity, Piety grows so pleasant and delightful, that were it left to his choice, he would certainly embrace it as the Beauty, Health, Dignity, and Perfection of an intelligent Being. I shall conclude this Discourse with a Citation from Archbishop *Tillotson*, pertinent to this Occasion.

"There are two Bridles or Restraints, which God hath put upon Human Nature, Shame and Fear. Shame is the weaker, and hath place only in those in whom there are some Remainders of Vertue. Fear is the stronger, and works upon all who love themselves, and desire their own Preservation. Therefore in this degenerate State of Mankind, Fear is that Passion which hath the greatest Power over us, and by which God and his Laws take the surest hold of us. Our Desire, and Love, and Hope, are not so apt to be wrought upon by the Representation of Vertue, and the Promises of Reward and Happiness, as our Fear is from the Apprehensions of Divine Displeasure; for tho we have lost, in a great measure, the Gust and Relish of true Happiness, yet we still retain a quick Sense of Pain and Misery. So

"that Fear relies on a natural Love of
"our felves, and is complicated with a
"neceffary Defire of our own Preferva-
"tion. And therefore Religion ufually
"makes its firft Entrance into us by this
"Paffion: Hence, perhaps it is, that *So-*
"*lomon* more than once calls, the Fear of
"the Lord the Beginning of Wifdom."

AN ESSAY
UPON THE
IMMORTALITY
OF THE
SOUL.

AN ESSAY UPON THE IMMORTALITY OF THE SOUL.

THIS Mortal Life in its full Bloom and Vigor, is so precarious, and in its utmost Extent so short and transient, that in the Opinion of Men of Prudence and Reflection, it mightily abates the Value of the most desirable Enjoyments of this World; and it is just Matter of Astonishment, that since all Men have a perfect Assurance, that their

State of Existence here is so uncertain, and flies away with such Rapidity, that the present Satisfactions and Delights, which they must leave so soon, and for ever, should not fall under greater and more universal Contempt.

The longest Life is a fugitive and inconsiderable Duration; but if we abstract from it those Parts, in which we have but a naked, or undelightful, or miserable Being, and therefore not to be valu'd, upon such a Calculation, how great must the Discompt be? If we do not reckon the Life of Man to begin till he is in Possession of himself, and can exercise the Faculties and Powers peculiar to his Species, we must not only cut off the Stage of Infancy and Childhood from it, but likewise that of old Age, which for the greatest part is only the flat Leavings of Life, decay'd and drawn off to the Lees; when, tho the Animal survives, the Man does scarcely exist. And yet by how many other ways is our short Time contracted? Acute Pains, languishing Sickness, and wasting Labour, besides tormenting Envy and anxious Care, uneasy Malice, and exquisite Grief, the violent Perturbations and Tempests of the Soul, arising from a thousand various Causes, by the numerous Gaps and Breaks which they

they make in Life, reduce its Duration to very fcanty Limits. Add to thefe Refts and Interruptions, the neceffary Returns of Sleep, which fufpends the Exercife of our intellectual and fenfitive Faculties; and it will appear, that all together they defraud us of two Thirds of our Time: If thefe Allowances are made, and the Accompt is juftly ftated, what a mean Ballance will remain, as the Claim of Life, if taken in the View before defcrib'd?

So fhort is the Extent of our prefent Exiftence, if confider'd in an abfolute Senfe; but how momentary will it feem when compar'd with Ages that never end? What is this Span of Life, when we reflect upon interminable Duration? What is Time but a little Rill, or Drop, compar'd with the boundlefs Ocean of Eternity?

As this Terreftrial Globe is reduc'd to a defpicable Spot, when we contemplate the immenfe Body of the Sun; and as the Sun it felf loofes his Magnitude, and is no more than a glowing Atom, when we confider the amazing Circumference of the Univerfe; fo the whole Syftem of the Univerfe is contracted to the minuteft Size, if fet in competition with the Gulphs of Space that lie beyond it, and the unlimited

Heights and Depths, and still increasing Lengths and Breadths of vast Immensity. In like manner should the Life of Man continue many Ages, even as long as the Sun and Moon endure; yet when measur'd with Immortality, it would shrink to an unextended Point. What is Man but the Tenant of a Mould of Clay, endow'd indeed with Angelick Faculties, but a perishing Wight and an Insect in Duration? What is this intelligent Creature, who thus dissolves like the Morning Cloud, and as the Evening Dew vanishes away? And what is Life, but a tender Flower that unfolds its Beauty and dies in its Bloom, an empty Vapour of the Air, that as soon as kindled, glances by our Sight, and expires in a sudden Flash? So short is the Continuance of Man in this mortal State, if compared with endless Duration.

It must therefore be a Matter of the highest Importance to make Enquiry, whether by Death the Life of Man is totally extinguish'd, and the Body complicated with the common Mass of Matter, never again to be collected and reunited; or whether it will be continu'd in different Circumstances, and another Mode of Existence, and tho the Frame of the Body be ruin'd, and its Parts dissipated and blended with

IMMORTALITY *of the* SOUL. 297
with the common Mafs of Matter, whether that which we call the Soul or the Mind, fhall furvive in a feparate State, and never know Corruption.

If the Soul is diffolv'd, and perifhes with the Body, and no future Exiftence is to be expected, then the Foundation of all Religion and Obligation to Moral Duties, if they are not deftroy'd, will be render'd infignificant and ineffectual; for no Temporal Confiderations will reftrain degenerate Mankind from following their vicious Inclinations, as if they had an unlimited and arbitrary Power over their Actions. But on the contrary, if it be eftablifh'd by convincing Evidence, that the Soul is Immortal, and out-lives Death in a State of Separation from the Body, this will naturally lead a prudent and confiderate Man to befpeak himfelf in this manner: Since after this Body is buried in the Grave, I fhall ftill remain in Being, nor will my Exiftence be difcontinued in any Period of Duration, it is of the higheft Concern to know, whether I fhall be Happy or Miferable in that Everlafting State. I am a Creature and a Subject of the Supream Ruler of the World, and by the rational Faculties with which I am endow'd, I can eafily difcern there are many
natural

natural Laws and moral Duties which I am bound to obey; and that therefore I am an accomptable Being, and shall be rewarded or punish'd, according to my Observance or Contempt of those Divine Precepts and Rules of Life; and how terrible will be the Sentence, should I be condemn'd to endless Sufferings and Despair? Would not that Man be look'd on as uncapable of Reflection and deserted of common Sense, who should chuse, for the sake of one Hour's Pleasure, to endure unremitting Torment and Anguish of Heart, during the whole remainder of his Life? But how infinitely greater an Instance of Folly and Distraction is it, for the sake of the short-liv'd Enjoyments here, to draw upon one's self Divine Displeasure and endless Misery hereafter?

This Point then of the Soul's Immortality being of such great Consequence, it is no wonder that it has exercis'd so many excellent Pens, as well in the Pagan as the Christian World. *Plato*, *Plutarch*, *Avicenne*, and *Nemesius*, are celebrated Authors on this Subject: and since the Evangelical Revelation has brought Life and Immortality to Light, many have writ with great strength of Reason on this Article of our Belief, but none with so much Force and Perspi-

IMMORTALITY *of the* SOUL. 299

Perspicuity, as some late Writers of our own Nation.

But since so great and important a Doctrine cannot be too much illustrated and confirm'd, especially when we reflect on the present prevailing Power of Impiety, which maintains its ground against the most vigorous Assaults of Reason, spreads its Contagion, and makes Proselites in defiance of the Religion and the Laws of the Kingdom, I have thought it useful and seasonable to publish this Essay, in which I have endeavour'd to add some new Arguments, and to give greater Force and Clearness to those that have been already urg'd by others, to support the Belief of the Soul's Immortality, by casting them in another Form that may heighten the Evidence of the Demonstration. The great Spring, whence the deplorable Decay of Piety, and the universal Corruption of Manners that threaten this Nation with Ruin, are deriv'd, is the disbelief of a Future State of Life, or a Fluctuation of Mind about its certainty, or an indolent Inattendance to it. Nor can the Vertue of this Nation, which must be allow'd to our great Dishonour, as well as Danger, to be in a very languishing Condition, if not at the last Gasp, be recover'd to a vigorous and healthful State, till a warmer and more general Belief of a Future Life of Happiness or Misery, shall take Possession of our Minds, determine the Choice of our Ends, and govern the Course of our Actions; for without the Motives drawn from the Certainty of the Rewards that attend the Practice of Vertue, and the Punishments decreed to Irreligion and Vice in the next State of Life, powerfully apply'd to our Hopes and Fears, the Strength and Support of Piety and Moral Goodness fall to the Ground.

THAT the Passions are the Blemish and Disgrace of Human Nature, the Distemper and Diseases of the Mind, and therefore entirely to be subdu'd and eradicated, was the absurd and extravagant Opinion of the *Stoick* Philosophers. Hence they infer'd, that Hopes and Fears were not only unnecessary, but inconvenient and hurtful; and therefore should not be the Springs and Principles of our Actions. That we should not be deter'd from Vice and Immorality by the Apprehensions of consequent Shame and Punishment, nor pursue any good and generous Design from the expectation of a Future Reward; but in short, that Vertue should be esteem'd and embrac'd for its native Beauty and
intrin-

intrinsick Perfection. In conformity to this erroneous Sentiment they endeavour'd, tho with fruitless Labour, wholly to extinguish the natural Emotions of the Soul, and pretended to court Vertue under no Views of Advantage, but for its own inherent Excellence.

About two hundred Years before the Incarnation, one *Sadoc*, a Disciple of *Simon the Just*, and the Founder of the *Sadducees*, the first Sect among the *Jews*, profess'd and propagated the same Doctrine; tho some affirm, that he only asserted, that if indeed there were no Future State of Retribution, yet an innocent and pious Life ought to be pursu'd as good and delightful in it self, and Vice to be resisted and avoided as ignominious and detestable from its own intrinsick Turpitude; upon which his unwary Scholars mistaking their Master, as if he had taught that no Future Recompence was to be expected, took up this Doctrine, and maintain'd it against the *Pharisees*.

To excite a Man to the Esteem and Love of Vertue, by the sole Representation of its excellent and amiable Properties, abstracting from all Prospects of present or future Recompence, at first sight
seems

seems to heighten its Idea, and makes us believe, that those who thus adhere to it, act from a more generous and sublime Principle, than they who court her under mercenary Views, and are more in love with her Fortune than her Beauty.

But if this be examin'd it will soon appear, that by thus refining and exalting the Notion of Vertue, they have destroy'd its Force, and dismiss'd its Followers: For tho it is true, that setting aside the Consideration, that Vertue and Religion expose Men to the Loss of Liberty, Estates, and Life it self, during the Violence and Persecution of cruel Tyrants, the Dictates of Reason would determine us to the Choice of a just and religious Life; yet if we reflect on the innate Depravity and corrupt Habits inherent in the Minds of Men, by which they are powerfully sway'd to gratify their Passions and inordinate Appetites, it must be allow'd, they will not be attracted by the naked Charms of Vertue, nor affrighted by the meer Deformity of Vice from their criminal Enjoyments. We find, by constant Experience, that all the Arguments drawn from the amiable Nature of Vertue, and the temporal Advantages that arise from the Practice of it, tho back'd and enforc'd by the Encourage-

IMMORTALITY *of the* SOUL. 303

couragements and certain Expectations of endless Felicity hereafter, engage but few, if compar'd with the Race of Mankind, heartily to espouse her Cause; how then can we expect she should have any Votaries, if she had nothing to bestow upon them but her self, and what she confers in this Life? Hence the *Stoicks* and *Sadducees*, that persuade Men to be vertuous, abstracting from Hopes of Reward, or Fear of Punishment, lay the Ax to the Root of Piety, and exterminate moral Goodness from the World.

I SHALL now Attempt to give such Proofs of the Immortality of the Soul, as will leave in the Mind no reasonable ground of doubting.

The IMMORTALITY *of the* SOUL *demonstrated by natural Arguments.*

AS at the command of the Omnipotent Creator, to whom to Will and Execute is the same, all the Beings that compose and adorn the Frame of Nature, started out of Nothing and stept up into Existence; so the Conversation, which is a prolong'd Creation of those Beings, is owing to a constant Communication of
Power

Power from this exhaustless Source of Energy and Motion. Should he no longer Will its Continuance, but suspend his preserving Influence, the whole Creation would immediately dissolve and disappear. Streams may sooner renounce their dependance on their Fountains, and Light subsist without fresh Emanations from the Sun, than the most excellent and perfect Creatures can remain one Minute independent on their Maker.

AND since the Author is a free and arbitrary Agent, the Duration and Futurity of Being must absolutely rely on his Pleasure; and we are no farther capable of knowing whether any of his Creatures shall have the Privilege of Everlasting Existence, than he either by the Light of Reason or Revelation has signify'd his Will concerning it.

To know then if the Soul of Man shall for ever exist, it is necessary to enquire, whether the Divine Author has made any Declaration of his Will always to uphold its Being; and setting aside Revelation, I shall attempt to show by the natural Dictates of Reason, that he has made known his Pleasure, that Human Souls shall always continue.

He has signify'd this Intention, by framing the Soul of a Substance, not obnoxious to Corruption or Dissolution: Artificers express by the Nature, Properties, and Capacities, which they give to their Works, what those Works are design'd for; and by the Frame, Springs, and Movements communicated to their *Automata*, they shew how long they intend their Motion shall endure. Thus by making the Soul of a Substance, that is not Matter, nor liable to Waste or Disunion, the Author has declar'd that he design'd it for an unlimited Duration.

That the Soul is incorporeal will be the sooner granted, if an immaterial Substance be not thought to imply a Contradiction, and none but the Atheist, with whom I am not at present concern'd, will maintain that Assertion, for all others acknowledge a Divine omnipotent Mind not compounded of material Parts, and therefore the Notion of an incorporeal Substance, cannot be repugnant to Reason, nor rejected by any but the profess'd Patrons of Impiety.

The Soul is discover'd to be Immaterial by its Operations. That Sensation,

An ESSAY upon the

as Atomists affert, can be the Effect of the Organ from its Renitence or Elastick Spring, by which it strives to free it self from the material Object that strikes upon it, is an inexplicable Explanation of sensitive Perception; for Instance, When the Corporeal Image, says Mr. *Hobbes*, enters into the Organ of the Eye, the nervous Fibres implanted there to resist its Progress, spring back against it, and from that Effort Vision results.

Now let any Man try if he can conceive how the Impulse of one material Thing, and the Resistance and Re-action of another can produce Sensation; we must solve this Difficulty our selves, for the Philosopher does not pretend to inform us. But entirely to subvert this Hypothesis, it is evident that Perception is not perform'd in the Organ, but in the Head, since it often happens that Men are entirely depriv'd of Sight, tho the Eye has no defect, and the visible Image has free admittance there, as oft as the Optick Nerve is so obstructed, as not to suffer the Spirits acted upon by the Object, to propagate their Motion, and carry the Impulse from the Eye to the Brain.

It

It is yet harder to conceive, how meer Matter by its own Power, can recoil upon it felf, contemplate its own Nature, Reafon and Philofophize upon its own Properties and review its own Actions: How, in Argumentation, it can affent to two Propofitions, between which it difcerns an Agreement, and by quite another Motion deduce from them a Third. That Matter fhould be able to begin its own Motion, to ftop or change it to another at Pleafure, as it muft do in Contemplation and Reafoning, is to afcribe Powers to Matter, which are acknowledg'd inconfiftent with all the Properties obferv'd in corporeal Beings. The Formation of Ideas in the Brain by Imagination, the ranging and Difpofition of them by the Judgment into regular Schemes and Trains of Thought, muft be allow'd the Effect of an Immaterial Principle. If meer Matter could, by its peculiar Figuration, Purity, and Motion, be rais'd to the Dignity of a Thinking Subftance, fuppofe, fince Matter is divifible, that when it has form'd a Thought, it fhould be feparated into Parts, the Confequence would be, that each Part muft retain its Portion of the Character or Idea; and thus you might divide a Thought into Halves, Quarters, or yet minuter Portions, which founds a a little odd in the Mouth of a Philofopher.

Nor is it poffible to account for Memory any more than for Reflection, Calculation, and Reafoning from mere Matter and Motion; as for many other Reafons, fo for this, That Matter being in continual Flux, and therefore the Limbs of our Bodies and the Organs of our Senfes being not the fame now as they were fome Years ago, the old Materials perpetually fleeting from the Body, and new ones fucceeding in their Place; the Particles of Matter being loft that form'd our Spirits feven Years ago, and were endow'd and ftamp'd with the Characters produc'd at that Time, muft have carry'd away thofe Impreffions with them, and the new Matter that came in the room of the former being naked and unfigur'd with thofe Ideas, could not poffibly preferve the Memory of paft Tranfactions. If a Ship, on which are carv'd, for Ornament, various Figures and Signs, fhould ftay out at Sea till every Plank and Piece of Wood, by degrees, were gone, and their Places fupply'd by frefh Timber, as it is reported of *Drake*'s Veffel, would this Ship retain thofe Images and Ornaments which it carry'd out?

Nor

IMMORTALITY *of the* SOUL.

NOR is the Self-determining Power or free Choice, which the Soul enjoys, a less convincing Evidence of its immaterial Nature, than its Reflection, Argumentation, and Memory. This Capacity of designing an End, of deliberating and ballancing about the Fitness of the Means to attain it; and at last, upon the Comparison of chusing one in preference to the rest, is so plain a Discovery that the Soul is not Corporeal, that the Opposers of its immaterial Nature acknowledge this to be the most difficult of all the Powers of the Mind to be accounted for upon their Hypothesis: and it is indeed so difficult, that in their Attempt to explain it, they are driven to the most extravagant Absurdities. Can any thing be more inconsistent and ridiculous than the Invention of *Lucretius*, who to solve this Difficulty, supposes, against the Foundation of the *Epicurean* Scheme of Philisophy, a declining Motion of his Atomes; that is, neither strait nor oblique, but *quasi* oblique. But I shall not pursue this Subject here, having fully expos'd that idle and incoherent Hypothesis in another Writing.

IF the Soul were a System compounded of refin'd and figur'd Matter, agitated by a rapid Motion, it would furmount the reach of Human Underftanding to imagine how it fhould fo far tranfcend the Sphere of its own Activity, as to have any Notion of immaterial Subftance; that it fhould doubt of its being Corporeal, difpute againft its own Nature, fufpect its own Properties, and grow ambitious of being rang'd among fuperior Creatures, even thofe of angelick Endowments and immortal Duration. Yet this is the Cafe before us; if the Mind of Man is made of Matter, it is, I fay, unaccountable whence it fhould be capable of forming the Idea of an intellectual Spirit, and how it came to be univerfally prejudic'd againft the right Conception of its own Nature, and prepoffefs'd with the contrary erroneous Opinion.

ANOTHER Argument of the Soul's Immaterial, and therefore Immortal Nature is this; that it enjoys Pleafures and Satisfactions peculiar to the Capacities and Tafte of a fpiritual, intelligent Being; of this Nature is the Delight that a Philofopher perceives in contemplating the beautiful Syftem of the World, in fearching the hidden Springs and Caufes of Things, and tracing Nature through the Varieties of her fecret and admirable Operations, of this fort likewife is the Pleafure of a Mathematician, taken up in the Purfuits of Knowledge by an infinite Series of coherent Deductions and Demonftrations. Nor is the Poet's Delight of a different Kind, that arifes from the Operations of a fpiritful, fertile, and vaft Imagination. Thefe Pleafures, that are plainly Intellectual, are fo much fuperior to thofe of Senfe, that fometimes they tranfport Men out of themfelves, and fo far fufpend their Relifh and Defire of fenfitive Enjoyments, that they forget to refrefh themfelves with Meat, Drink, and Sleep. Yet the Satisfaction and Complacency of a religious Mind, flowing from Acts of Piety and Devotion, from the ardent Efforts of Divine Love, Gratitude, Joy, and Admiration, from the Contemplation of the infinite Perfections of the Supream Being, and the Foretaft and Preoccupation of Future Felicity, are yet of a more excellent and exalted Nature: Thefe are refin'd, elevated, and fpiritual Joys, of which the Animal Nature is entirely incapable. Nor are thefe the Delights of Men of an odd and whimfical Complexion, but of Perfons of fevere Judgment, clear Heads, ftrong Reafon, and inur'd to the clofeft manner of arguing; Men unbiafs'd and difinterefted, and as much

deliver'd

deliver'd from a superstitious Turn of Mind, melancholy Delusions, and splenetick Dreams, as their Opponents are from the Impressions of Religion, and the Prejudices of Education. But if the contrary were true, that the Divine Pleasures that arise from the Exercise of pious Habits were imaginary and groundless, yet still the Argument holds good, that they are of a peculiar Kind, proper to the Soul, and distinct from those sensitive Satisfactions that only affect corporeal Organs. A Man of Reflection will easily acknowledge they are above the Sphere of Sense, and of so pure celestial, and sublime a Nature, as to be adapted only to spiritual Beings. And hence it will appear, that there is the very same Reason to conclude that the Soul of Man is Incorporeal, and therefore an incorruptible Substance; as that any created Being is so, whose Immaterial and Immortal Nature cannot be infer'd from any other Principles than those, which will as well demonstrate the same Properties in the Soul of Man.

The Happiness then which the Soul enjoys peculiar to its Faculties, and distinct from the Pleasures of the Body which it inhabits, will facilitate to Men of Reason the Belief of its Immortality. Brute Creatures

tures, not being made for endless Duration, have no Taste or Desire of the Felicity of an intelligent Mind, which arises from the Acquisition of Knowledge and Wisdom, the Practice of Vertue, and the sweet Reflection on a useful and innocent Life: For this Happiness is proper to the Soul, which it is evident it may possess in a State of Separation; for the Animal Part of Man has no more Relish or Perception of these superior intellectual Delights, than the same low Nature has in the Beasts that perish.

And if the Soul is capable of this Felicity and Perfection, and has Pleasures peculiar to its own Nature, and is capable of enjoying them when disunited from the Body; and if the Creator of the World did not endow it with that Capacity in vain, it should not, methinks, be difficult to discern, that therefore he design'd it for a happy Immortality.

Nor is the Argument less conclusive for the Soul's Immortality, when we urge, that it is capable of Pain and Misery appropriated to it self. It can discern the Deformity and moral Turpitude of its Actions, and reflect on Guilt with Shame and Remorse; it is startled and terrify'd

at

at the Apprehensions of Divine Displeasure, can anticipate the awful Solemnity of the Day of Accompt, and to avoid an endless miserable Existence, can desire to go out of Being, and wish for Annihilation. These Operations are so far above the Capacity of the Animal Nature, that one would think they should convince any Man, that the Soul is Spiritual and Immaterial, and therefore fram'd for endless Duration: For he may be as well satisfy'd from what has been alledg'd, that the Animal Part of Man is as uncapable of that intellectual Happiness or Misery which have been describ'd, as we are sure that a Tree, notwithstanding its vegetable Life, cannot feel, see, or hear, while we observe that it expresses no sensitive Perceptions, nor has any proper Organs for such Purposes.

BESIDES, let it be consider'd, that Mankind even in their deprav'd State, notwithstanding the Obscurity of their Thoughts and the Confusion of their Ideas, as well as their moral Corruption and Degeneracy, have universally expres'd a strong Inclination to believe the two great Articles of Religion, The Existence of a God, and the Immortality of the Soul. These Notions bear such a Conformity to their
Intel-

Intellectual Faculties, that as soon as ever they exercis'd their Reason, and were left to the Freedom of their Thoughts, they readily assented to the Truth of them. The first of these Articles, the Existence of a God, is suppos'd to be granted in this Discourse: And as the general Consent of Mankind to the Notion of a God, is justly us'd as an Argument of great Weight against the Atheist; so the same universal Voice of Nature is of no less Validity against the Infidel, that disbelieves the Immortality of the Soul; for those Notions which the whole Human Species readily assent to, must be allow'd to be the Declaration and Opinion of Nature; or in plainer words, the strongest, clearest, and most early Dictate of Reason, otherwise it will be impossible to account for the general and ready Belief of such a Notion. It must be granted, that the powerful Disposition and Bent of Mind, in all Nations and Ages, to receive this Proposition as true, That the *Soul is Immortal*, will make it evident, that it must be a natural Idea, agreeable to the Inclination, and suitable to the Frame and Faculties of the Mind. The common People, conducted only by the Biass and Light of Nature, believ'd that the Soul did not perish with the Body, but that after the

Diffolution of that Tenement, it continu'd in Being, and pafs'd into a State of Happinefs or Mifery, agreeable to its Behaviour in this Life.

Their Deifying of deceafed Men, who had been eminent Benefactors to Mankind, and peopling Heaven with Colonies of Heroes, their Kingdom of *Pluto*, and the variety of Torments fuppos'd to be inflicted on the Impious and Flagitious, and the Pleafures of their *Elyfian* Fields, the Reward of the Juft and Innocent; and in fhort, their whole Scheme of Theology, however furperftitious and abfurd, were evidently founded on this Principle of the Soul's Immortality.

The greateft part likewife of the moft eminent Philofophers held this Opinion; the Primitive *Pythagoreans*, the *Platonifts*, and the *Stoicks*, at leaft for the moft part, were Affertors of it: and that this was the general Notion of their wifeft Men, we have the clear Teftimony of *Cicero*, who with great Care had ftudy'd their Writings, and was admirably vers'd in the Doctrines of all their different Sects. That great Man having freely declar'd his Belief of the Soul's Immortality, fays thus; *Nor has Reafon only and Argumentation compell'd*

compell'd me to receive this Opinion, but the Judgment and Authority of the most eminent Philosophers. And elsewhere he affirms, That this *Notion of the Soul's Immortality, was supported by the Consent of all Nations.* Tho *Socrates,* the most excellent of the Pagan Sages, who never roundly and positively affirm'd any thing, spoke with Diffidence and Fluctuation about a Future State after his modest manner; yet his Belief, tho it did not exclude all doubting, was so prevalent, that it over-power'd and controul'd his Diffidence to such a degree, that upon the Hopes and Prospect of a happy Immortality, he laid down his Life with Alacrity and great firmness of Mind. And as in moral Habits, that degree of Vertue that is powerful enough to bear down the contrary evil Inclinations, and engage us in predominant Obedience to its Precepts, is in a Christian Sense real and sincere; so that Belief of a Future State that prevails with any Man, in spite of all Opposition, to act in conformity to that Principle must be allow'd to be genuine; and what could have been expected more from *Socrates,* to have manifested his Integrity and the victorious Degree of his Belief of the Soul's Immortality, than that which with great Courage and Constancy he express'd. But of all the learned and
wise

wife Pagans none have more openly, and in ftronger Terms up and down his Writings, acknowledg'd his Belief of this Article, than *Cicero*. Thefe are his words: (a) *The Souls of all Men are Immortal, but thofe of the Good and Valiant are not only Immortal, but Divine.* (b) *There is nothing fublunary, but what is mortal and perifhing, except the Souls that the Gods have beftow'd on the Race of Mankind.* (c) *Death is not the Deftruction of our Being, and the Extinction of all our Enjoyments, but a fort of Tranflation or Change of Life.*

(*a*) Omnium quidem Animi Immortales funt fed fortium Bonorumque divini. *De Leg.*

(*b*) Infra Lunam nihil eft nifi Mortale & Caducem, præter Animos generi Hominum numero Deorum Datos.

(*c*) Mortem non interitum efle omnia tollentem atque delentem, fed quandam migrationem & commutationem Vitæ. *Tufcul.*

Animus feipfum movet atque idcirco non eft Natus fed Æternus. *Tufcul.*

Mors iis terribilis eft, quorum cum Vita omnia extinguntur. *Parad.*

Mors aut meliorem, quam qui eft in Vita, aut certe non deteriorem allatura eft ftatum. *Pro Flacc.*

Incorpore inclufus tanquam alienæ domi, propria emin ejus fedes eft Cœlum. *Tufcul.*

Sic habeto te non efle mortalem, fed Corpus hoc. *De Som. Scip.*

Bonorum mentes mihi Divinæ atque Æternæ videntur, & ex Hominum Vita ad Deorum Religionem Sanctimoniamque migrant. *De Leg.*

Impii apud inferos pœnas luunt. *Ibid.*

But he declares his Mind upon this Subject moſt clearly, and in the moſt noble and pious Expreſſions, in the latter end of his excellent Book *De Senectute*, where he ſays, That he firmly believ'd that the famous *Romans*, his deceas'd Friends, were ſtill alive, and that they enjoy'd a Life which only deſerv'd that Name. And afterwards he aſſerts, that he collected the Immortality of the Soul from its Operations and immaterial Nature. *I perſuade my ſelf*, ſays he, *ſince the Soul is endow'd with ſuch Activity, ſuch a Remembrance of Things paſt, ſuch a Foreſight of Events to come, ſo many Arts, Sciences, and Inventions, that a Nature, which contains in it ſelf ſuch Perfections, cannot be Mortal; ſince the Soul is always agitated, nor has any beginning of Motion, becauſe ſhe moves her ſelf; nor will have any end of Motion, becauſe ſhe will never deſert, or be wanting to her ſelf; and ſince the Nature of the Soul is ſimple, nor contains the mixture of any Thing that is unlike or incongruous to its ſelf, it can never be divided, and therefore can never periſh.* ———— *My Soul exerting her ſelf, always look'd upon Futurity in this View, that when it ſhould part with Life, it ſhould then Live.*———— *I have an ardent Deſire*, ſays he to *Scipio* and *Lælius*, *to ſee your Fathers, whom I honour'd and lov'd*

320 *An* ESSAY *upon the* *lov'd, nor do I long only to converse with those whom I knew, but with those likewise of whom I have heard and read, and of whom I my self have written.* —— And a little after, transported with the Prospect of a happy Immortality, he breaks out into this triumphant and celebrated Exclamation —*O glorious Day, when I shall be admitted into the Council and Assembly of Souls, and be deliver'd from this tumultuous and polluted World, when I shall not only meet with the great Spirits before-named, but with my lov'd* Cato *also, the bravest and best of Men!* ——And after, *If I err in this Belief of the Immortality of the Soul, I err willingly, nor shall any thing while I live wrest this Error from me.* —— What an excellent and divine Mind had this noble *Roman*, tho a Heathen, compar'd with the Professors of Impiety and the Christian Libertines of these degenerate Times?

THERE remains yet another Argument to prove, that the bravest and wisest Men in all Ages thought that the Soul remain'd alive after the Dissolution of the Body, and that is, their earnest Desire of Glory and Immortal Fame. That the greatest and most generous Spirits among the Heathens, coveted above all Things Applause and a great Name, is evident from

their

IMMORTALITY *of the* SOUL. 321

their own Writings, in which they express this Passion in the warmest manner, and acknowledge, that this was the Spring and impulsive Principle from which their indefatigable Labours and worthy Undertakings had their Rise. And to the same Desire of Renown, perhaps, the far greatest part of the Productions of famous Wits and the illustrious Atchievements of Heroes among Christians owe their Birth. *Cicero* says, that this Passion is always found in the greatest and finest Spirits. (d) *The Minds of the best Men,* says he, *chiefly aspire after immortal Glory.* And elsewhere he says thus : (e) *There is scarce any Man, who by the Labours he undertakes, and the Dangers to which he exposes himself, does not desire Glory, as the Reward of his great Actions.* — And in another place he gives this Reason of it : (f) *The Life of Man is short, but the Course of Glory is Eternal.* In another thus : (g) *Of all the Rewards of Vertue Glory*

(*d*) Optimi cujufque Animus maxime ad immortalem Gloriam nititur. *De Sen.*

(*e*) Vix invenitur, qui laboribus fufceptis periculifque aditis, non quafi Mercedem rerum Geftarum defideret Gloriam. *Off.*

(*f*) Vita brevis, curfus Gloriæ fempiternus. *Pro Seft.*

(*g*) Ex omnibus præmiis Virtutis ampliffimum effe Præmium Gloriam, effe hanc unam, quæ brevitatem Vitæ Pofteritatis Memoria confolaretur, quæ efficeret, ut abfentes adeffemus, mortui viveremus. *Pro Mil.*

is the greatest; it is only this that can afford Consolation for the shortness of Life, by causing us to be remember'd by Posterity, that can make us Present while Absent, and preserve us alive after Death. This universal desire of Praise and Admiration, and to be spoken of with Honour in the Ages to come, must suppose, that those who covet and pursue it, must believe as I have suggested in another Discourse, that they shall continue in Being after their Decease, or else that Passion is very idle and unaccountable; for what Satisfaction can the Applauses and Panegyricks of Posterity afford a Man that is not in Being, and therefore entirely uncapable of enjoying them?

Thus the best and wisest Persons in all Times and Nations, have look'd on the Human Soul as incorporeal, except those of the *Epicurean* School, who with great Zeal and Labour endeavour'd to elevate their Nature to the Rank of intelligent Engines, and self-moving *Automata*; but the Reasons they us'd were so frivolous and inconclusive, and the Explications they have given, how Matter may be dispos'd to Think, Reason, and acquire a self-determining Power and Freedom of Choice, are so inept and ridiculous, that to name them

IMMORTALITY *of the* SOUL. 323

them is enough to confirm the Reader in the contrary Opinion. Let any Man consider how these little Philosophers solve the Operations of the Mind upon the foot of mere Matter and Motion, and I assure my self, he will reject their Notions with Contempt.

If then the Body of the common People, and the far greatest part of the wisest and most learned Men in all Ages, have declar'd their Belief of the Soul's Immortality; this will amount to the universal Approbation of Mankind, notwithstanding some Individuals have express'd their Dissent; of which more in the next Argument. And this is so agreeable to *Cicero*'s Sentiment, that notwithstanding he had acknowledg'd that *Democritus*, *Epicurus*, *Dichæarchus*, and others affirm'd, that the Soul was Corporeal and Mortal, yet he declares his Sense thus: (h) *It is my Judgment that the Soul is Immortal, by the Consent of all Nations.*

The no less universal Desire of Immortality which is found among Mankind, if well attended to, should induce

---

(h) Animos permanere, arbitramur consensu omnium Nationum. *Tuscul.*

Y 2

us to receive this Article; for if this Desire be universal, it must be an Instinct of Nature; and if so, must be implanted in the Mind, like other inbred Propensions and Appetites, by the Author of Nature, who, I imagine, no one will believe mixt in the Constitution of Man any Desires, Faculties, or Appetites, for which he had provided no suitable Objects; for this would be to suppose, that either infinite Wisdom acted without an End, or that infinite Goodness design'd a Delusion; of which more when we come to MORAL ARGUMENTS. Now that the Desire of Immortality is as really universal as other natural Appetites, will appear thus.

THAT Impulse or Propension must be allow'd to be Natural, which is felt by all Nations in all Ages, and especially by those whose Nature is most perfect, and whose Faculties are most refin'd and improv'd, which is the Case before us. All People, tho most remote from each other, and most different in their Language, Customs and Inclinations, agree in their Desires and Expectations of Immortality, and feel something of a secret Assurance, that their Lives will not be extinguish'd by the Dissolution of the Body, but only change its State and Circumstances. And

it

it is not only Death, of which by the strong Principle of Self-preservation they express an Abhorrence, but the Soul shrinks and starts back on her self at the Thoughts of Annihilation; and this Instinct is so general, that it must be concluded it was originally interwoven with our native Complexion.

It will be in vain to contend, that the Desire of Living always is not universal, and therefore not a natural Impulse, because several Persons are so far from wishing an Immortal State, that they decline it, and dread nothing more. Let this be granted, yet it does by no means overturn my Position; for the Idea of Universality, in this Case, does not include the Desires of every Individual, but the ordinary Temper of Mankind, and the Instincts of infinitely the greatest Number of Persons; for that is said to be natural, which in the customary Series of Nature's Operations generally is produc'd, tho sometimes she may deviate from her common Path, and surprize us with irregular and extraordinary Productions. Deprivation of Sight and incapacity of Hearing or Speaking, which some owe to their first Formation in the Womb, will be no convincing Argument, that Seeing, Hearing, and Speech are

are not natural to the Human Species. Nor is it a Demonstration that the Shape, Number, and Connexion of Members, which are commonly obferv'd in Man, is not the natural Order requir'd in his Structure, should it be alledg'd, that in some this Symetry is neglected, that the *Fœtus* comes into the World rumpled and mishapen, with more or fewer Limbs than usual, and in its Growth still keeps its monstrous Figure and Deformity. Besides, it must be consider'd that those few Persons, in comparison, who instead of desiring, would avoid Immortality, are generally such, whose evil Habits and vicious Manners make them obnoxious to the dreadful Apprehensions of Divine Punishments in another Life; and therefore they tremble at the Thoughts of a Future State of Existence. In this Case these Men act agreeably to Reason, while they chuse rather to perish, to be dissipated and mingled with common Matter, and to go quite out of Being, than to live in Pain and endless Misery. And when by their immoral Behaviour they have made it necessary to their Safety, that their Souls should perish with their Bodies, by degrees they bring over their struggling Reason to the side of their Interest, and deny, or pretend to disbelieve the Soul's Immortality.

Immortality *of the* Soul. 327

lity. And this will account for a surprizing Event; that is, why among Nations, whose Faculties are more cultivated and inlighten'd by the Christian Religion, the Disbelief of the Soul's Immortality should be more rife and prevalent than among ancient and modern Pagans. For these not being so certain of incurring, by their evil Actions, Divine Displeasure and suffering Future Misery, did not lie under so strong a Temptation to reject the Opinion of a Future State, as a loose and vicious Christian, who being instructed in the Conditions of Happiness hereafter, is assur'd, that his dissolute Life is inconsistent with those Conditions; and therefore if after Death there is an everlasting State, he must expect to be for ever miserable.

And this Assertion is supported by the following Observation. Men that have been bred in loose and ignorant Families, not being thoroughly made acquainted with the Nature of Vertue, and the necessary Terms of Future Felicity, seldom become so impious in Principle as to renounce the Belief of a Deity and a Future State; for these can make their disorderly Life, and the Hopes of a happy Immortality, agree well enough together, not knowing that they are really repugnant and never to be reconcil'd; while those who have had the Advantages of liberal and vertuous Educations, and are convinc'd of the Necessity of a regular and sober Life to the attainment of Immortal Bliss, and the avoiding of endless Sufferings; while these, I say, who are endow'd with a good Share of religious Knowledge, which however is unoperative in their Lives, being overpower'd by the Violence of evil Habits and vicious Inclinations, are very sensible, that by their irregular Actions they become obnoxious to Divine Displeasure, whence they are constantly disturb'd in their guilty Enjoyments by secret Terror and Remorse, it is no wonder that they use the most effectual means in their Power, to remove the perpetual Anguish and Disquiet of their Minds; and since they labour under a moral Impotency, and are not able to restrain their inordinate Appetites, what can they do, but attempt to efface the Notion of a Future State of Immortality, that they may pursue their dissolute Course of Life without troublesome Reflections, and keep their Breasts from being a miserable Seat of War, between their immoral Habits and the Dictates of Vertue? This is the Reason, why those, who in their Youth have been well instructed in the Principles of Religion, and bred

bred among great Examples of Piety and Vertue, and of which themselves once exprefs'd some Taste and Esteem, if they afterwards become Libertines, are more inclin'd than others to renounce the Belief of a Future Immortality.

IF then the Soul be an immaterial Substance, and more than a dissipable System or curious Web of attenuated Matter, it discovers the Will of the Author, that he design'd it for immortal Duration.

Of Moral Arguments.

THE Belief of the Existence of God, and the Immortality of the Soul, are Articles of Religion so closely connected, that he who acknowledges the first will soon be induc'd to embrace the last: For from the infinite Perfections of the Divine Being, namely, his Goodness, Wisdom, Justice and Faithfulness, the eternal Life of the Mind is so evidently infer'd, that it scarce needs any other Demonstration.

IN the first place, I will attempt to deduce this Conclusion from his infinite Goodness. All who acknowledge a supream Being, the Maker and Moderator of the World,

World, conceive him as endow'd with unlimited Power; and that therefore he is able to produce all Things, the Notion of which does not contain any inconsistent Ideas that destroy each other; that is, which does not imply a Contradiction: for such repugnant Things are justly allow'd to be out of the Sphere of Omnipotent Activity. It must then be granted, that an Almighty Cause has Ability to create an immaterial and incorruptible Mind like himself, who is an Incorporeal and Spiritual Being, since that Conception does not include contradictory Terms. Infinite Power and unlimited Fruitfulness can, with the same Ease, make a Seraph as a Worm: nor can an incorporeal Substance, yet unproduc'd, any more disobey the creating Word, or delay to put on Being and step forth into Existence, than a Peble or an Insect. This being premis'd, it will follow, that if we have a just Conception of the Divine Goodness, we may thence deduce the Immortality of the Soul.

Goodness is a generous Disposition of Mind, to diffuse and communicate it self to others, in proportion to the Agent's Ability, and the Receiver's Capacity. This Notion is so just, that tho a Man should possess an Affluence of all Things requir'd for

IMMORTALITY *of the* SOUL. 331
for the Gratification of his Senses and the Endowments of his Mind, yet his Felicity would be incompleat, were he without an Ability of being Beneficial to others; no excellent and exalted Spirit can be easy, tho he enjoys whatever his Desires demand for himself, unless he is capable of supplying the Wants of those about him; nor will he esteem himself happy, while it is out of his Power to make others so.

This Idea of Goodness strikes us with such Pleasure and Admiration, that we presently ascribe it in the highest Degree to the great Creator, and adore him as the Best and most Beneficent Being. And therefore the Philosopher said well, That those Men were most like the Gods, who wanted least for themselves, and did most Good to others. The Supream Being then, who is endow'd with all possible Perfection, and therefore possesses this Attribute of Goodness in its utmost Extent, must have boundless Propensions to communicate it self, and impart Felicity to others. And since he has brought into Existence Corporeal Creatures of an inferior Rank and of different Degrees of Perfection, and has diffus'd one common Nature with amazing Variety, through innumerable Kinds of Insects and superior Animals, in a beautiful

ful Subordination to each other, it is not to be imagin'd, why his Fertility should stop here, and not proceed to form more excellent Beings; we may then safely conclude, that since he is able, his infinite Desire of communicating his Goodness has actually inclin'd him to create Substances of an immaterial Nature, and of a higher Order than his visible Productions; such are the various Ranks or Classes of Spirits, dignify'd with Reason and Freedom of Choice. This therefore amounts to a Demonstration, that God has made Creatures of a more excellent Nature than those compounded of Matter; and that such as are distinguish'd by the Faculty of Reason, Judgment, and Self-determining Power, must be concluded to be these immaterial Beings, on whom the Author, who envies no Happiness of his Creatures, has bestow'd such high Endowments.

AND when we contemplate the infinite Wisdom of the first Cause, the beautiful Method and Order that he has observ'd in the various Productions of his Power, it will appear very reasonable that he should have made such a compound Being as Man, in whom the spiritual and Angelick Nature is vitally blended and combin'd with that of a Corporeal Animal. This, I say,

Immortality *of the* Soul.

is reasonable to believe, if we observe the Subordination of the different Kinds of his Creatures, and the gradual Ascent from the lowest to the highest, contriv'd with such admirable Art, that it is difficult to assign the Limits where one Species ends, and another begins. Some rais'd above inanimate Things possess only a vegetable Life. The next Order are Insects, whereof some besides a Principle of Motion, have a low sensitive Perception, imperfect organical Frames, and are of short continuance. Others have more Sensation, more perfect Bodies, and a greater Principle of Local Motion, but in various Degrees, and of various Duration. The Class above this is that of brute Animals, which have sensitive Perception, Appetites, and Local Motion in a Superior manner, but destitute of Choice and Reason: If now from this Rank of irrational Animals, we should step immediately into the superior World of Angels and immaterial Spirits, would there not appear a great Chasm and want of that Subordination and Connexion, which the wise Creator has manifestly observ'd in the gradual Ascent, from the inferior to the higher Ranks of his Creatures? And is it not congruous and suitable to his Steps and Progress in Creation, and very becoming his Divine Wisdom,

Wifdom, that before we go from Beafts to Angels, that Gap fhould be fill'd up, and the ordinary Gradation be maintain'd by a Species of Creatures, that are partly one and partly the other, that is, Mankind, who by their participation of both Natures, beautifully preferve the Connexion between the Animal and the Spiritual Angelick World? If then the fupream Caufe is able and willing to produce an immaterial Mind; and if it becomes his Wifdom, and is agreeable to his Providence and the Rule and Manner of his acting, to embody fuch a Mind in a corporeal Frame, one may fafely conclude that his Creature Man is fuch a Production.

Another Moral Argument for a Future State, may be deduc'd from the joint Contemplation of the Divine Goodnefs.

The Author of this wide and magnificent Theater of the World, did not act by a Neceffity of Nature, in producing his wonderful Works, otherwife he muft always have exerted his utmoft Energy and Art, and had given Exiftence to no Creatures but thofe of the higheft Perfection, who approach'd neareft to his own Divine Nature; but he has fhewn himfelf a free
and

Immortality of the Soul.

and arbitrary Agent, by creating Beings of infinite Variety; all which, tho diftinguifh'd by different Degrees of Excellence, are perfect in their Kind, and by their Connexion and regular Subordination to each other, confpire to produce the Symetry, Beauty, and Harmony of the whole. And tho fometimes there appear Deviations and Errors in the Production of fublunary Beings, which are call'd the Sport or Play of Nature diverted from her firft Intention; yet this happens but to a few Individuals, while the Kind is preferv'd regular and compleat. Now all this wonderful Diverfity of Creatures arrive at a finifh'd State; Stones and Minerals, Vegetables and Animals, by degrees, grow up to the Perfection of their Species: But this cannot be affirm'd of Man, who in this Life never arrives at confummate Felicity. The moft learned Philofopher knows nothing of the Works of Nature, in comparifon of what he is intirely ignorant. The moft Pious and Devout will own they are very defective, and come vaftly fhort of that height of Vertue, at which they aim. All forts of Men complain of Delufion and Difappointment; when by prudent Schemes and induftrious Application they have attain'd the Poffeffion of Wealth or Power, or Pleafure, for which they contended,

tended, they are so far from acquiring the Rest and Satisfaction they expected, that they renew their Pursuits after the same Enjoyments with as great Vehemence as before. Place a Man in any Circumstances which himself shall desire, he will still be uneasy. The *Indies* will not satisfy the avaricious Miser, nor the vastest Empire the ambitious Monarch. Vain Man imagines, that in the tempting Object which he now seeks, he shall find his Happiness; but when he possesses it, the beautiful Phantom mocks his Embraces, and proves in his Arms an empty Cloud. The World is a Scene of unsatisfy'd, complaining Men; for such are the Faculties and Capacities of Human Nature, that no Objects here can compleatly gratify them. Hence justly is infer'd a Future State of Life, where Man shall attain the Felicity and Accomplishment of his Being; for otherwise the Author must be deficient in Wisdom, Benevolence, or Power, who has made an intelligent Creature, that he either is unable, or unwilling, or knows not how to carry on to Perfection. And he that by this Argument is induc'd to believe a Future State, will soon embrace the Opinion of the Soul's Immortality.

Immortality *of the* Soul.

The next Medium I shall use to demonstrate the Soul's Immortality, shall be drawn from the Truth and Faithfulness of the supream Lord and Governor of all Things.

It has been already prov'd, that this Article of Belief has been universally receiv'd and profess'd by the Race of Mankind in all Ages of the World; nor can the different Opinion of some impious Philosophers among the *Gentiles*, and the *Sadducees* among the *Jews*, before-mention'd, or a few modern irreligious Persons, any more invalidate this Assertion, than the appearance of some irregular and deform'd Productions can be pleaded against the common Course of Things, and the general Custom and Law of Nature; for tho particular Individuals have been so stupid as to maintain, that the Soul perishes with the Body and mingles with common Matter, no more to be reviv'd; yet Human Nature was never so infatuated, as to suffer this malignant Contagion to spread far among the Species. From the beginning of Time none ever read, or heard of a Nation of *Epicureans*, *Scepticks*, or *Sadducees*, who disbeliev'd a Future Existence; which must therefore be an Opinion establish'd

blifh'd by the general Confent of Mankind.

It is very certain that *Juvenal*, *Cicero*, *Plutarch*, *Epictetus*, and many other Moralifts, have afferted, that many defperate Malefactors, tho they efcap'd the Cognizance and Sentence of the Magiftrate, have however been arraign'd and condemn'd at the fecret Tribunal of Confcience in their own Breafts, and that Mankind in general, reflecting on their Guilt, felt inherent Terror and Remorfe, and lay under tormenting Pangs and frightful Apprehenfions of Divine Anger and Future Sufferings. They believ'd there was a Place of Punifhment, where the Gods, by feveral ways, did execute their Wrath on impious Criminals ; where Furies, Wheels, Vipers, and Vultures, a fad variety of Pain and Vengeance, tormented the Unjuft and Irreligious: While, on the contrary, it was their Opinion, that good and vertuous Men fhould, after Death, forget all their Sorrow, ceafe for ever from their Labours, and be convey'd to Seats of Happinefs and endlefs Delight. And the Hopes and Expectations of this Future Felicity, infpir'd them with the love of Piety and fober Manners, and excited them to undertake many illuftrious and heroick Actions,

Actions, that in the next Life they might attain the Favour of the Gods and the Reward of Vertue. Since then by this Principle of the Soul's Immortality, Mankind have been mov'd and guided in their Actions, and this has been the chief Foundation of Religion and Vertue in the World, I thus argue, That Principle or Article of Belief, by which God has actually govern'd the Race of Mankind from the Beginning of Time, cannot be falfe: Now it is evident, that God has actually and conftantly govern'd the World by this Belief and Expectation of a State of Immortality to come, and therefore that Principle muft certainly be true: For fince Mankind in all Times have been acted upon and excited by Arguments and Motives drawn from a Future State of Life, and the Supream Being has all along ruled the Minds of Men by the Belief and Expectation of Immortality; if notwithftanding this there fhould be no fuch State, then it will neceffarily follow, that God has govern'd the rational World in all Ages by a Falfhood and a meer Delufion. And thus to mock Mankind and act upon their Paffions by an imaginary and feign'd State of Life in another World, is inconfiftent with his perfect Truth and inviolable Faithfulnefs; and yet, if this impious Abfurdity

dity be not fwallow'd, a Future State muſt be allow'd as certain.

If it be objected, that the Supream Being does not rule the Minds of Men by the Expectations of Rewards and Puniſhments in another Life, but only permits Men to deceive themſelves; I anſwer, Firſt, that the Perſons who thus deceive themſelves, if indeed they are deluded, have always been the wifeſt, the moſt vertuous and excellent Men; for the Truth of which Aſſertion I appeal to the Hiſtory and Obſervation of all Ages. Now it is not conſiſtent with the Honour and Faithfulneſs of the Divine Being, to ſuffer thoſe who moſt reſemble his own excellent Nature, and do him the moſt eminent Service, to be conſtantly mov'd by a Deluſion, to do thoſe Actions by which they ſtrive to imitate, ſerve, and pleaſe him.

And from hence may be form'd a ſtrong Argument againſt the *Scepticks*, with whom I am engag'd in this Diſputation; for to any Man that reflects with Attention, it will appear incredible, that if the Immortality of the Soul be an imaginary and falſe Notion, that a God of infinite Goodneſs and Love to Mankind ſhould not, by his gracious Providence, protect Men of Wiſdom,

Immortality *of the* Soul.

Wisdom, Piety, and Vertue, that bear the nearest Conformity and Similitude to his own Perfections, and are most obedient to his Laws, from constantly falling into this Error, of believing a Future State, while the vilest and most flagitious Part of Mankind, whom from the perfect Purity of his Nature his Soul abhors, should be inlighten'd in this important Point, discover the Truth, and escape the great Mistake of the Soul's Immortality. It will be difficult to tell what is inconsistent with the infinite Goodness of the Supream Being, and his Regard and Benevolence to good Men, if this Supposition we have made be reconcil'd to that Divine Attribute.

From the Justice of God I thus argue, Those who believe that the Creator is likewise the Lawgiver and Supream Judge of the World will agree, that Man is an accomptable Creature, and that one time he must appear before the high Tribunal of this Sovereign, to be absolv'd or condemn'd, and rewarded or punish'd for his Observance or Contempt of the Divine Laws. Now, as in Fact, there appears nothing in our present State like an equal Distribution of Rewards and Punishments, so it is impossible that a Man can be brought to an Accompt for the Actions of his

his Life, till his Life is ended. While we exift here we are under a State of Trial, nor can it be judg'd whether we have done our Duty till the Term of our Probation is expir'd; feeing then it cannot be decided how any Man has pafs'd the Courfe of his Life, till Death puts an end to it, and yet fometime or other he muft come upon his Trial, it is evident, that there muft be a State of Life after this, in which the Moderator and Judge of the World will vindicate the Honour and Juftice of his Government, by an impartial Sentence upon all Men, according to their paft Demeanour.

If it appears by the Reafons which I have urg'd for the Soul's Immortality, that there is but a bare Probability of a Future Exiftence; the Inference will be ftrong and evident, that it is the Duty and Intereft of every Man to act in Conformity to this Opinion, and fo to demean himfelf that he may be happy, and not miferable, in this Eternal State that is likely to come. For fince this Tranfient Life in Duration is but a Moment compar'd with vaft Eternity, all Men who can reflect, will pronounce it highly reafonable, that fince the Difproportion between this fleeting Life and endlefs Ages is fo immenfe and unconceivable,

Immortality *of the* Soul.

ceivable, every one should be mov'd and govern'd by the probable Prospect of Everlasting Happiness and Misery, rather than by the Pleasures or Sufferings in this State of Mortality. And this is what is constantly practis'd by wise and considerate Men, who in various Instances part with some Things of Value, only from the Hopes of reaping a far greater Advantage; if it be prudent in the Affairs of this World, thus to govern our Actions, then we are evidently more oblig'd to neglect the Enjoyments of this World, from a probable Expectation of unlimited Felicity. Now if this be a clear Dictate of Reason, that a Man should, in the Course of his Life, be influenc'd by an Opinion of the Soul's Immortality, then he is bound by a Law of Nature, which is nothing else but the Will of the Supream Being, reveal'd to Man by the Light of Reason for the government of his Actions, so to regulate his Life, as if he were well assur'd of a Future State. Hence it will clearly follow, that if there be but a bare Probability of a Life to come, that the Author of our Beings has made it our Duty to act in conformity to that Opinion. And since by his infinite Perfections he is uncapable of deceiving his Creatures, and making it their Duty to act upon imaginary and ground-

groundless Views, may not the Certainty of the Soul's immortal Duration be hence infer'd?

Objections *against the* Soul's Immortality.

AGAINST the Immateriality, and consequently the Immortality of the Soul, some superficial Philosophers, and loose Wits their Admirers, bring this Objection, That an incorporeal Substance implies a Contradiction; so Mr. *Dryden* says it appears to him, in a Dedication to Sir *Charles Sedley*: And if these Gentlemen had vouchsaf'd to have given any Proof of their Position in a Matter of such Importance, it could by no means have been look'd on as an unbecoming Condescension. How it came to pass that they thought they should be believ'd upon their bare Assertion, without offering the least Evidence, I must acknowledge I cannot imagine.

It is plain, that these low Pretenders to Reason take the Idea of Substance and Matter for the same, looking on those Words as Synonymous; and if it were so, it would plainly follow, that an incorporeal Body would be an inconsistent Conception, and one
Term

Term would destroy the other; but why will they produce no Argument to evince the Truth of their Opinion, and make it appear that all Substance is Body. In this Discourse the Existence of a Deity, the Maker of all Things, is suppos'd to be granted; and unless they infist, that the Supream Being is a Material and not a Spiritual Substance, then the Idea of an Incorporeal Substance has nothing in it absurd and impossible, as I have had an Occasion to mention before. And should it be granted, that the Soul is a Corporeal Being, yet this would not hinder but that it might still be Immortal; for if their Master *Epicurus* or *Aristotle* are of any Authority in this Debate, it is evident, that both these look'd on the Gods as Corporeal, and yet affirm'd they were Eternal. And if these Gentlemen, their Followers, allow a Corporeal Deity, they will notwithstanding grant that he is Immortal. But there is no reason to carry this Argument farther; for what is advanc'd with great Confidence, but without Proof, ought to be rejected as unworthy of an Answer.

ANOTHER Objection to the Doctrine of the Immaterial and consequently Incorruptible Substance of Human Souls, is this, that the Souls of Brute Animals are Incorporeal,

poreal, and notwithstanding are not Immortal, but are allow'd to be of a perishing Nature. It has been the almost universal Opinion of Men of Learning and celebrated Judgment in past Times, that the Bodies of Brutes were enliven'd by a vital Principle of a superior Nature to that of Matter. And those ingenious *Corpuscularians*, who of late thought fit to revive and polish the obsolete and decry'd Hypothesis of *Democritus* and *Epicurus*, and will not allow to Brutes an incorporeal, vital Spring of Sensation, seem rather to affect a Sport of Wit and Imagination, than a solid Scheme of Philosophy.

I MUST acknowledge, that I look upon the Souls of brute Creatures as Immaterial; for I cannot conceive how an internal Principle of Sensitive Perception and Local Motion can be fram'd of Matter, tho ever so subtile and refin'd, and modify'd with the most artful Contrivance. And I challenge the most accute Philosopher to assign any specifical Character, that will essentially diversify and distinguish an Animal from a Watch, a Puppet, or any other curious Engine, if the vital Principle that informs the Animal be not Incorporeal; for the implex Contrivance, the curious Disposition and Minuteness of the Parts, will by no means

means vary the Species; a Clock of the smallest Size, with wonderful Diversity of minute Springs and Movements, and great Variety of lasting Motions, does not differ in Kind from a plain one of the largest Dimension, that has but one simple Motion, and that of short Continuance.

Whence it will follow, that according to the Philosophy of the Atomists, and their manner of accounting for sensitive Operations by the Impulse of outward Objects made upon the Organs of the Body, and the Collision, Conflict and Reaction of Matter upon Matter, an Animal is nothing else but an admirable Machine and a curious Invention, that imitates exactly the Principle of Sensation in Man; but in reality is nothing but an excellent Piece of Mechanism, that represents and mimicks in a surprizing Manner the Perceptions of Human Souls: and indeed the Imitation is so perfect, that we may be as sure that a Beast has as real Sensation, as we are that any other Men besides our selves are endow'd with that Principle: For what can be alledg'd to demonstrate the Truth of other Mens Sensation, which I my self do not feel, than what will as effectually prove, that Brute Animals are likewise sensitive Beings, the Operations of such Powers being

being as fully evident as they are in Man, and often more perfect?

Tho the Souls of Brute Animals are allow'd to be Incorporeal, yet they are plainly of a bafe and low Nature, and deftitute of thofe intellectual Faculties and free Choice that fhould make them Subjects of Moral Government, enable them to difcern the Obligation of Laws and the Diftinction of Vertue and Vice, and underftand the Notion of being an accomptable Creature, and receiving Rewards and Punifhments. Hence it follows, that they are entirely incapable of the Felicity of a Rational Soul in the Fruition of the Divine Being, whom they are unable to contemplate, love, admire, and adore: and from this it is evident that the Author and Lord of Nature has fignify'd his Will, that he does not intend them for perpetual Duration, in that Senfe which we mean, when we fpeak of the Soul's Immortality, that is, its eternal Continuance in a State of Happinefs or Mifery; for to what purpofe can it be fuppos'd, that the Souls of Brutes fhould be deftin'd to endlefs Duration, if after the Diffolution of the Body they have no Faculties, Capacities, or Operations, like thofe of the Soul of Man, that can give them the like Delight and Felicity? But

Immortality *of the* Soul.

But I answer, in the second place, That supposing the Souls of Brutes are Immaterial, and that they continue after Death, since they are endow'd with no nobler Principle than that of Sensation, and since that must depend upon the use of proper Organs, it being impossible to conceive an Idea of Seeing and Hearing, if one divests it from its Relation to an Eye or an Ear, it will follow, that the Souls of Brutes after Death, must remain inactive and insensible, for want of those necessary Organs by which they exerted their Operations when vitally united to the Body, on whose Frame and Disposition it was wholly dependent in its Actions.

But whether the Animal Souls in a State of Separation remain stupid and asleep, or whether they are dispers'd thro the Creation and employ'd to animate other Beings, or return to one common Element whence they were at first deriv'd, is unreveal'd; but this is certain, that, which ever of these is true, the Souls of Brutes are not design'd by the great Creator for such a Life of Pleasure and Happiness as that of Human Souls in a State of Immortality and Perfection, for the Enjoyment of which they have no Dispositions and Capacities.

pacities. And tho we should not be able clearly to account for the Nature of Brute Animals, and how their Souls are dispos'd of by their Maker after Death, yet our uncertainty in this Point will by no means weaken the Force of those Demonstrations that have been produc'd for the Immortality of Human Souls.

It is farther Objected against the Immortality of the Soul, that it plainly relies in its Operations on the Temper and Disposition of the Body; that its Faculties are exerted with different Degrees of Vivacity and Perfection in the feeble State of Infancy, the Vigor of Youth and the Decays of old Age; that they are suspended or disturb'd by Sleep, and quite subverted by Lunacy or the stroke of an Apoplexy; that they are enfeebled by languishing Sickness, and interrupted by Fury and other violent Passions; and therefore must be allow'd to be dependent on the Body which it animates. To this I answer, that during the vital Complication of the Soul and Body, the first uses the instrumental Assistance of the last; but this does not prove that the superior essential Faculties of the Mind are incapable of exercising their Operations in a State of Separation; for those do not depend on Corporeal Organs, as the Principle

*

of

of Sensation does; what mechanical Frame is necessary to Understanding, Reflection, Argumentation, and Memory? What secret Wheels, what Re-active and Elastick Springs and Movements communicate to the Soul its Self determining Power, or Liberty of Will? Can the organical Contrivance be explain'd, by which a Man is fram'd a Moral and Religious Animal; by which he discerns the Beauty of Vertue and the Turpitude and Danger of Vice, and by which he is mov'd to aim at the Felicity and Perfection of his Nature, in his Resemblance and Fruition of the Supream Being? It cannot be deny'd, but these Operations may be perform'd without the Body, since our Conceptions of these does not, like that of Sensation, include the Idea of any material Organ to which they relate; and therefore tho the Objection proves a vital Union of the Soul and Body, it cannot be thence infer'd, that the superior Faculties of the Mind are incapable of acting in a State of Separation.

AN
ESSAY
UPON THE
LAWS of NATURE.

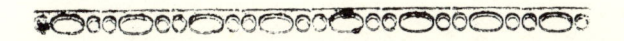

AN ESSAY UPON THE LAWS of NATURE.

IT would have been an acceptable Performance to the World, if the Gentlemen of the prefent Age, who own a Caufelefs Supream Being, but do not acknowledge the Authority of Revelation, and the Divine Inftitution of the Chriftian Religion, yet at the fame time complement one another with the refpectful Titles of Philofophers and Mafters of unprejudic'd Reafon, had publifh'd a Scheme of Natural Religion, or a Syftem of thofe Laws which all Men, who believe the Exiftence of a Deity, are bound to obey; and had shewn whence those Moral Obligations arise, and by what Sanctions they are enforc'd; which, in the Preface to *Creation*, I have urg'd them to attempt: Had they done this, they would not only have wip'd off from their Character all suspicion of Impiety, and have demonstrated that they did not, to avoid that infamous Imputation, shelter themselves under the Profession of Deism; but they would likewise have acted an honest part in respect of those Persons, whom with great Art and Industry they labour to convert from Christianity to Paganism. For since from our native Degeneracy the Difficulty of paying Obedience to the Rules and Precepts of the Redeemer, and not the Articles and Mysteries of Belief, is the most frequent Cause why Men at length renounce his Religion; these Apostles of Infidelity, that with great Diligence strive to replant the World with the exploded Doctrines of the Heathen, ought to acquaint their Disciples with the whole Scheme of their Antichristian Maxims, and not promise to deliver them only from the hard and abstruse Points enjoin'd to be believ'd, while the harder and more disagreeable Vertues still remain to be practis'd, which is the most discouraging Difficulty in the

Christian

Chriftian Syftem. Thus while the Unbeliever, to engage the Chriftian on his fide, undertakes to eafe him in Points of Faith, he conceals, out of Ignorance or Defign, thofe Moral Duties which the Deift is oblig'd to, as well as thofe who own a Reveal'd Religion.

There is great Reafon to believe, that many are induc'd to renounce the Chriftian Religion by a falfe Notion, that if they are free from the Reftraints of its Precepts, they fhall enjoy a more extenfive Liberty, be lefs control'd in the Courfe of their Actions, and being deliver'd from the Strictnefs and Severity of Manners which that Divine Inftitution enjoins, they may gratify their Paffions, and indulge their Senfes, without Guilt and Fear of Punifhment. But thefe Perfons fhould confider, that there is nothing new in the Chriftian Inftitution, but Matters of Faith. There are no new Vices forbidden, nor new Vertues commanded; the Prohibition of the one and the Injunctions of the other are again indeed enforc'd by Revelation, but without that, we are by the Moral Law under the fame Obligations, and the fame Confinements. And 'tis obfervable, when the Scriptures recommend Chaftity, Temperance, Juftice, and Mercy, they never give

give any Definition of thofe Vertues, but barely name them, fuppofing the World was acquainted with their Nature, and that the Obfervance of them, as well as the Forbearance of the contrary Vices, were the Dictates of the Light of Reafon, and the Refult of the Moral Nature of Things. It is in vain therefore to reject the Chriftian Religion, in hopes of being deliver'd from the Reftraints it lays upon us; for we fhall ftill lie under the fame Limitations from the Laws of Nature, whofe Obligations will ftick infeparably to us, and make us altogether as much accomptable. And to make this evident, I have undertaken to demonftrate the Obligations we are under by thofe unwritten Laws.

IN profecuting this Defign, I fhall firft make it clear, that in Fact there are fuch Moral Obligations, which are term'd Laws of Nature. And, Secondly, that thefe Laws neceffarily arife from the various Relations between God and Man, and derive their binding Force from Divine Authority. In order to this, I fhall fhew what thofe Relations are, and in what they are founded ; and then fhall demonftrate how the Laws of Nature or Moral Duties muft unavoidably refult from thofe relations.

Laws *of* Nature.

Before we enter upon this Province, it is necessary to observe, that the Assertors and Patrons of Impiety use this Expression, *The Law of Nature*, in an equivocal Sense, and mean by it nothing but the Order and Course of Things, or the Series and Connexion of Causes and Effects in the visible World; as, for instance, the Diurnal and Annual Revolution of the Sun, the Circular Motion and various Appearances of the Moon, the Propension of heavy Bodies to descend and of light ones to rise, the Flux and Reflux of the Sea, and the like Phænomena, are said to be the Laws of Nature, as indeed they are in a Physical, tho not in a Moral Sense; that is, the Author of all Things has made that Disposition and Connexion of active Principles and passive Natures, that such a Course and Order of Events shall of Necessity be preserv'd. But then these false Philosophers and Pretenders to Reason declare their impious Opinion, that Man is mov'd in the same manner as Brutes and Inanimate Beings, by a necessary Impulse, and will not allow the Deity to rule his Rational Creature according to his Nature, and in as high and honourable a way as the Civil Magistrate governs his Subjects, that is, by a Rule prescrib'd to their Actions.

ons. 'Tis plain, that by the Laws of Nature as they regard Mankind, thefe Men do not mean the Precepts or Commands of God, fignify'd and directed to a Moral Agent, one capable of determining himfelf to Compliance or Difobedience, which is the only Senfe in which I take the Expreffion.

I SHALL now undertake to evince, that there really are Moral Obligations, which we term Laws of Nature.

THAT the Power we have over our Actions is bounded by natural Limitations, which make it our Duty to do fome Things and to forbear others, antecedent to the Authority of Human Laws, is a Truth confirm'd by the general Confent of Mankind. Men feel in their Breafts a fecret Senfe of Religion and Vertue; and when they act in conformity to the Rules of Piety and Juftice, they are rewarded with an inward Pleafure and Satisfaction: And, on the contrary, when they violate thofe Precepts by enormous Tranfgreffions, they are ftartled by Reflection on their Guilt, and fill'd with Remorfe and Terror. And this the Pagan World, who had not the Advantage of Revelation, did always acknowledge. *Juvenal*, in the beginning of
his

his thirteenth Satire, affirms, "That every Man is difpleas'd with himfelf for being the Author of an evil Action, and that guilty Perfons are condemn'd by their own judicial Sentence." *Cicero*, in his Book of Laws, fays, *Furies purfue and torment the Wicked, not with fabulous Firebrands, but with the Anguifh of Confcience and Tortures of inward Guilt*. And in another Book he affirms, That *a Mind confcious of Wickednefs, is tormented with the Expectation of all kinds of Punifhment*.

It is the univerfal Opinion of Mankind, that Humanity, good Nature, Benevolence, Gratitude, Modefty, Friendfhip, and Heroick Zeal for the good of our Country, are eminent Vertues and the Ornaments and Perfection of our Nature. And are not Infolence, Pride, Impudence, Ingratitude, Cruelty, Avarice, and a narrow Self-interefted Spirit, as much condemn'd and detefted? On this Subject *Cicero* thus argues, "If Juftice is "not eftablifh'd by the Law of Nature, all "Vertue is gone; where would Liberality, where would Charity, where would "Piety, where would Beneficence and "Gratitude Exift? If only the Fear of "Punifhment from the Magiftrate, and "not its evil Nature and Turpitude deters us from a flagitious and wicked "Life,

" Life, no Man could be vicious or un-
" juſt: Nor could a Man ſo properly be
" call'd Wicked, as Unwary. —— If,
" ſays he, the Laws of the People, the De-
" crees of Princes, the Determinations of
" Judges, conſtitute the Goodneſs of our
" Actions; then would it be lawful to rob,
" to commit Adultery, to forge Deeds and
" Teſtaments, if theſe ſhould be autho-
" riz'd and approv'd by the Voices of the
" ruling Multitude? But can the Power
" of ignorant Men change and invert the
" Nature of Things? If ſo, they might,
" by a Law, make Good Evil, and Evil
" Good. If in *Rome* there had been no
" written Law againſt a Rape, in the
" Reign of *Tarquin*, would not therefore
" *Tarquin* have offended againſt the Eter-
" nal Law, when he offer'd Violence to
" *Lucretia?* There was in this Caſe a
" Dictate of Nature, which did not then
" begin to be a Law when it was firſt
" written, but was Coæval with the Di-
" vine Mind;" and therefore he calls it
the Law of the Supream God: And ſays
farther, That the Laws of the Civil Magiſtrate are then good, when they bear a
Conformity to the Law of Nature; otherwiſe they are no Laws.

PLATO

Plato prepares the People to be good Subjects, by inculcating on them the Obligations they are under by the Laws of Nature, to yield Obedience to the Civil Magiftrate. And *Cicero* in imitation of him, expreffes himfelf in this divine manner: "Let Citizens be firft perfuaded that there "are Gods, who are Lords and Gover- "nors of all Things; that all Things are "adminifter'd and directed by their Wif- "dom and Providence; that they obferve "what every Man is, what he does, and "what he entertains in his Breaft; with "what Temper of Mind, and what De- "votion he pays Divine Worfhip; and "that they make a Diftinction of the "Pious and Impious: And then fays, Who "will deny thefe Opinions to be ufeful, "when he reflects how many Things are "confirm'd by a folemn Oath, how much "religious Leagues contribute to our Safe- "ty and Advantage; how many are re- "duc'd from Wickednefs by the Fear of "Divine Punifhment, and how facred the "Society of Citizens muft be, while they "look on the Immortal Gods both as "Judges and Witneffes of their Deeds?" This acknowledgment of a moral Diftinction between Good and Evil, and the Fear of Divine Difpleafure and Punifhment from enormous Guilt, is so universal, that many affirm Divine Laws are born with us, are written in our Hearts, and, as *Cicero* speaks, implanted in our Nature.

The Legislative Authority of Civil Magistrates cannot extend to the Secrets of the Heart, which fall not under their Knowledge and Observation; and therefore they do not pretend to prescribe Laws to regulate our internal Actions. If then we are under no Limitations from any Divine Precepts, we have an absolute and uncontrol'd Dominion over our Thoughts and Passions, and are accomptable to no Tribunal for any secret Transactions of the Mind. And hence it will follow, that no Obliquity, no Guilt, no Dishonour can attend any Emotions of the Heart, tho it is indeed the Source and Spring of all Morality. Excessive Anger, Malice, Hatred, Envy, Ill-will to our Neighbour, secret Joy at the Ruin of our Benefactors, or the Misfortunes of our Country, or the Destruction and Calamity of Mankind, would be innocent and lawful: Ambition, Pride, Haughtiness, Self-admiration, Contempt and Scorn of others, Avarice, Dissimulation, would not deserve the least Blame or Reproach. But was any Nation ever known so stupid and barbarous, as to believe there is no Turpitude, nothing to be censur'd or detested in such Passions? Have not the Heathen World express'd their Abhorrence of them; and the more civiliz'd and enlighten'd they were, did they not the more condemn and inveigh against them? Have not the wisest of them left excellent Writings, wherein they persuade and excite Men to the Government of the Passions, and lay down Rules and Directions by which they may attain this Perfection? Were not *Socrates*, *Plato*, *Aristotle*, and *Plutarch*, *Cicero*, *Seneca*, *Antonine*, and *Epictetus*, besides many others, famous for their Instructions on this Head of Morality? And if the secret Operations of our Minds and the Regulation of our Thoughts, the Restraint of our Appetites, and the Conduct of our Passions, are Moral Duties, they must be denominated such from the Obligations of Divine Commands, that is, from the Laws of Nature.

All Laws must be the Laws of some Person invested with Legislative Authority; and therefore if there be any antecedent to, or besides those of the Civil Magistrate, they must be the Precepts of the Supream Being. I must acknowledge, that the Moral Goodness and Beauty, the Wickedness and Deformity of Actions, which some great

great Divines derive from the intrinfick Nature of Things, without any Confideration of a Law that commands or prohibits them, is what I am not able to conceive. The Diftinction of Good and Evil feems to me to refult from the Difagreement or Conformity of our Actions to the Precepts that enjoin them. If there be no Law, where is Difobedience? If no Rule, where is Error or Deviation? If no Limits prefcrib'd, where is Tranfgreffion? I believe, upon Examination, it will appear, that all the celebrated intrinfick Good and Evil Things which is faid to be unalterable and eternal, without any regard to their being commanded or forbidden, muft be taken in a phyfical Senfe; and fo Things are term'd Good or Evil, as they are advantageous or hurtful, ufeful or prejudicial to Mankind. But this Convenience or Inconvenience, Comodity or Difcomodity of Things, is not their Moral Rectitude or Obliquity, which of Neceffity includes the Notion of a Law obferv'd or tranfgrefs'd.

Thus having fhown that there are Divine unwritten Laws, to which all Men ought to yield Obedience, I fhall now demonftrate their Authority and obligatory Force, and fhow in particular what they are.

Laws *of* Nature.

The Existence of a God and the Administration of his Providence, I have already asserted and prov'd in another Writing, which likewise has been done by many excellent Philosophers and Divines. I shall therefore take this Proposition, *An Eternal, Uncreated Mind, of Infinite Power, Wisdom, and Goodness, the Maker of Heaven and Earth, does exist,* as sufficiently evinc'd and granted; which shall now be the Principle whence I undertake to deduce my following Conclusions.

Whoever acknowledges the Being of this Independent and Self-existent Cause of Things, will easily discern the various Relations between God and Man, which flow necessary and immediate from this Principle.

If the Origin of Human Nature is deriv'd from God as the first Efficient, it follows that Man is related to him as his Creature, and he to Man as his Creator. And since 'tis a plain Contradiction, that there may be a self-sufficient, independent Creature; for then it must be granted, that the Supream Being has made a Creature equal in Perfection to himself,

that

that is, another God, the Consequence will be, that a Man who has a precarious and supported Existence is related to his Maker, as the continu'd Cause of his Being, and his Confervator. The Ideas of Creator and Preserver, of necessity include those of good Will and Beneficence: Whence the Inference will be clear, that Man is related to his Divine Author, from whom he has receiv'd all the Enjoyments and Perfections of his Being, and to whom he owes their Continuance, as his chief Benefactor. It will also be an undeniable Deduction from what has been laid down, that God is related to Man as his sole Proprietor; no Maxim being more easily and more universally allow'd than this, That what any one has entirely made is entirely his own, and no Right in any Workmanship can possibly be so full and extensive as that of a Creator.

AND whoever reflects on the Nature of Man, as endow'd with Reason, and a Faculty to will and chuse, whereby he becomes a Moral Agent, will pronounce him capable of being govern'd by Laws; and if he contemplates the Attributes of the Divine Being, his Almighty Power, Omniscience, Goodness, and Omnipresence, will, without hesitation, conclude, that
God

LAWS of NATURE.

God is perfectly qualify'd to be his Governor; and that he only is capable of governing the whole Race of Mankind: And if he confiders his absolute Propriety in Man as his Creature, he will clearly difcern the Right he has to exercife Dominion over him. The Creator then by giving Man Faculties to know and difcern his Will, and making him apt to be mov'd to Obedience by Hopes of Reward, and deter'd from Tranfgreffion by Fears of Punifhment, has made him a governable Creature; and fince it cannot be fuppos'd he gave him thofe Faculties in vain, nothing can be more agreeable to Reafon, than to conclude, that God intended and defign'd that Man fhould be govern'd according to his Nature; that is, as an intelligent and rational Being ; And fince every one has a Power to rule his own, as far as his Propriety extends, and the Supream Being has an unlimited Propriety in his Creature Man, and is likewife capable, only capable, of ruling the whole Species, it will moft evidently follow, that God is related to Man as his Governor, and Man to him as his Subject.

AND if Man is fubject to his Maker, as his Soveraign Lord and Ruler, 'tis clear,

that

that he muſt be an accomptable Creature, and that his Creator is the Judge to whom he muſt accompt; who will one Day bring him before his juſt Tribunal, and condemn or acquit, reward or puniſh him according to the Meaſure of his Obedience or Tranſgreſſion.

There have been many warm, but unneceſſary Diſputes manag'd by learned Men, about the Title of God to his Government of Mankind; but laying aſide Terms of Art, and avoiding Oſtentation of Learning and a diſputing Temper; from what has been ſaid, I imagine, the Divine Title, or the Foundation of God's Right to rule by his Laws the Rational World, will eaſily and clearly appear. His Relation to Mankind as univerſal King, that is, his Soveraignty or Supream Power, reſults from his abſolute Propriety in his Creature. Man is his own, becauſe he made him; and ſince he is made a governable Being, his Maker, as his abſolute unlimited Lord and Owner, muſt have the ſole Right or Authority to govern him. So that this Point, that has made ſo great a ſtir, and exercis'd ſo many Pens, does not ſeem ſo abſtruſe and difficult. I think it is very plain, that the Divine Right of Supream Government is founded in, and
reſults

results from God's plenary Propriety, in a Creature apt and qualify'd for Subjection and Obedience; and this Government he has ever exercis'd, and continues to do so, by making and declaring Laws to regulate the Actions of Men.

Of the LAWS of NATURE, how promulgated.

SINCE it is clear, that God is the Governor of Man, 'tis as clear he must govern him by Laws, that is, by Rules that settle his Duty. Let us therefore enquire what those Laws are, and how made known to Mankind.

IN order to this it must be consider'd, that a Law in general is nothing else but the Will of the Legislator declar'd to his Subject, as the Rule of his Actions. This is a full Definition, and tho the Sanctions of Rewards and Punishments are usually annex'd, which by acting on our Hopes and Fears enforce the Observance of the Law-giver's Command, yet is it no essential part of the Law; for the Will and Pleasure of the Soveraign Ruler, when made known, constitutes the Duty of the Subject, and binds him to obey.

The

The Threats and Promises superadded are only Incitements to the Subject to pay that Obedience, which before by virtue of the Lawgiver's Authority he was oblig'd to do.

Could it be suppos'd that God had made no Laws for Man discernable by the Light of Nature, that is, deducible by Reason abstracting from Revelation; Man being intirely free from Restraints would have an unlimited Power over his Actions, and there could be no such thing as Religion in the World; no Obligation on Princes to protect, or on Subjects to obey: No Duty from Parents to Children, or from Children to Parents: No Friendship, no Justice, no Faithfulness; in short, no Moral Distinction of Good and Evil. Man would be unable to Sin, and utterly uncapable of Guilt, or of recommending himself to the Favour or Good Will of his Maker by Obedience; and these are the Maxims which irreligious Philosophers would fain establish. But it will appear, that God has not in this case left himself without Witness, nor Mankind without proper Means to discover the Divine Will concerning their Duty. A conscious tho imperfect Light still remains in degenerate Nature, by which Men

Men difcern a difference between Vertue and Vice, the Regularity and Obliquity of their Actions, and by unavoidable Reflection condemn or applaud themfelves for what they have done. By the Guidance of this Light, without the Affiftance of Divine Revelation, many excellent Perfons in the Pagan World, carefully attending to its Dictates, made fuch Improvements in Moral Knowledge, and fuch Difcoveries of their Duty, that many fince, who have enjoy'd the vaft Advantages of Revelation, to their great Difhonour, have fallen fhort of the like Attainments.

Tho this be the Cafe, if the wifeft and moft vertuous of the ancient Philofophers are compar'd with the moft ignorant and vicious among Chriftians, yet they are infinitely inferior even in Moral Science to our learned and more accomplifh'd Men. Since the Saviour of the World has publifh'd his Divine Revelation, and brought Life and Immortality to Light, his Followers being inftructed in his heavenly Doctrines, were the better enabled to difcover the Duties of natural Religion, which otherwife they would not have done but in a very lame and imperfect manner; fo that in this Senfe we owe in a great meafure the rational Demonſtration of Moral Duties to the Revelation in the ſacred Writings.

I come now to define a Law of Nature, which is the Will of God ſignify'd to Man by the Light of Reaſon, as the Rule of his Thoughts, Paſſions, Words, and Actions. The Matter of this Law is ſomething enjoyn'd or forbidden. Its Generical Difference, as the Schools expreſs themſelves, is the Legiſlative Authority of the ſupream Being, who has the Right of a Governor to our Obedience. The Divine Pleaſure muſt be ſignify'd or declar'd before it becomes a Law; for no Man is oblig'd to perform any thing impoſſible, which he would be, were he bound by Precepts which he had no means to know. The ſpecifical Diſtinction of it conſiſts in the promulgation or diſcovery of the Divine Will by the Faculty of Reaſon, by which it is diſtinguiſh'd from his poſitive Precepts, which are made known by ſupernatural Revelation. I ſhall now undertake to ſhow, by what Steps and clear Inferences human Reaſon may trace and diſcern the Origin of our Duty preſcrib'd and dictated by Nature as reſpecting God, Man himſelf, and his Neighbour.

Man,

Laws *of* Nature.

MAN, as an intelligent Being, has the Power of perceiving the Truth of a first, self-evident Principle, to calculate, compare, and by inferring one Proposition from another, to form a coherent Train of Conclusions. By virtue of this Faculty he can contemplate God, as a causeless, independent Mind, and therefore All-sufficient in himself; and as the Author of all Beings in the Universe, which he created out of Nothing: And then by Force of this Self-evident Maxim, that nothing can give to another, what it has not in it self to give, he must easily infer, that all the Goodness, Energy, Life, and Intelligence, communicated to his Creatures, must be found in an eminent way collected in this Uncreated, Self-existent Mind, who must therefore be possest of all possible Perfection. It is therefore the Duty of Man to form just and right Conceptions of his Author, *First Law of Nature.* and entertain the most honourable and elevated Idea of the Divine Being, that it is possible for his Faculties by their utmost Efforts to conceive. He ought to contemplate, admire, and adore the ineffable Dignity and Excellence of his Nature: To bow down his Soul in the profoundest Submission, at the Thoughts of his Greatnefs and unapproachable Majefty. To celebrate his Praifes, and magnify his unlimited and independent Power, Wifdom and Goodnefs; in Converfation with others to fpeak of him and his glorious Attributes with the higheft Efteem, and moft religious Veneration. To propagate and fupport the Belief of his Exiftence, and his infinite Perfections: To confute and difcountenance the petulant and prophane Deriders of Religion, and expofe the unreafonable Principles of impious Pretenders to Reafon and Philofophy. It is evident that this is the Will of God, that we fhould think of him as he is, and not reprefent him to our felves or others under a falfe Idea. This then is the firft Law of Nature difcover'd by the Light of Reafon.

Thus much is due to God confider'd in an abfolute Senfe: But if we contemplate him under the feveral Relations he bears to Man, we fhall fee with Admiration the Streams of Moral Duties refulting, as natural Emanations, from thofe Fountains, and propagating their Branches in diftinct Order and beautiful Variety.

When a Man reflects, that he has received his Exiftence from the Deity, and all

Laws *of* Nature. 377

all the Faculties and Accomplishments of his Being, he will readily grant that God is his absolute Owner, as said before; and if so, that it is the Will of God, that his Creature should acknowledge his Maker's Right in him, and Dominion over him, as his Proprietor, and his unlimited Power to dispose of him at his Pleasure; this being an uncontested Maxim of right Reason, that every one may do whatever he pleases with any thing entirely his own. That Man should submit himself to the Divine Will, and by an humble and absolute Resignation of himself, acquiesce with Patience and Content in all the various Dispensations of Providence. That he should not complain or murmur against his Lord and Owner, and arraign him as a severe or unjust Master, if he allots him but a mean and narrow Fortune, afflicts him with Sickness, Losses, and Calamity, suffers his Estate to be wrested from him by Fraud or Violence, or his good Name and Reputation to be blemish'd and violated by the Malice of his Enemies. That, on the other hand, if he is possess'd of a plentiful Estate, of Health, Beauty, Power, and Esteem, he should acknowledge he owes these Blessings to the Divine Good-Will: That he has but a subordinate and dependent Right, and is possess'd of them but

but in Trust for the Honour, Interest, and Service of his Soveraign Master, to whom he is accomptable for his Management.

And when a Man considers that God is likewise the Creator of all other Rational, Animate, and Inanimate Natures, and that he upholds their Beings by his constant Aid and Concurrence, as the universal Cause, he will with ease discern, that by his Titles of Creation and Conservation, he has the absolute and plenary Right of a Proprietor in all other Things, as well as in Man himself. That he is the Supream and sole Lord of the Universe without Limitation or Circumscription, and that all his Creatures are wholly his own. What we mean by saying any Thing is one's own, is perhaps better understood by that simple Term, as it happens in many other Instances, than by the most labour'd Definition: A Power to rule and dispose of a thing at one's Pleasure and Discretion, is imply'd essentially in the Notion of Propriety, or results immediately from its Nature.

And therefore tho the inherent Goodness of the Divine Nature inclines him always to do good to Men, and not to treat them

them hardly, or make them miserable; yet however he should dispose of them, they being absolutely and without Restriction his own, they could not justly complain of any Wrong done them. This, I say, had been their Case, had not their Maker accepted to be their Governor, and thereby declar'd he would rule them by Laws as Rational Creatures; by which he has signify'd his Pleasure, that he will not use and dispose of Men as he is their unlimited Lord and Proprietor, but will deal with them as a Magistrate and Judge, and reward and punish them according to their Submission or Disobedience to his Precepts.

From this Relation of God as universal Proprietor of the World, the following Duties evidently arise; That we should acknowledge his Soveraign and unrestrain'd Dominion, as he is the Owner of all Things. That we should acquiesce and remain satisfy'd, however it pleases him to make the Repartition of States and Kingdoms, to canton the World among his Creatures, and confer Dominion, Possessions, and Honour on whom, and in what measure he thinks fit. We should not be uneasy, or look with an envious Eye on others, who are Wealthy, Great, and

and Prosperous, tho we see no Distinction of Parts, Vertue, or Merit, that should entitle them to such Advantages, or ever made it probable they should be so happy and successful: We should sit down contented with the Distribution made by Divine Providence, when we consider that our Maker gives nothing but what is entirely his own; and that therefore we receive no Injury from his Conduct. He has Authority to allot to every Individual what Portion of the good Things of this Life he pleases, and to continue them as long in their Possession as he thinks convenient; and therefore we should not by Fraud or Violence invade the Fences of another's Right.

Tho the Property of Men in respect of God is delegated and precarious, yet in respect of Men it is protected and guarded by the Law of Nature against the Encroachments of Force and Deceit. This Property is originally founded in the Distinction or Individuality of Persons; for every Particular having a Right to his own Life, and it being the Will of God that he should maintain and preserve his Life, he has a just Claim to so much as is necessary to attain this end. And this general Right is sometimes determined by seizing

seizing on that which was not appropriated or enjoy'd before; and that Seizure will give a Man a Title and justify his Possession; for by not dispossessing any other Person, he does no body any Wrong, and is therefore a lawful Owner. And this is the Case of the Planters of any Country that was not inhabited before, or of those who make Settlements on Places, where there is immensely more waste and desolate Territory than will suffice for a few wild and vagrant Natives. Or else Property is determin'd by Consent and Agreement, and the Boundaries set by Compact; which being done, Man by the Law of Nature, is forbidden and restrain'd from taking what is another's without his Consent. On the contrary, it is his Duty to assist and protect his Neighbour against all Oppression and fradulent Encroachments, as far as the Rules of right Reason or the Laws of the Society, of which he is a Member, will bear him out.

Farther, if we consider that God is the sole Author of our Existence, and that with his constant and powerful Concurrence, as a continu'd efficient Cause, he upholds our needy and dependent Being; that he bestows upon us out of his free and undeserv'd Bounty, all the Necessaries,

ries, Conveniencies, and Enjoyments of Life; that he commiferates our Calamities, relieves our Wants, prevents our Fears, fupports our Hopes, and removes or mitigates our Pain and Trouble; the Inference will be unavoidable, that we fhould efteem and love him as our Father, our Patron, our Protector, and greateft Benefactor: That we fhould admire and praife him for his Goodnefs, his gracious Difpofition and Benevolence, and make all poffible Returns that become a grateful Mind to one that has done us fo much Good; to whom we are indebted for whatever we poffefs, and on whom we depend for all Things that we hope to enjoy. That we fhould thankfully acknowledge him as the Author of our flourifhing and profperous Condition, and of all the Succeffes and happy Events that have attended our Induftry and Endeavours, and fhould employ our Power and Plenty, and Intereft among Men, for the Honour and Service of our great Benefactor. That we fhould rely on his gracious Nature and readinefs to do us good, even under the fevereft Difpenfations of his Providence; invoke him in Danger, truft him in Diftrefs, and in the midft of Trouble and Calamity caft upon him the Burden of our Sorrow; and by the unfhaken shaken Belief of his Compassion and Goodness, and that he is able and willing to relieve those that confide in him, as well as from our Experience of his merciful Nature and paternal Pity, we should make him our Refuge and the Foundation of our Hope.

The Author of Nature has implanted in our Minds so great a disposition to be grateful, and the Judgment and Determinations of Reason are so full and positive about it, that nothing which we are oblig'd to perform appears so clear, easy and reasonable a Duty. Hence all Mankind in all Ages have condemn'd and detested Ingratitude, as the most unnatural, most unbecoming, and odious Crime [*].

Hence some have made it a Question, whether a Man does not lie under a Moral Obligation to esteem, love, and praise a Benefactor, without respect to any Law or Precept concerning it; and if it were possible for me to conceive how there can be any Duty which does not result from

---

[*] Quæ natio, non Comitatem non benignitatem, non gratum animum, Beneficiique memorem non diligit ? Quæ superbos, quæ maleficos quæ crudeles, quæ ingratos non aspernatur, non odit ? ---- *Cic. de Leg.*

some Command of a Governor who enjoins it, or that any Guilt can be contracted without Disobedience to some Rule prescrib'd, I think Gratitude would appear a Vertue, and Unthankfulness a Crime in a conspicuous manner. But since it is so just, so natural, and so laudable a thing to be thankful for good Offices done, and Favours receiv'd; upon this account we may justly assert, that it is one of the clearest and most early Dictates of Reason; whence it appears to be a plain Declaration of the Mind and Will of God; and therefore Gratitude is a most evident Law of Nature.

Of Moral Obligations respecting our selves.

I Come now to the Duties which respect our selves, and shall establish them on their natural Foundations. The Idea of Creator unavoidably implies the Notion of Goodness and Benevolence to his Creatures; and therefore when we consider him as such, that is, as one that wishes well to Mankind, intends good to them, and desires their Happiness, we may infer with the clearest Evidence, that it is his Will that Man ought to do good to himself, and to use all Means in his Power

Laws *of* Nature. 385

Power to promote his own Felicity. This Conclusion is with some a Self-evident Principle, and they look on it as unnecessary to prove so clear a Proposition, *That all Men should do what is best for themselves.* But I have demonstrated this to be a Moral Obligation, that it may plainly appear that Piety and Happiness are not only inseparable, but that in Effect they are the same Thing, and distinguish'd only by various Modes of Conception and a different Appellation. The assertion of the Schools, that *Bonum Morale fundatur in Bono Convenientiæ,* that Moral Duty is founded in Convenience, that is, in a Physical Good, is very right, if understood in the Sense that I have given : That is, when a Man discerns that any thing is advantageous and beneficial to him, that it conduces to the Health of his Body and the Quiet of his Mind, to his Improvement in Knowledge, or the Acquisition of the good Things of this Life, he may thence discover it is the Will of God he should endeavour to attain it by all warrantable Means; and therefore what was his Interest before, now becomes his Duty. This is so evident that I shall hereafter take this Proposition as granted, *That it is the Will of God that Man should desire and pursue every thing beneficial to himself, and conducive to his*

C c *Hap-*

Happiness; and without repeating it often, I shall use this as a Principle of my following Conclusions, and whenever I have shown that any thing is commodious and promotes his Felicity, I shall take it as allow'd, that Man is under a Moral Obligation to pursue it.

THE highest Interest and first Duty of Man, that respects himself, is to discern and make choice of the true final Object of his Happiness, which can be no other than the Supream Being; who, to speak in conformity to the Manner of Human Conception, design'd and intended himself as the ultimate End of Man; and accordingly dignify'd his Mind with Capacities to know, chuse, love, and enjoy his Maker, whence his perfect Felicity would effectually result. It is a plain manifestation of the Will of the Creator, that his Creature should act in Conformity and Agreement to the Principles implanted in his Constitution, and pursue the Purposes for which he gave him suitable Powers and Dispositions. That Man should behave himself as becomes a reasonable Being, that he should exercise his Faculties on their most excellent and proper Objects, and contemplate, admire, love and adore the Supream Efficient and final Cause of all Things.

Things. That all his Defires, Aims and Endeavours fhould in a due Subordination be directed to his Honour and Service; and that the Chain and Connexion of inferior and fuperior Ends fhould be kept unbroken, and never terminate till they reach the higheft, that is, the bleft Creator. That he fhould not debafe the Dignity of his Nature, and proftitute his elevated Capacity, by forming any mean Defigns and Schemes of Life unbecoming and unworthy of a Being endow'd with Thought, Reafon, and a Self-determining Principle, created and qualify'd to make his Divine Author his chief Felicity; for that would be to rob God of his Honour, by feparating his Creature from that dependance and fubferviency to himfelf, in which he has plac'd him, and as much as in Man lies to difappoint him of his Defign in Creation.

And it is farther evident, that Man fhould own and chufe the Author of his Being as his chief and ultimate End from this Confideration, That the Felicity and utmoft Perfection of his Nature confifts in this Choice. The fupream Being only has Goodnefs fuitable and adequate to the Faculties of an intelligent Nature, commenfurate to his wideft Capacities and moft most extensive Desires, always present and at hand, and lasting and durable as his Being: In short, since the Divine Being only is able and willing to succour and support him, to prevent his Dangers, relieve him in Distress, supply his Wants, and raise his Nature to a State of Perfection, he only can be the final Object and the supream Good, the Possession of which must be his Happiness.

And we are in possession of this supream Good when our Faculties bear a perfect Conformity to his Will, and we attain the highest Similitude to the Divine Nature that our own can bear; which, tho unattainable here, is the reasonable and delighful Expectation of good Men in a Future State of Life; for when we have all the Knowledge of the Creator which our Understandings are capable of receiving, we enjoy the Beatifick Vision; and when we love him with all the Powers of the Soul, we are in Heaven, or a State of Perfection. From the Operations of our Faculties about their supream Good, results that strong, serene, and pure Pleasure, that ineffable Complacency and Fullness of Joy, which produce consummate Bliss: and this is what we mean by the Possession or Fruition of the Supream Being.

And

Laws of Nature.

And indeed the sincere and solid Satisfaction, the intellectual, divine, and spiritual Delights, which proceed from the Practice of Vertue, from a conscioufnefs of having done well, and the self-applauding Reflection, which all good Men experience, and some excellent and elevated Minds more fully and constantly perceive, will convince the Possessors, that were those Pleasures perfect and without interruption, they would want nothing to make their Happinefs compleat. Tho I have before demonstrated, that God is the ultimate End of Man from the Design he had in creating him, which could be only to please himself; and have now made the same Conclusion evident, by shewing, that he is the supream Good, the Attainment of which can only constitute our Felicity; yet these are in effect the same thing, and differ only in the Mode of Conception: For the Creator's Design in making Man is accomplish'd, when to his Honour he manifests his Power, Wisdom, and Goodnefs in the higheft Degree of which our Being is receptive, in which the Happinefs of Man does likewife confift. So that the Glory of the Divine Attributes exhibited in the Perfection and Felicity of Human Nature, muft be the supream Good and principal End of Man.

There was a strange variety of Opinions in the ancient Schools of the *Greek* Philosophers about the *Summum Bonum*, or supream Good. Some contended with Vehemence, that nothing could be esteem'd Good but what was vertuous; and others warmly disputed for the Goodness of other Things, as Health, Honour, and Possessions. *Cicero*, as Moderator, endeavours to accommodate the Matter, and reconcile the Parties, by stating the Controversy in this manner: Those, *says he*, who maintain nothing is Good but Vertue, take Goodness in a Moral Sense, and so their Notion is right; and those who contend for the Goodness of other Things are to be understood in a Physical Sense, as meaning, that such Things are convenient, useful, or advantageous to Mankind; and thus, *says he*, their Controversies are more about Words than Things. Another Sect asserted, that Pleasure was the chief Good, which they plac'd in the Indolence of the Body, and Tranquility of the Mind. But it is certain that human Felicity cannot consist in Inaction, otherwise Men in a Swoon, a deep Sleep, or a senselefs Lethargy, would be extreamly happy. But had their Assertion been, that Pleasure was the supream Good, and had they made that

that Pleasure arise or result from consummate Piety and Vertue, and the highest Operations of the Mind endow'd with perfect Faculties, they had given a good Account of the Happiness of Man.

Having thus clearly shewn, that God is the chief Good and ultimate End of Man; it does as clearly follow, that Man should acknowledge and chuse him as such. That we should prefer him in our Esteem and Desire above all other Things. That we should make him the Object of our most ardent, sincere, and exalted Love. Think on him with that Delight and Complacency with which Men contemplate the Things in which they place their Happiness; maintain a sacred Commerce and Correspondence with him; and by imitating his Perfections, strive to resemble him; that from a Similitude of Natures he may appear most amiable to us, and we agreeable and pleasing to him.

When the Understanding directs and approves, and the Will is fix'd and determin'd in the Choice of the Divine Being, as the *summum Bonum* and the final Object of our Happiness; when all the inferior Powers of the Soul, the Passions,

Appetites, and the Senses, are mov'd and govern'd by the superior commanding Faculties, in conformity to the Divine Precepts dictated by right Reason: When this end, I say, is principally and prevalently intended in all our Designs, Aims and Endeavours, and constantly and regularly pursu'd through the whole Series of onr Actions, in all the Stages and Schemes of Life, there arises in the Mind such inexpressible Satisfaction and Divine Pleasure, as are far better felt by the Possessor, than express'd by the most lively Representation of Words. The Tranquility and Delight that flow from the Harmony and moral Rectitude of the Faculties, and pious Emotions of the Mind, are like the Pleasure and Alacrity which are felt from a Sense of Life, Health, Strength and Vigor, resulting from the Abundance and Vivacity of the Spirits in a happy Constitution of Body. When a Man is conscious that he pleases the Author of his Being, he cannot fail of being pleas'd with himself: when he is sure that he esteems, desires and seeks the Possession of him as the final Object of his Felicity, that he does in a prevalent degree direct his Actions to this End, and has therefore a reasonable Expectation of acquiring at last the enjoyment of his Wishes; when, I say, a Man

is

Laws of Nature. 393

is in such Circumstances, he must needs be at ease, and feel himself very happy. And thus it appears that Religion is our greatest Interest, and that Vertue in this Sense is its own Reward: For what greater Recompence for his good Actions can a Man ask or receive, than the Perfection of his Nature? And in what is That to be found, but in the most religious Regularity of his Faculties, and their purest and most exalted Operations towards the Divine Object of our Happiness.

All the Goodness of Human Nature consists in its being refer'd and becoming subservient to this great End; and when we cut off our Relation to the Creator as the final Object of our Felicity, we destroy all that is valuable in our Being, and while other Creatures conspire in constant Harmony to attain the Ends for which their Natures are fitted and design'd, and by no deviation, reluctance, or seditious opposition, dissolve the Union or disturb the Tranquility of the Universe, degenerate Man only opposes the Intention of his Creator, and breaks the Connexion and Order of Things. Besides, by making himself a deform'd and irregular Part, he grows the Dishonour and Reproach of the Creation, and by crossing the Design of his Existence, he annihi-

annihilates the ufefulnefs of his Being; and becoming an impertinent and infignificant Creature, he is in a moral and fpiritual Senfe look'd on as deceas'd, and is number'd among the Dead. And is it not more defirable to lie mould'ring and corrupting in the Grave, than to carry about a putred Mind inter'd in a living Body?

Nor do Men by not chufing the Supream Being for their final Good, make themfelves only ufelefs Parts, exorbitant and lifelefs Excrefcences of the World, but they likewife become hurtful and pernicious; if they are not for God they are againft him, if they are not his Friends they are his Enemies; and if they do not promote the End and Purpofe of their Exiftence, of neceffity they muft thwart and oppofe it. And what a Figure muft a Being make in the Creation, that declares himfelf an Enemy to his Maker, refifts and traverfes his Defigns, and as much as in him lies difturbs the Peace and fubverts the Foundations of the Divine Government? And is it not eafy to fee that fuch Enormities are forbidden by the Dictates and Laws of right Reafon; and that to avoid them we are oblig'd to efteem, love, and feek the Enjoyment of our Maker as our final Felicity.

MEN

Men are therefore oblig'd to direct all their Aims and Endeavours to this Mark, and to propose no Scheme of Life that does not maintain a due Connexion of each inferior with the supream End.

He that stops short in his Esteem and Love, destroys his subordination and dependance on his Author, as his soveraign Good and Happiness; deposes his Lord and Benefactor, and advances some created Thing, which he values more, and loves better, to his Throne and Dignity; he either idolizes his own Qualifications, or deifies his Gold, or pays divine Adoration to the Pleasures of Sense.

As God is the first efficient Cause from whence proceed all the Powers and operative Principles, which are propagated through the long Series of second and subaltern Causes; so likewise he is of necessity the final Object, to which, after all their long Circulation and Variety of Motion and Mutation, they must return: And as in a Physical manner all the Beings of the animate and inanimate World, all Energy and active Springs conspire to promote this purpose; so the noble Principle of Thought, the Power of Perception and Self-determinamination in Man, fhould be fubfervient and directed to the fame End. If our Actions therefore do not flow from a pious Principle of Obedience to the Divine Laws, and are not alfo aim'd and directed to him as our chief Good and ultimate End, let the Matter of them be ever fo fpecious and illuftrious, they cannot pretend to any Moral Goodnefs, as wanting their relation to the chief End, which is the vital and effential Principle that quickens and informs them, and whence they are conftituted Moral and Religious.

AND fuppofing the regular Chain and beautiful Connexion of final Caufes is interrupted, before it reaches our Divine Author as the ultimate End, not only no Piety, Vertue or Goodnefs will be found in thofe Actions, but on the contrary, they will be morally Evil, being irregular and repugnant to the Rules and Dictates of right Reafon. If my Neighbour careffes me with great Expreffions of Kindnefs, does me good Offices, and conftantly heaps new Favours upon me, but in the mean time has only his own Intereft in view, and intends no good to me, but in the end to make me ufeful to himfelf, can he be accounted my Friend or efteem'd my Benefactor? In like manner if a Man by

his

his Actions, which are denominated religious or virtuous only in respect of their Matter, designs not in the first place the Honour of his Maker and the Enjoyment of him as his final Happiness, but principally seeks some inferior End, whether Riches, Honour, or the Pleasures of Sense, can such a Person be look'd on as a good Man, and sincerely devoted to the Service of his Creator?

Those celebrated Heroes and Leaders of Armies, who in their great Undertakings chiefly aim at Fame, Popularity, Possessions or Dominion, and do not carry their Design farther, that is, to advance the Honour and Service of their Divine Soveraign, acquire no Trophies or Laurels but what are the ignominious Marks of their Immorality and want of Piety; for while impell'd by an irregular Principle they defend their Country against the Violence and Oppression of ambitious Neighbours, and so far merit the Applauses of the People, they themselves break in upon the Frontier of Religion, and encroach on the Rights and Prerogatives of Heaven.

We admire a great Philosopher that is able to solve the most difficult and abstruse

Appearances, and with unwearied Application has fearch'd and laid open all the Springs of Motion, and form'd an admirable Syftem of Natural Science; we applaud the Poet, who entertains and inftructs the World with good Senfe and beautiful Expreffion, recreates the Reader with an Effufion of Wit and Humour, and fhews the greateft regard to Decency and Vertue, arifing from his true Tafte and right Judgment of Men and Things: Nor do we lefs commend the Moralift, who teaches the People the unwritten Precepts of Religion and the Obligation of natural Duties, with clear Arguments and perfuafive Eloquence; yet if either of thefe chiefly aim at Efteem, Honour, and the Reputation of a Man of great Genius, refin'd Parts, and uncommon Erudition, he only makes his court to himfelf and complements his own Perfections; and tho the Matter of his Actions be ever fo fhining and amiable, yet being perverted from their right End, and principally intended to footh his own Vanity, they become evil and irreligious. I have enlarg'd on this Subject in the ESSAY upon FALSE VERTUE, to which I refer the Reader, and fhould not repeat any thing here, did not the Ground-work and all the Strength that fupports our Religion and Happinefs
                          *
                                            rely

rely on the right Choice of our ultimate End. This is the first true and necessary Step in our way to Blessedness; and if this is not taken right, all our Motions, Designs, and Schemes of Life will not only be an impertinent Train of Errors; but not having our chief End in view, whatever we do in the whole Course of our Actions, we shall go backward and obstruct and oppose our Duty and Interest.

Besides, if we aspire after the greatest Accomplishment of our Being, which is but another Expression for our consummate Felicity, we shall see our selves oblig'd to contemplate the Divine Nature, and to imitate his Perfections. For since the Notion of a God implies a Possession of all possible Perfection, the nearer we approach to him, and the greater our Resemblance of him is, the more exalted must be our Minds; and when our Conformity to his Nature is as full and great as our Faculties are capable of receiving, they have then attain'd their greatest Perfection. Hence the imitation of the Divine Purity, Justice, Mercy, Compassion, Forgiveness, Patience, and Beneficence, which tend to form in us a God-like Temper of Mind, conduces directly to our compleat Happiness; and hence the Moral Obligations

tions to perform thofe Duties is very manifeft.

And as our Similitude to the Supream Being in the Exercife of Vertue, raifes and ennobles our Nature, fo it is a neceffary Means to qualify us for the Fruition of him, that is, of becoming Happy; for Love being the Faculty by which we enjoy any Object, if our Natures are wicked and flagitious, they are oppofite and unlike to that of the Deity: And fince the effential Idea of Felicity confifts in the Delight and Complacency that refults from the pureft and ftrongeft Operations of Love to our Maker, and the reciprocal Senfe of his Benevolence to us, no Man without a Likenefs and Conformity to the Divine Being can poffibly be happy; and thus too the Obligation of the Moral Duties abovemention'd is very evident.

This Pofition being fully demonftrated, That the Fruition of God by the moft perfect Operations of the Mind, the cleareft Knowledge, the higheft Admiration, and moft intenfe Love, whence Extafies of Joy and Divine Pleafure will conftantly flow, is the chief End of Man; it follows with the plaineft Evidence, that Man fhould delight himfelf in the Contemplation

tion of this Object of his Happiness, and pursue it with the most vehement Desire, and ardent Affection. When any Man, determin'd by an erroneous Understanding and distemper'd Inclinations, makes some inferior Good, either Riches or Dominion, Fame or Pleasure, his superior and prevalent Choice, how amiable does the Idea appear in his Imagination? How eagerly, how constantly, and with how much Satisfaction does he revolve it in his Mind? It attends him by Day, accompanies him to his Bed, and if waking, entertains him by Night; it is the last Object of his Evening and the first of his Morning Thoughts. And if he approaches to a nearer View, and has reason to believe he shall, in a short time, possess his Wishes; how charming is the Prospect? How chearful is his Temper, and how delightful are his Hopes? In like manner, when a Man has chosen the Author of his Being for his final Felicity, he ought to value, admire, and love him with all the Powers of his Soul. To think on him constantly, desire him above all Things, applaud, congratulate, and please himself with frequent Reflections on his happy Choice; and from the reasonable Prospect of attaining his Happiness, anticipate the Possession by his joyful Expectation.

As the chufing our Maker for our chief Good, directly and immediately regards our Perfection and Happinefs, fo the inferior Duties which refpect our felves plainly promote the fame End, as they procure the Health of our Bodies, as they have an apparent tendency to make us eafy in our Fortunes, and are conducive to the Content and Satisfaction of the Mind.

Temperance and Sobriety in the Ufe of the Pleafures of Senfe, greatly contribute to the Health and Indolence of the Body, and to keep it in an active and vigorous Conftitution; and by preventing many dangerous and fatal Diftempers, they prolong Life, as they make it eafy. While the contrary Vices, Riot, Luxury, and immoderate Gratifications of voluptuous Defires, diffipate and exhauft the Spirits, enfeeble the Body, and fhorten the Days of the inconfiderate Libertine; who not only brings upon himfelf many wafting Diftempers and Death it felf, but propagates and conveys his Difeafes to his Children, and fettles a fad Inheritance of Pain and Sorrow on his miferable Pofterity. From a right Judgment, that the Vertues above-nam'd greatly conduce to our Health and Eafe, *Epicurus*, who plac'd all Happinefs

Laws of Nature. 403

nefs in the Pleafures of Senfe, prefcrib'd a moderate and reftrain'd ufe of them, as neceffary to the attainment of that End.

Besides, Sobriety and Temperance promote our Happinefs, by keeping the Spirits lively, the Brain clear, the Imagination free and undifturb'd, by which means the Mind has always apt Inftruments for its operations; while Excefs in eating, drinking, and other Delights of Senfe, weaken, opprefs, and dull the Spirits, and fo cloud the Head with Fumes, or fill it with Pain, that the Exercife of our intellectual Faculties is almoft fufpended; by which means we are for that Seafon degraded and funk to the low Rank of meer Animals, and lofe the Dignity, by lofing the ufefulnefs of intelligent Beings: And if all thofe Breaks and Chafms of Life, which in this Senfe are occafion'd by the Moral Errors of Men, were fum'd up, by a juft Calculation it would appear that their Vices have robb'd them of more Hours than they now imagine.

Moreover, their exceffive Purfuits of voluptuous Entertainments defraud them of a great deal of Time, which might have been happily employ'd in their ufeful Callings; or if they are Men of Leifure

D d 2

sure and plentiful Fortunes, in improving and adorning their Underſtanding with variety of Knowledge, or managing their Eſtates, or ſerving their Country, and in ſhort, in doing much good to themſelves and others.

These Vertues, together with Frugality and Induſtry, greatly contribute to the Eaſe and Well-being of Men, in procuring or preſerving their Poſſeſſions by reſtraining their Appetites, and bounding their Pleaſures; whilſt by a prudent Management they ſave, and by good Oeconomy augment their Subſtance, on which their own Comfort and the Proſperity of their Families ſo much depend. But on the other hand, how does Luxury and a vicious Courſe of Life promote the contrary Ends? How ſoon does it ruin a ſmall Eſtate, and what Havock does it make in the moſt plentiful ? And by this Waſte and Diſſipation of their Treaſure, how uneaſy does it make them in their Fortune? How often are they pinch'd and ſtreighten'd in their Circumſtances, and compell'd to deſcend to mean and ſordid, and ſometimes evil Practices, to ſupport their Expence, and ſupply the Demands of their tyrannical Appetites? Hence their diſconſolate Families are impoveriſh'd, their

their Children depriv'd of Education and Maintenance, and left to struggle with Want and Misery.

That the Moderation and Government of the Passions conduces to the Felicity of Human Nature, has been allow'd by all the *Pagan* Philosophers, who have taught Morality, and search'd after the *Summum Bonum*, or Happiness of Mankind; and for this they have left many excellent Precepts. This Duty is indeed absolutely necessary to the Peace and Tranquility of the Mind, without which it is impossible to be happy. If violent and exorbitant Emotions, that have shook off the Yoke of the superior Faculties, and are no longer obedient to the Dictates of Reason, are convenient, useful, or delightful, then Storms and Tempests are more desirable than fair Weather; and Uproar, Confusion and Distraction, should be prefer'd to Peace, Beauty and Order. If unbridled Anger and brutal Rage do not interrupt our Happiness and abate the Perfection of our Nature, then a Fever is no Disease of the Body, nor a Phrensy of the Mind. If Pride, Self-admiration, Haughtiness, and an insolent Contempt of others, are desirable Qualities, then to be always disappointed of our End, and to feel the constant

constant Resentments of real or imaginary Affronts, Neglect and Injuries, is to be very happy. Are Envy, Hatred, and a malicious revengeful Temper to be fed and cherish'd, as not only unhurtful, but conducive to our Good ? Then to be stung to the Heart, to be torn to pieces, and devour'd with inward Cares, anxious Designs and self-tormenting Thoughts, has been unjustly represented as a miserable Condition. If any Man can possibly believe these inordinate Passions are not very painful and uneasy to the Mind, it must be one who never felt their lawless Power. Whoever has experienc'd their Dominion will readily complain, that he has extreamly suffer'd, and been very ill us'd by these unreasonable and cruel Masters. Whence it appears, that in order to Happiness, we are under no less Obligations to regulate our Passions, than to restrain our Appetites.

Besides, licentious and ungovern'd Passions are very prejudicial to the Mind, by clouding the Understanding, perverting the Judgment, and putting a wrong Biass on the Will : They raise such thick Mists and *Egyptian* Fogs before the Eyes of our intellectual Guide, that it constantly loses its way, and becomes guilty of the great-

greatest Errors. These heady Perturbations fill the Mind with Tumult and Uproar, assault with Violence the Tribunal of Reason, compel it to reverse the Judgments and Determinations made in cool Blood, and pronounce new Decrees in favour of the contrary Side. During this Disorder and Insurrection of the Passions, the Mind holds unsteadily the Reins of Government, till at last her Authority is insulted and suspended; and in this Interregnum, for so this Interval of Confusion may be stil'd, the Dictates and Operations of the superior Faculties being either suppress'd or disregarded, the Man dishonours and vilifies the Dignity of his Nature, and acts like the Beasts of the Field from an unreasonable Principle, and a brutal Instinct. And if the Violence of Passion is not arriv'd at so great a Degree, as quite to subvert the Exercise of Reason, yet in whatever Measure it gains upon us, it will in proportion disable the Understanding, and misguide the Judgment, whence our Actions will become irregular: Anger, Resentment, and Love rais'd to excess, by being an over-match for the Prudence and Discretion even of wise Men, often make them act below the Superiority and Gravity of their Character, and bring them down to the ordinary Rank and Level of Mankind.

That exorbitant and unruly Emotions of the Mind pervert the Judgment, and cause Disorder and Confusion in the Operations of the upper Faculties, is plain from hence, That when the Tide subsides and the Storm is blown over, our Minds in this calm and sedate Season condemn and rescind the Decisions, which, during the Rebellion of the turbulent Passions, they were mov'd by Violence and Constraint to make.

Of Moral Obligations *in respect to our Neighbour.*

As to the Duties incumbent on Man in his Relative Capacities, their Moral Obligation comes now to be demonstrated. We cannot contemplate the Author of our Being, but we must conceive him full of Good-Will, and desirous of the Welfare of Mankind; and he that makes this Reflection will unavoidably discern, that it is the Will of his Maker that he should contribute to the Good of others, and promote their Happiness. And will further see himself oblig'd to this, if he considers, that because God wishes well to Men, and heaps Blessings and Favours upon them, he ought

Laws of Nature.

ought to do the same; since he cannot reach the Perfection of his Nature, in which consists his Felicity, except he imitates the supream Being, as before-mention'd. Hence it will appear, that the Government of Families is of Divine Institution, that Parents ought to rule their Children, and Masters their Servants; that they ought to instruct their Understandings, and adorn them with Divine and Human Knowledge; to direct their Wills in their Choice, and restrain their immoderate Appetites; to teach them the Government of their Passions, and give them all the Advantages of good Education.

Man's Title to this Government arises from his imperfect Propriety in his Children, and from his Qualifications for Government, and theirs for Obedience, as well as from his Obligation to exercise this Authority, which he cannot omit without Guilt, proceeds from the signification of the Will of God, by placing Man in such Circumstances and endowing him with such Capacities; as likewise, by making it a necessary Means to promote the Happiness of Mankind, that Parents should rule, instruct, and provide for their Families. And the like may be said of Masters in respect of their Servants, tho their Propriety in these is in a lower Degree. The

The Order of this Discourse requires, that I should now enter upon the Moral Obligations that Men are under, consider'd as Members of a Civil Society, and make those Duties appear which Soveraigns owe to Subjects, Subjects to Soveraigns, or one Subject to another; but I have reserv'd the two first for a distinct Dissertation, and shall only in this place insist on the last.

Of Relative Duties *from one Subject to another.*

THERE are many Duties from one Member of a Society to another, which do not result from Human Laws, but flow immediately from the Fountain of Morality, the Light of Reason.

Of these I mention'd several in the beginning of this Discourse, where I asserted, that *de facto* there were Divine Laws antecedent to all human Authority, and acknowledg'd as such by all Nations of the World; and from their Conformity to these Laws, many Qualities or Habits derive their Moral Goodness, for Instance, Humanity, Candor, Benevolence, Integrity, and Faithfulness, of which the Civil Magistrate giftrare is no Judge. I shall now endeavour to demonstrate the Natural Obligation we lie under to exercise these and the like Vertues.

One Neighbour is bound by the Dictates of Reason, to pity the Sufferings of another and to mitigate his Sorrow, to be touch'd by his Misfortunes, and rejoice at his Prosperity and Success. It is his Duty to supply his Neighbour's Wants and Necessities, to acquaint him with his Danger, and give him Assistance to prevent it; to instruct him, if Ignorant, of what relates to his Happiness, dissuade him from a vicious, idle, or pernicious Course of Life, and excite him with convincing Reasons and important Persuasions to embrace the Ways of Religion and Vertue. It is his Duty to do him good Offices, to express Affection, Beneficence, and Generosity; to forgive Unkindness, Affronts, and Injuries, upon the Submission and Entreaty of the Offender; to avoid Envy, Malice, and Revenge; to love his Neighbour as himself, and an Enemy too, as far as to endeavour to make him a Convert, and promote his Happiness. All these Precepts are the Dictates of Right Reason, and they are deduc'd from this Maxim, That every Man ought to do to another, as he would be be done by in the like Circumstances. Can a hard-hearted and cruel Person, who is not touch'd with the Sufferings and Calamities of another, but shuts up the Bowels of Tenderness and Compassion to his Brother in want and nakedness, with reason expect, that if by the Vicissitude of Human Affairs he himself should be brought to the like Extremities, that his Neighbours should express their Commiseration of his Calamity, be troubled for his Misfortunes, and administer Comfort and Supplies to his Necessities? Can any Man reduc'd to a low Condition, with reason, complain of Wrong and Violence, who when in Power and Plenty, oppress'd his Inferiors, trampled on their Rights, wrested from them their Goods, and with an iron avaricious Hand griped the Widow and the Fatherless? Can he expect to be forgiven, who is himself deaf and inexorable, and will never pardon? Can he who delights in Censoriousness and Detraction, in justice hope that his Honour and good Name should be guarded by others? This Axiom, that every Man should so use another as he would be us'd himself, is allow'd by general Consent to be a Rule of Action that all Men ought to observe. And its Reasonableness or moral Obligation is clearly deduc'd from its

Apti-

Aptitude and Tendency to promote the Welfare and Happiness of Mankind: For if Men behav'd themselves in Conformity to this Precept, they would not only forbear Violence, Oppression, and Defamation, but would assist, comfort, and relieve their Neighbours, and protect the Persons, Estates, Rights, and Reputation of one another; and how far this conduces to the common Good and Felicity of Mankind, need not be express'd.

Thus I imagine I have, with clear and convincing Evidence, demonstrated Morality, and the Distinction between good and evil Actions, according to their Conformity to or Deviations from the Divine Rule of Right Reason.

And from the same Principle, and by the same manner of arguing, the Natural Obligation of other Duties which I have not nam'd, most of which are more minute and remote than those I have mention'd, may be deduc'd. By which means a compleat System of Ethicks would be compil'd, and establish'd on the certain Foundation of Divine Authority; whence Morality and Piety, Vertue and Religion, would appear the same Thing under different Conceptions and Appellations, arising
from

from the same Spring, regulated by the same Divine Will, and respecting the same ultimate End, the Honour of the Supream Being, and the Felicity and Perfection of Human Nature.

SINCE by the natural Dictates of Right Reason it is evident, that the Supream Being is the Governor of Mankind, and rules the World by declar'd Laws; and since Judgment is a necessary Branch of Government, it follows with the clearest Evidence, that God, by being the Governor of Man, becomes his soveraign Judge, and therefore will bring to an Accompt the Creature whom he has made accomptable, and will acquit or condemn, punish or reward him in proportion to his Obedience, or Deviation from the Rule of his Actions.

Now it is very plain, that in this Life God erects no Tribunal for the impartial Distribution of Rewards and Punishments; he, by no solemn Sentence clears the Innocent, or condemns the Criminal, nor consigns them to a State of Happiness or Misery, according to their Demeanor; which I have taken notice of in another Essay.

Laws of Nature.

It has been the Observation and Complaint of many wise and good Men, besides *Job* and *David*, that the impious Contemners of Religion, and Men of an immoral and dissolute Life, not only go unpunish'd in their impudent and enormous Vices, but thrive and prosper in an eminent degree; and after a long Life in Health, Plenty, and Pleasure, go down to the Grave in Peace: While, on the other hand, those who have exprefs'd the sincerest Zeal for Religion, and deserv'd well of their Country by their excellent Examples and constant Course of vertuous and great Actions, have been defam'd, opprefs'd, and expos'd to all the Sufferings and Calamities that the Wit of their Enemies could invent, and their Cruelty inflict. Now to vindicate the Justice of God, the Honour of his Government, his Love to Vertue, and the Purity of his Nature; what can be alledg'd but this, That he has referv'd for another World the great Day of Accompt, when all Men shall appear before his Judgment-Seat, there to be consign'd by an impartial Sentence, to a State of Misery or Happinefs, according to their past Demeanor.

And indeed the Remorse and Trouble that wicked Actions leave in the Mind of the Criminal, as well as the Chearfulness and inward Pleasure that follow the Practice of Vertue, very much facilitate our Belief of a Future Day of Accompt. Men who dishonour and vilify their excellent Nature, by overturning the Government and despising the Divine Authority of Right Reason, and suffer themselves to be led away and rul'd by their animal Instincts and vicious Passions, not only reflect on their Guilt and Pollution with Shame and Dissatisfaction; but more, they are often affrighted with the Apprehension of Divine Displeasure, fill'd with secret Fears and terrible Expectations of Future Punishment. And tho perhaps some few hard and desperate Libertines, by frequent Affronts and Insults offer'd to their Reason, repeated Violations of the Laws of Nature and a long Course of Vice, have, perhaps, fatally succeeded in their Attempts, and in a great measure stifled their inward Light, and suspended the Admonitions of their Reason, yet the generality of Mankind, upon their Commission of great and enormous Crimes, are haunted with an inward Remorse, and a dreadful Prospect of Future Vengeance.

This

Laws of Nature. 417

This is so true, that *Epicurus* and *Lucretius* declare, That to free Men from the terrible Apprehensions of Future Punishments, which were inconsistent with that Ease and Tranquility of Mind they propounded to themselves, they invented their irreligious Scheme of Philosophy.

On the other hand, the Men, who by obeying the Dictates of Natural Light and the Divine Canon of Reason, do Justice and Honour to the Rank and Character of intelligent Creatures, when they reflect on the Rectitude of their Faculties and the Moral Improvements of their Minds, the regular Government of their Passions, and their vertuous Actions, not only feel an inward Satisfaction arising from that review, but likewise cherish a delightful Expectation of a suitable Reward from the just Governor of the World; who, as he has made us accomptable Beings, so at last he will make a distinction between obedient and rebellious Subjects. Hence the wisest and best Men among the Heathens nourish'd in their Minds a comfortable, tho uncertain Hope of a Future State of Happiness, and believ'd, that a good Man had great reason to please himself

E e with

with the Opinion of the Favour of the Gods; and that they would, in the end, assert the Justice of their Government, by appointing a different Issue to a vertuous and wicked Life.

If the universal and righteous Governor of the World must convene all the Nations of his Subjects before him as their supream Judge, to reward the diligent observers of his Laws, and punish those who liv'd in Guilt and Disobedience; then it plainly follows, that there must be a State of Life after this, in which all Degrees and Ranks of Men must be brought upon their Trial.

And if there be a Future State of Life and a Day of Accompt, it will be a clear Dictate of Natural Light, that Mens Minds should be more taken up with the Thoughts of this great Day, and the Consequences of it, than with all the Affairs and Concerns of this World. That Men should either find out some way to annihilate their Beings, or conceal their Crimes, or elude the just and irreversible Sentence of the Supream Judge; or if that cannot be done, to enter upon such a vertuous Course of Life as will alone avail them in such an Hour, and is alone able to secure them from

from Divine Displeasure. If those, who constantly indulge themselves in sensual Pleasures, or the Pursuits of Wealth and Power, and never reflect on a Future State, would deliberate and cast Things together, would lay in one Scale of Reason their present uncertain and transient Enjoyments, and in the other, the immortal State of Pain and Misery, which will be the certain Punishment of their Sin and Folly, they must be infinitely stupid, and their Judgments must be biass'd and overpower'd to Amazement by the violence of their Passions, or disabled and blinded by their vicious Habits, if they cannot in such a Case see where their Safety and Interest lie.

AN
ESSAY
UPON THE
ORIGIN
OF
CIVIL POWER.

AN ESSAY UPON THE ORIGIN OF CIVIL POWER.

WERE Mankind disengag'd from the Obligations and Restraints of Political Government, the World would become a deplorable Seat of Uproar and Confusion; Cruelty and Injustice, Avarice and Ambition set at Liberty, would make the Kingdoms of the Earth

Earth such Scenes of Calamity and Desolation, as would more resemble the Habitations of salvage Beasts, than the Dwellings of Reasonable Beings. As the Lives and Estates of Men in such a Case would be precarious and always lie open to Insults and Rapine from a more powerful Aggressor, so their Minds would continue barbarous and uncultivated, without the Improvements of Science, and the Ornaments of Polite Arts, which are highly beneficial to Mankind. To prevent these Evils and advance the Felicity of Man, the Pleasure of the Supream Being, who wishes the Happiness and prosperous State of his Creatures, is apparent that Men should form Societies and institute Civil Government.

As the Divine Being has made Mankind sociable, and fit for Government, so the Individuals depend so far upon one another for mutual Assistance, and the Supply of each other's Wants, that no Means can be found for their Subsistence without Political Combinations, where Multitudes of Particulars contribute in their several Capacities to the Safety and Happiness of the Whole. If then the wise Creator intended the Preservation and Good of Men, he must likewise intend

tend the necessary Means to acquire that End.

WHENCE it appears that Men are not at Liberty in this Point, but are under the Obligation of the unwritten Divine Law, to institute Civil Communities for their mutual Defence and Concurrence to each other's Benefit. It is true, there is no Divine Command that prescribes any particular Form of Government into which they shall enter; but here they are free and unlimited, and only lie under the general Obligation of doing what is best for themselves; and therefore they are bound to chuse that Species of Government, whether Monarchical, Aristocratical, or Popular, which, according to their Circumstances, they shall judge most advantageous and subservient to the End of Civil Institutions, that is, the Welfare and Prosperity of the whole Society.

THERE have been abundance of warm but unnecessary Disputes about the best Frame of Government; while some argue with great Zeal for an Absolute, Despotick Power, some for limited or divided Soveraignty, and others for a Republican or Democratical Constitution, in opposition to both the others. But this is as if the
Engineers

Engineers should sharply contend for any one Plan or Model of Fortification, as necessary or most convenient for every Town or Place of Defence, let the Disposition or Nature of the Ground be ever so unlike. That Form of Government which may be most useful, and therefore most eligible to some Nations, may be very improper and inconvenient for others, who, in respect of their Situation, their neighbouring Potentates, the Temper of the People, the Extent of their Territories, and their Traffick and Commerce, are in very different Circumstances. For this Reason all Species of Government are lawful; and it is the Duty of Men, if at liberty, to chuse that which is most expedient, if they have Time to deliberate; and to do what they are able, if they are forc'd, as it often happens, to huddle up a Constitution in haste for their immediate Security.

When any Species of Government is chosen and consented to, 'the Divine unwritten Command, that made it the Duty of Men to enter into Societies, will oblige them to pay Obedience to it.

The Divine Being, as the Supream Governor of Mankind, and of all Civil Societies, gives to those Communities, that

that is, to the governing Part, Authority to make Laws for the Subject, which are as By-Laws in respect of the King of Kings; as those of Corporations and Companies are in respect of the soveraign Magistrate of any Nation. The Commission or Charter of the Moderator of the World to human Legislators, by which they are empower'd to make Orders and Rules for the People, is demonstrated from his Precept, reveal'd by the Light of Reason, that Men should form Societies: which cannot be done, unless some or one govern, and the rest are oblig'd to obey; and if there must be Governors, they must be endow'd with Authority to make Laws; for they must be allow'd a sufficient Power to perform their Duty, otherwise they would be oblig'd to do something impossible. This Power they cannot have but from the uncontested Fountain of all Legislative Authority, that is, the supream Monarch of the World; for he being the sole, universal, and absolute Lord and Ruler of Mankind, it is as impossible to have the least governing Power any other way than from his Charter and Commission, as it is for a Constable, a Justice of Peace, or Corporation of Men, to possess any Civil Authority but what is communicated to them from the supream Magistrate of the

the Country. Let us contemplate the Divine Being as a Governor, and all the People of the Earth as his Subjects in the great City of the World, and then confider particular Kingdoms and Soveraign States, as Parts and Members of his unlimited Empire, and we shall presently see that all these Potentates are but his inferior Officers, Delegates, or Vice-roys, and therefore can have no Power but what they derive from their supream Lord and Magistrate. Under this View all Princes and Legislative Powers in this universal Monarchy of the World, are such inferior and subaltern Officers as their own subordinate Ministers of State, Generals, and Lords Deputies are in respect of them. Whence the Demonstration is clear, that earthly Soveraigns being no more than Subjects in this Divine Constitution, can have no legal Authority but what they derive from the supream independent Lawgiver. This Position that appears so very evident, will serve to demonstrate many important Conclusions, and therefore I have discuss'd it the more largely. But tho it will be allow'd, that the Legislative Authority of Potentates is delegated and deriv'd from the Divine Being, yet the Mode of Communication or Conveyance of this Power to earthly Monarchs and Magistrates is sharply disputed. SOME

Origin *of* Civil Power.

Some deduce the Authority of Princes and States from *Adam*'s Paternal Power, which they say contain'd likewise that of a Civil Magistrate; upon which Hypothesis that Soveraignty which at first was only over one Family, as fast as Men multiply'd, extended it self over all, and the eldest Father became sole Monarch of Mankind, and were he still alive must be the absolute Ruler of the whole World, a pretty difficult Province to manage. Upon *Adam*'s decease the Right of Soveraign Power, say they, descended to the next of Blood; and the Patriarchs were the supream Civil Magistrates, as well as the Lords and Masters of their numerous Families; and whatever Power any Prince is now invested with is deriv'd from that of a Father, descending to him by uninterrupted Succession from our first Parent. This Opinion is attended with great and manifest Absurdities, that offer themselves at first sight to Men of Reflection; as for Instance, that it confounds the Notions of the Magistrate's Power with that of a Master of a Family, and that it makes it impossible for any Prince to prove his Title to his Crown; since it is impracticable to deduce the Descent of *Adam*'s Paternal Power upon him, without which
he

he has no legal Authority: And suppoſing he could make good his Claim from that pretended Origin of Dominion, he muſt by that Evidence have a right to the Government of the World, as our firſt Parent had, and all other Rulers would be diveſted of their Power, and be oblig'd to ſurrender their Monarchies to the Heir of *Adam*; Tho it is true, Princes may be at eaſe in the Poſſeſſion of their Thrones, if they are not interrupted till this Heir be produc'd. But notwithſtanding theſe and a long Train of falſe Concluſions will follow from this Principle, which may be ſeen in one of our celebrated Writers, who has fully expos'd this Doctrine; yet it was once ſo much in Faſhion, that Patriarch and Monarch were ſynonymous Appellations, and thoſe who believ'd otherwiſe, were look'd on as diſaffected Subjects, and no Orthodox Chriſtians.

The unwary Perſons, who with great vehemence propagated this Notion of the Origin of Dominion, ſeem'd willing to extend the Power of the Prince to an abſolute and deſpotick Degree, ſuppoſing they ſhould always be able to unſheath the Magiſtrate's Sword, and with that keen Argument effectually confute all their Adverſaries,

versaries, while they were sure to have the Executioner on their side. Many of these express great Reverence to Kings, not as Kings, but as the Heads of their Party, that are ready not only to secure their Rights, but to augment their Power. And that this is the Spring whence their Zeal in maintaining these Principles proceeds, is very plain; for when a Prince fills the Throne that touches their Interests, that is, refuses to be the Vice-gerent of a Faction, and will not employ his Authority as they direct, their celebrated Passive Obedience becomes active Resistance, and Prayers and Tears are turn'd into Preparations of War and open Rebellion; and whenever their Party-Interests are in Danger, we may always expect from them the same uneasiness and opposition; for to do them Justice, I cannot believe they advance the Doctrines that favour Despotick and Arbitrary Power, with any Design of enslaving themselves; but they do it for the Reasons above suggested, that is, that they may share with the Prince his unrestrain'd Authority, and oppress those whom they esteem their Enemies. They would be contented that their Monarch should be as unlimited as the Emperor of the *Turks*, or the great *Mogul*, provided they are his Bashaws and Mandarines, to rule the Provinces, and execute his exorbitant Power; and without this Limitation I believe they are ready to enter their Protestation against absolute Government.

OTHERS make the People the Origin of Civil Authority, and affirm, that each Individual, by giving up into the Hands of one or more Persons, the Power which they have over their own Actions, and that of Self-Defence against an Assailant or Invader, constitutes the Power of the Magistrate; and their Opinion is, that God conveys to Princes and Potentates their Legislative Capacity by this concurrence and union of all private personal Rights; which Collection, say they, produces the Publick Right of Governing. Among the Assertors of this Opinion we find the famous Mr. *Hooker*, in his *Ecclesiastical Polity*. But neither do these rightly account for the Rise of Civil Authority; since Personal and Magistratical are distinct Powers, and the People by this Scheme must be suppos'd to convey to the Magistrate a Power of governing, which, in my Opinion, they never had to give, particularly that of putting a Subject to Death. On the contrary, upon Examination, it will appear that God conveys to the Magistrate all his

Origin *of* Civil Power.

his Authority by his unwritten Charter or Commission, expres'd and manifested by the Light of Reason, that is, the Law of Nature.

If we consider the supream Being as the unlimited Ruler of the World, and the numerous States and Kingdoms of the Earth as the several Branches or integral Parts of his unconfin'd Empire, in the same manner as various Provinces and Cities compose any one of those States and Kingdoms; how can we suppose that a dependent and subordinate Governor can have any Authority in the Divine Monarchy, which includes all human Dominions, but what must be deriv'd from the Head of the Government? Now God, by the Law of Nature, that obliges Men to enter into Societies for their common Good, declares his Will, that the chosen Magistrates of each Society should be endow'd with sufficient Power to discharge their Duty, and procure the Ends of Government; for the Law of Nature that commands the End, enjoins also the necessary Means to attain it. And thus the Commission of the Supream Being to human Magistrates, constituting their Office and investing them with Civil Power to execute that Office, is drawn up, ratify'd, and publifh'd by the Light of Nature with the fame Force and Authority, as if it had been convey'd by Revelation. Let us fuppofe, for farther illuftration, that the Moderator of the World had, by a written pofitive Ordinance in a fupernatural way, reveal'd his Will that all Men fhould combine for their common Safety in publick Communities; that the Magiftrates fhould be empower'd by fuch a meafure of his Royal Authority, as will render them capable of difcharging their Truft, and ruling their Subjects for their Good ; That he left them at liberty to chufe what Form or Species of Government they thought beft; and that they might reftrain by Fundamental Laws and antecedent Covenants, the Power of the Monarch if they confented to that Form of Government, and the Monarch confented to fuch Limitations ; and that when they had chofen their Magiftrate or Magiftrates, he did, as fupream Ruler, declare they fhould be commiffion'd by him as his Royal Deputies and Vice-roys, whom he, their Sovcraign, invefted with fuch a degree of Authority as fhould enable them to procure the Ends of their Government: would it not then appear very plain which way the publick Magiftrate came by his Civil Power? And fince I have demonftrated

Origin *of* Civil Power.

strated all this to be the Will of God declar'd by the Law of Nature and the Exercise of Reason, is not this as Valid and Canonical as if it were written and signify'd by Revelation? When the Freemen of the City of *London* have, by their Suffrages, chosen their Mayor and Aldermen, who, tho subordinate to their Soveraign, are the supream Magistrates in that Corporation, do not those Magistrates derive their governing Power from their Prince's Charter, or the whole Legislative Power, if their Charter has receiv'd that Confirmation, and not from the collected personal Power that each Inhabitant casts upon them? Suppose a King of *Great-Britain* should, by a Royal Grant, authorize the People of each County to elect their Lord-Lieutenant, or Sheriff, and declare what measure of Power they should have when they were chosen; will the People's Election amount to any thing more than a determining of some Branch of the Regal Authority to such particular Persons? And when they are elected, would not the Power they should claim and exercise in each County, flow from the Prince's Grant, and not the People's Nomination? In like manner, if the People of any Country have a Right to elect their supream Magistrates, whether

Princes or States, that Country being but a Part and Branch of God's univerſal Monarchy, when they have nominated and choſen their Magiſtrates, whether Monarchs or Soveraign States, they being no more than inferior and ſubordinate Officers in reſpect of the Divine Being, tho ſupream in reſpect of their own People, or any other earthly Potentate, they muſt receive all their Civil Authority from the chief Magiſtrate, who is God himſelf; and the way by which he conveys it, is his Grant or Commiſſion expreſs'd and ſignify'd by the Light of Nature, and diſcover'd by the Exerciſe of Right Reaſon in the manner before explain'd.

WHEN Men have form'd Civil Societies, which, as has been ſaid, are ſo many Companies and corporate Bodies in the Kingdom or City of the World, whereof God is the unlimited Governor, the Meaſure and Extent of Power with which the Rulers of thoſe Societies are inveſted, is preſcrib'd and aſcertain'd by the Commiſſion granted them by their Soveraign, which is their Warrant to govern, and the Rule of their Subjects Obedience. As the Lord Lieutenant of a Province, or the General of an Army can lawfully exerciſe no more Power than they are warranted and autho-

Origin *of* Civil Power. 437

authoriz'd to do by the Commiſſion of their Soveraigns, no more can thoſe Soveraigns who are under Officers of State in the Divine Monarchy, tho High and Mighty in their own Kingdoms, claim any Juriſdiction, or legally execute any Power but what is contain'd in their Commiſſion.

It is then very evident, that as Miniſters and inferior Magiſtrates, for Inſtance, a Juſtice of Peace or a Lord Lieutenant, cannot bind the Subject to Obedience, by commanding any thing out of his Commiſſion, and much leſs, if againſt the Laws of his Country, which contain the declar'd Will of the chief Magiſtrate; no more can the Commands of Princes oblige their Subjects to compliance in things which are contrary to the Laws of God, the chief Magiſtrate. Nor can they reſtrain the natural Liberty and Power that Men enjoy over their own Actions, if they are not authoriz'd by the declar'd Will of the chief Ruler ſo to do, tho there ſhould not appear in ſuch Commands any contrariety to the Divine Pleaſure; and they are yet more unwarrantable, if they enjoin Things hurtful and prejudicial to the Publick; for ſuch Reſtraints will exceed the Bounds and Meaſures of their Commiſſion; and how the

Subject is oblig'd to demean himself in such Cases shall be afterwards explain'd.

Moral Obligations on Civil Powers.

As the chief Ministers of Kings and Potentates, their Judges and other subordinate Magistrates, are bound to promote the Honour of their Princes; to maintain the Peoples Esteem of their Persons and Zeal for their Government; to discountenance and punish the Turbulent and Seditious, and protect the Loyal and well-dispos'd Subject; so it is the Duty of Potentates, who are Ministers, Judges, and Delegates of State in the Divine Monarchy, to take care of their Master's Honour; to manage with Industry and Fidelity his Interests; to promote and preserve in the Minds of the People, the most honourable Opinion and the highest Veneration of his Person, and the greatest Esteem and Affection to his Government; to discourage and deter profane and flagitious Persons; to suppress and exterminate the Atheist and Blasphemer, the impious Scoffer and petulant Derider of Religion, as the declar'd Enemies of Heaven and contumacious Opposers of Divine Authority. On the other hand,

Origin of Civil Power.

hand, it is their Duty to defend and reward the Good and Vertuous, who reverence and honour their supream Lord, are well affected to his Government, and express a sincere and warm Zeal for his Service.

And this is no more than they themselves expect from those of their Subjects, on whom they confer Posts of Power and Dignity, and whom they intrust with the Administration of Publick Affairs. And when Princes act in this manner, and thereby promote the Felicity and Good of their Subjects, as well as their own, they act in Conformity to the Dictates of Reason, or the Law of Nature.

But more particularly it will hence appear, that Princes and Potentates are oblig'd to take care that their Subjects should adore and worship the Divine Soveraign in publick Assemblies; that they should restrain and punish those that profane his Name by impious Swearing and detestable Execrations; that expose sacred Things and Persons by raillery and ridicule, and by their vicious and profligate Manners dishonour God, and teach others to do the same. What would earthly Potentates think of their immediate Ministers and Officers of State, if they certainly knew that thefe Men did conftantly hear their Royal Perfons revil'd, their Actions expos'd, their Title to their Crowns queftion'd, and their Government affronted, while they patiently conniv'd at fuch enormous Offences? And is it not as unnatural and misbecoming the immediate Servants and Vicegerents of the fupream Being, to fuffer thofe Perfons to efcape with Impunity, who by their diffolute and flagitious Lives, offend againft his Laws with Contumacy and Infolence, defy his Juftice, and by propagating impious Opinions and loofe Manners, declare themfelves Traytors to Heaven and Haters of the Divine Government.

It is further evident that Princes are oblig'd to reftrain and punifh fuch licentious Criminals, becaufe nothing more advances the common Good, and promotes the End of entring into Societies; for as Impiety and Profanenefs deform the Mind, efface the Similitude of the Divine Nature, and fo deftroy the Perfection of our Faculties; fo Vice and Luxury not only bring Difeafes on Mens Bodies, but impoverifh and ruin their Families: And befides their prevailing Power to bring down Judgments upon a People, they have a natural Tendency to deftroy the firmeft

Conſtitutions that the Wiſdom of Man can invent.

It is to be remark'd, that ſince the Obſervance of Vows, Promiſes and Contracts are abſolutely neceſſary for the Preſervation of Societies; that when a Potentate has conſented to any Limitations and Reſtraints in the Exerciſe of his Civil Power, and has bound himſelf by Covenants and Compacts with the People, to govern them according to the Fundamental Laws of the Conſtitution, he cannot without tranſgreſſing the Law of Nature, exceed thoſe Limitations and Boundaries of his Power; and it will be Illegal and Tyrannical in ſuch a Potentate to exerciſe a Juriſdiction of an unlimited Extent, and to make any Encroachments on the Rights and Privileges of the People, which are ſecur'd by ſuch Original and Fundamental Contracts; tho the Caſe is different where the Subjects have conſented and ſubmitted to an arbitrary and unlimited Monarchy.

Of Obedience *due from Subjects.*

THE Law of Nature that obliges Men to form Communities, and conſent to ſome one Species of Government for the common Good and Felicity of the Whole,

Whole, must likewise lay the Subjects under a Moral Obligation to observe the Laws of their Magistrates, whether the Civil Power be lodg'd in the Hands of one or more Persons. For since their mutual Safety and Happiness are promoted by Civil Government, it is for that Reason an evident Law of Nature, that as Subjects they should pay Obedience to it, without which no Community can be supported: They are therefore for their own sakes, and for the general Good, oblig'd to reverence and honour the supream Magistrate; to maintain the Esteem and Credit of his Administration; to yield a chearful Submission to the Laws, and prevent and suppress all publick Disturbance and seditious Attempts.

It is true indeed, if the Orders and Injunctions of God's Vice-gerents are contrary to the Laws of the supream Ruler of the World, it is plain in that Case the Divine Being who is the chief Magistrate must be obey'd, and not his under Officers; for it cannot be imagin'd that he has intrusted any of his Delegates with a Commission to act against himself, and oblige his Subjects to break his establish'd Ordinances, any more than it can be suppos'd that the Civil Magistrate has warranted any

any inferior Officer in the State to compel the People to transgress the declar'd Laws of their Country: And therefore should the Prince enjoin any Thing contrary to the Divine Precepts, he manifestly exceeds the Bounds of his deputed Power, and usurps an Authority to which he has not the least claim; and for this Reason it is an evident Dictate of natural Light, that the Subject has an undoubted Right to exercise a Judgment of private Discretion: When he receives the Commands of the Magistrate, it is his Duty to consider, whether they contradict any previous Command of the supream Ruler, because he is as much oblig'd not to yield Obedience to Commands which are contrary to those of the Divine Being, as he is to submit to them, if the Matter of them is not forbidden by Him: And since the Subject is not bound to obey without Reserve, but on the contrary, must in some Cases refuse Obedience; how is it possible that this can be done if he is not allow'd to reflect, examine, and judge whether the Injunctions of the Magistrate are repugnant or agreeable to the Divine Laws? If an inferior Officer in any human Government, should issue out Orders to those under his Jurisdiction, that contradict the known Statutes of the Land; must

must not the Subject refuse Obedience? If so, he must be allow'd a Judgment of Discretion to weigh, compare, and determine whether they are opposite or suitable to the establish'd Laws of the Chief Magistrate.

In like manner if a Potentate, who is a dependent and subordinate Officer in the Monarchy of the World, in which the Divine Being is supream, should enjoyn any Thing forbidden, or forbid any Thing enjoyn'd by the Soveraign of Mankind, are not the Subjects oblig'd to disobey? And if they are, must they not exercise their private Reason in the Case, and consider whether the Commands of Potentates oppose any Divine antecedent Precept? It is therefore a natural Dictate of Reason, or a Moral Law, that Subjects should deliberate and judge whether the Commands of their Rulers are conformable to the Divine Ordinances, that is, whether the Magistrate exercises his Legislative Power about such Actions as are not already settled and determin'd by Divine Precepts or Prohibitions.

If the Question should be ask'd, whether in those Things where we are left at Liberty by the supream Governor, that is, where

where we are not reftrain'd by any Divine Prohibition or Command, the Civil Magiftrate has Power to oblige his Subjects to Obedience? I anfwer, that the Magiftrate in Things indifferent and undetermin'd by any particular pofitive Law of God, is by the general Law of Nature confin'd and bound to command nothing but what is conducive to the Ends of Government. The merciful and indulgent Lawgiver of Mankind cannot be fuppos'd to have conftituted Vice-roys and Deputies to rule any particular Provinces or Cities within his Dominions, for other Purpofes than to carry on his Defign in Creation, which is his own Honour and the Felicity of his Subjects; and all human Subaltern Officers under the fupream Moderator of the Univerfe, are oblig'd to make fuch Laws only as are conducive to this End; they are bound to deliberate and chufe out of a great Variety the fitteft Means for the Ends of Government, and their Duty is to reject what is infignificant, and much more what is inconvenient or hurtful. When the Rulers have found out what is ufeful and proper to be the Matter of a Law, the general Precept of Nature becomes particular, and obliges them to enact it by their Authority, as much as if it had been exprefly commanded.

manded. But if from Error of Judgment, Negligence, or an ill Principle, they issue forth such Commands as are useless or prejudicial, and much more if destructive of the Ends of Civil Society, it is impossible that these Commands, which exceed the Bounds of their Commission, should operate by any binding Virtue. They are indeed the Commands of a publick Magistrate, but one acting without Warrant and beyond his delegated Power; and so not being enliven'd and inform'd by legal Authority, they have no more force of themselves than the Precepts of private Persons: And were there no other Law of Nature supervening to determine the Subject to submit, he is, as to the illegal Orders of the Magistrate, at his Liberty to obey or refuse Obedience; for where there is no Authority to command, no Obedience can be due. But where the Magistrate shall enjoin Things only impertinent or hurtful, but not in a degree that threatens Ruin to the Constitution, then the Law of Reason that directs us to preserve Peace and Union in Civil Societies, and to bear a less Suffering for the preventing of a greater, and always to decline that which will bring more Evil than Good, will oblige us to Submission.

The Subject therefore for the publick Good and Tranquility muſt bear Hardſhips with Patience, and acquieſce in Male-Adminiſtration, unleſs the Conſtitution of the Community, and the univerſal Welfare of the People are expos'd to apparent Danger. But in Caſe the Civil Magiſtrate ſhall, in a notorious degree, violate his ſolemn Compact, by which he conſented to be reſtrain'd and limited in the Execution of his Power; if he breaks in upon the Rights and Liberties of the People by violent Encroachments, and ſhakes the eſſential Foundations of the State, the Subject then is no longer oblig'd to ſubmit, becauſe now his Patience and Compliance will be more hurtful than beneficial, and will evidently contribute to the Deſtruction of the Community, which he is bound to preſerve and not betray. And even in Abſolute and Deſpotick Monarchies, tho the Soveraign is not reſtrain'd or check'd by any Contract or Stipulation with the People, yet is he under the Limitations preſcrib'd by the Law of Nature, which are altogether as obligatory, not to exerciſe his Authority for the Detriment and Ruin, but for the Good and Benefit of the Society. And where his Commands apparently contradict the Ends of Government, and ſo are

repug-

repugnant to the Dictates of Reason and the natural Law of God, they are only Commands, that is, they have only the Matter, but wanting Authority, they have not the essential Form that constitutes a Law. And therefore the most zealous and ablest Defenders of Monarchical Government (*Grotius, Barclay,* &c.) readily concede thus much, That it is lawful to disobey Princes, when they rage against their Subjects and destroy them with Violence and barbarous Cruelty; and if in such Cases Potentates meet with Resistance from their Subjects, those Subjects are justify'd to make such Opposition by their Right of Self-Defence and mutual Preservation, establish'd and supported by the Law of Nature.

FINIS.